# CONFLICTING PARADIGMS
# IN THE ECONOMICS
# OF DEVELOPING NATIONS

# CONFLICTING PARADIGMS IN THE ECONOMICS OF DEVELOPING NATIONS

*WILFRED L. DAVID*

New York
Westport, Connecticut
London

**Library of Congress Cataloging-in-Publication Data**

David, Wilfred L.
  Conflicting paradigms in the economics of
  developing nations.

  Bibliography: p.
  Includes index.
  1. Developing countries — Economic conditions.
2. Economic development. 3. Dependency. I. Title.
HC59.7.D335 1986     330.9172′4      86-16906
ISBN 0-275-92108-5 (alk. paper)

Library of Congress Catalog Card Number: 86-16906
ISBN: 0-275-92108-5

First published in 1986

Praeger Publishers, 521 Fifth Avenue, New York, NY 10175
A division of Greenwood Press, Inc.

Printed in the United States of America

The paper used in this book complies with the Permanent
Paper Standard issued by the National Information Standards
Organization (Z39.48-1984).

10 9 8 7 6 5 4 3 2 1

Dedicated to the memories of my friend
PROFESSOR RASHID HALLOWAY,
who understood the meaning
of the disjuncture between theory and praxis
in the development paradigm,
and of my father
PHILBERT CAESAR DAVID,
whose life was a quintessential example
of the development quest

# Contents

# *Preface*

The Bandung Declaration of April 1955 saw the birth of the so-called Third World nations, originally known in international circles as the "Group of 77." Associated with this development was a focus on the idea that there existed a group of nations whose economic status, power, prestige, and, indeed, interests, could not be defined primarily in terms of "East-West" ideological relationships, but, more important, in terms of the economic distance that seemed to separate them from the more industrialized capitalist and socialist nations. This shift in emphasis from "East-West" to "North-South" relations was a reflection not only of the aggregate and structural gaps existing between the developed and developing nations, but was also related to the general perception of developing countries that they should be allowed to participate more meaningfully in the international decision-making process. This, in turn, was seen as a means of enabling them to combine the prerequisites of political self-determination with the more pressing requirements of economic independence and sustained development.

From a historical perspective, therefore, the urgency underlying the contemporary development quest has been recognized for only about three decades. Of course, this should not be interpreted to mean that there were no problems of development and underdevelopment prior to the 1950s when colonialism was pervasive. However, paralleling the increasing concern for economic self-determination and development has been a tremendous growth in intellectual activity concerning the problems of development and underdevelopment. Contextually, the past three decades have witnessed a plethora of models, theories, and empirical investigations of the development problem and the possibilities offered for transforming Asian, African, Latin American, and Caribbean nations. This body of knowledge has come to be known in academic and policy circles as "Development Economics," and is termed in this study as the "Economics of Developing Nations."

As elaborated in Hirschman (1981) and Lall (1985), this corpus of thought and knowledge denotes economics with a particular perspective of developing countries and the development process. It has come to shape our beliefs about the economic development of Third World countries and the policies and strategies that should be used in this process. While this "Economics of Developing Nations" goes beyond the mere application of orthodox economic principles to the study of developing countries, it remains an intellectual offspring and subdiscipline of the mainstream economics discipline, or the "Economics of Developed Nations."

A major premise underlying this study is that the growth in economic knowledge—and the corresponding intellectual maturation of development thought and policy—has not been matched by equally significant changes in the living conditions and life chances of the majority of the people living in the developing world. This apparently antithetical situation can be explained in both general and specific terms. In general, it mirrors a disjuncture between accepted theory and development reality. At another level, it may be a reflection of the fact that the "Economics of Developing Nations" is both "rich" and "poor" at the same time. On the one hand, the presumed richness of the field is suggested not only by the sheer quantitative growth that has taken place in the development literature but also by the related advances in theoretical sophistication and analytical rigor. On the other hand, these intellectual achievements have been growing at a time when the needs and wants of the majority of the people in the developing world have been escalating, and in a larger world order defined by increasing polarization and inequality.

In the latter context, the evidence suggests that a basic contradiction has emerged in the development process at both national and international levels. From one perspective, several developing nations seem to have made substantial economic progress over the past 20 years. According to World Bank estimates (World Bank 1985), GDP growth of the developing countries averaged about 6 percent a year between 1960 and 1980. There has also been some visible progress in terms of the behavior of related quality-of-life indicators. For example, life expectancy in the developing world increased from an average of 42 years in 1960 to 49 years in 1982, infant mortality was halved, and the primary school enrollment rate rose from 50 to 94 percent. Needless to say, these average performance indicators are by no means representative and tend to mask several other important dimensions of the development problem.

First, average per capita real incomes in the large majority of developing countries, especially in African and Asian low income ones, are no higher than they were in the late 1960s, and many seem to have retrogressed. Second, at both national and international levels, successful aggregate economic growth performance has resulted in marked improvements in living standards of a powerful minority while the majority of the population still subsists in a vicious circle of poverty and underdevelopment. As mentioned earlier, this contradiction seems to have been heightening at a time when the needs and wants of the impoverished majority continue to grow. Third, the situation can be considered a reflection of the classic race between development and discontent. On the one hand, there is an increasing desire for rapid economic growth and improvements in material living standards. On the other hand, this seems to clash with the need to establish an equitable, free, and democractic society in the developing world.

Many scholars interpret this apparent dilemma in terms of a "failure," "poverty," or "disparagement" of Development Economics or the Economics of Developing Nations. In this context, the situation is also sometimes viewed as an integral part of an epistemological crisis that continues to plague the mainstream Economics discipline and its major subdisciplines. Others feel that there is nothing fundamentally wrong with the theoretical structure and domain assumptions underlying either Economics in general or the Economics of Developing Nations in particular. In the latter case, the perceived lack of socioeconomic progress in the developing nations is explained in terms of their failure to follow the sound economic principles and practices that are suggested by orthodox economics.

In many cases, differences of opinion can be traced not so much to disagreements about the scientific status of specific models, theories, or explanations of development and underdevelopment, but more to differences (explicit or implicit) in ideological postures, ontological commitments, theories of knowledge, and related value orientations. While economists and social scientists differ as to the amount of weight that should be attached to these factors in the search for truth, they must be considered important in the sense that they help to explain why certain paradigms, world views, or development ideologies maintain their dominance and tenacity. What is evident from the debate, however, is that the Economics of Developing Nations seems to have reached a crossroads. There is therefore a corresponding need to conduct more serious epistemological activity within the discipline itself. This is also true of the mainstream economics discipline. What seems to be called for is a critical examination and assessment of the validity of accepted development truths, dominant theoretical explanations, domain assumptions, analytical procedures, and related intellectual toolkits.

This study represents a very small step toward meeting such a gargantuan, if not impossible, intellectual challenge. Its general thrust consists of an attempt to juxtapose alternative world views or perspectives of thought on the theory and reality of development and underdevelopment. Contextually, the theoretical and analytical foundations underlying three broad paradigmatic typologies are highlighted. The first, or orthodox paradigm, comprises research programs or schools of thought that are basically concerned with applying the tenets of orthodox economics to the study of developing economies. From such a perspective, the principles underlying the Economics of Developing Nations are the same as, or can be considered extensions of, those governing the Economics of Developed Nations. This implies that meaningful epistemological activity within the

Economics of Developing Nations cannot be conducted without first determining its inextricable intellectual and analytical ties to mainstream economics, or the Economics of Developed Nations.

Second, and at the opposite pole, is the Marxian or radical heterodox paradigm that essentially views development in terms of a transition through stages of capitalist development to socialism. Both orthodoxy and Marxian heterodoxy are based on a universalist epistemology and a deterministic view of societal change and development. Under orthodoxy, the process is considered to be an evolutionary and harmonious one, while Marxian heterodoxy sees the process as being inherently conflictual and therefore requiring revolutionary modes of transformation.

Third, several eclectic and middle-range perspectives of thought lie sandwiched between the pure orthodox and Marxian poles. The most well developed is the "structuralist" perspective that emphasizes the need to analyze the problems of development and underdevelopment in terms of specific factors governing the historical integration of developing countries into the world economy, their continued dependency on the latter, the unique structural and institutional rigidities that have become endemic to the domestic development process, and related factors that help to perpetuate unbalanced growth and disequilibrium.

A related neoliberal or "egalitarian" perspective addresses at least three interrelated development concerns. A first, based on the historical development experience, suggests that the benefits of material economic growth have not sufficiently "trickled down" to the masses of the population in the developing world, in accordance with the expectations of the orthodox paradigm. A second strand emphasizes the need for a paradigmatic shift from the traditional concern for material economic growth and in the direction of human development, that is, the possibilities offered for growth with equity, poverty redressal, and basic human needs fulfillment. This is related to a third variant that views development as a moral problem. The underlying assumption is that value judgments would have to be made about the equity and efficiency components of economic welfare and therefore about the elements of distributive justice underlying alternative development paths.

A basic concern of the present study is to reinterpret the strengths and weaknesses of conventional development theory in the light of the challenges posed by the unorthodox or heterodox pespectives alluded to above. In this context, an effort is made not only to explain the ramifications of alternative development philosophies but also to suggest ways in which the conventional or accepted paradigm may be amended, extended, or otherwise completely revised. Further, while the focus is primarily on theory and analysis, and only indirectly or tangentially with policy questions, many of the issues discussed do carry important policy implications. As such, the present work takes one stage further some of the concerns about development philosophy raised in my recent study, *The IMF Policy Paradigm* (David 1985). The latter study specifically emphasized the need to integrate the tenets of standard macroeconomic and stabilization policy with relevant aspects of development theory.

While the present book is designed as a very general statement of alternative world views on economic development, it is by no means monolithic in orientation and can serve several purposes simultaneously. From one angle, it displays many of the features of a text, both in terms of the breadth of coverage and the emphasis placed on formal analysis. However, even from this perspective, the coverage is far from complete, and many topics of interest have been neglected or may not have been covered in sufficient detail. Nevertheless, the book does take some bold forays into several areas that are either totally neglected or dismissed, or otherwise only incidentally treated, in more popular works on development.

From another angle, and in a more important sense, therefore, the objective is to go beyond the more limited and confined textbook treatment of the subject matter. In this context, the book displays many of the qualities of a treatise. First, it tries to present an unbiased and undogmatic statement of alternative, and at times controversial, philosophical positions and world views. Second, the rigors of abstract theoretical analysis are combined with, and juxtaposed against, findings derived from empirical observation and development practice. Third, while the book falls short of presenting a new development paradigm, it raises many of the questions and pertinent issues that must be addressed if such an exercise were to be carried out on a systematic basis.

# Acknowledgments

The present study is an outgrowth of cumulative experience gained from two decades of teaching, research, and related policy work in the field of international economic development. A broad range of individuals and works have proved influential in shaping my interest and perspectives, and I have therefore accumulated innumerable intellectual and related debts.

My decision to devote some effort to the comparative analysis of economic paradigms and their epistemological ramifications has been encouraged by the work and example of Professor Bernard Williams, Provost of Kings College, Cambridge, and Professor Stuart Hampshire, Warden of Wadham College, Oxford. Sir John and Lady Ursula Hicks, and John Bamborough, Principal of Linacre College, Oxford, have contributed in different ways to my intellectual development and have always been generous with their encouragement and support.

Over the years, I have benefited from the writings of, and/or communications with, several scholars. A highly truncated list of names must include Samir Amin, George Beckford, Celso Furtado, Albert Hirschman, Irma Adelman, Arthur Lewis, Nicholas Kaldor, Thomas Balogh, Gunnar Myrdal, Gerald Meier, Paul Streeten, Dudley Seers, John Lewis, and Lance Taylor.

I am grateful to the following individuals who spared time either to read portions of an earlier draft or to discuss points of detail with me: Simon Jones-Hendrickson, Alfredo Sfier-Younis, Herman McKenzie, Cedric Grant, Carl Stone, Harold Lucius, Lloyd Best, Peter Hopcraft, David Flood, Manuel Diaz, and Jean Curling.

I also wish to acknowledge the invaluable contribution of my Praeger editors who monitored the book's production with the utmost efficiency and care.

Last but not least, my wife, Peggy Ann, has always been, and continues to be, a constant source of support and encouragement.

The usual caveat should be added that none of the individuals mentioned above should be held responsible for any views expressed or for errors remaining in the work. These are the author's sole responsibility.

# List of Tables

# List of Figures

# I

## PROLEGOMENA

# 1

## *Introduction and Overview*

From a development perspective, the nations of the world can be subdivided into two basic groups or sectors. One group or sector comprises the relatively developed and industrialized nations in the temperate zone (the North). The other constitutes a large mass of developing or less developed tropical or subtropical nations in Africa, Asia, Latin America, and the Caribbean (the South). This "North-South" distinction cuts across the traditional "East-West" ideological dichotomy and highlights the differentials in economic status, power, and prestige that exist between the two groups of nations.

The differentials in economic status can be defined in terms of absolute and per capita income attainment, levels of technological development, degrees of industrialization and urbanization, and other economic indicators. There is also a positive correlation between economic status and economic power, with the latter connoting a given country's technological maturity, its economic dynamism, its ability to exploit a wide range of technological and economic opportunities, as well as its capacity to penetrate, and maintain control over, world resources and markets.

Further, economic status and power tend to be highly correlated with political status and power, with the latter determined by a given nation's level of constitutional development. This, in turn, is defined by the degree of autonomy it has in formulating, and exercising control over, a wide range of decisions in its own interests and its capacity to respond to various political, social, and economic crises. Political status and power are sometimes influenced by forces of geopolitics, which determine a country's bargaining power in the world order and its ability to control its own political destiny. All the factors mentioned above ultimately determine a country's prestige which can be considered a broad measure of its international social status.

While the developing nations are a heterogeneous group, they are undifferentiated in the sense that they share a common lack of status, power, and prestige in the economic, social, and political spheres of the world order. The disparities in economic status and power can be illustrated by considering dimensions of the absolute and relative gaps in average incomes between the developed and the developing nations. In this context, we follow the standard practice of using Gross Domestic Product (GDP) and Gross National Product (GNP) as measures of aggregate economic status and therefore levels of economic development. As further defined in Chapter 3, GDP measures the total value of the final output of goods and services produced within a country's economy over a given period of time—usually one year. This output can be produced by both residents and nonresidents, regardless of its allocation between domestic and foreign claims. GNP measures the total domestic and foreign output claimed by residents of a country. To arrive at GNP from GDP, we add factor incomes such as investment earnings and workers' remittances accruing to residents from abroad and subtract the income earned in the domestic economy that accrues to persons and institutions abroad, for example, repatriated profits on foreign investment, interest on foreign loans, and so on.

On the basis of these aggregate income measures, the developed sector of the world consists primarily of the industrial market economies that are members of the Organization of Economic Cooperation and Development (OECD). This group of countries (excluding Greece, Portugal, and Turkey) had an average GNP per capita of over $11,000 in 1984, with the average ranging between $5,150 per head for Ireland to over $17,000 per head for Switzerland. Some Eastern European socialist countries such as the USSR can also be considered developed, although no firm or reliable statistics are available on their income levels.

The developing sector of the world is made up of both low and middle income countries. The World Bank defines low income countries as those with an average GNP per head of less than $410, and the middle income ones as having an average GNP per person of $410 or more. On this basis, the average GNP per person in low income developing countries was around $280 in 1984 compared to about $1,520 for middle income countries. However, the middle income developing countries represent a varied group and include countries at both the lower and upper ranges of the income scale as well as oil exporters and oil importers. Lower middle income developing countries have an average per capita income of $840, with a range between $440 per head for the Sudan and $1,500 for Colombia. In the case of upper middle income countries, the average is about $2,500, with a range between $1,680 for Syria and $6,840 for Trinidad and Tobago.

Table 1.1 presents some computations of the absolute and relative gaps in GNP per capita between developed and developing nations for the 1950–80 period. The absolute gap is measured by the difference in GNP per capita levels, while the relative gap shows GNP per capita in the developing countries as a percentage of that of the developed ones. These gaps are measured in terms of 1980 U.S. prices and therefore may conceal several problems of a purely statistical nature. Nevertheless, they do reveal some broad and stark dimensions of international inequality. First, while GNP per head in the developing countries more than doubled in the 30-year period between 1950–80, this has been largely due to the impressive performance, on average, of the middle income developing countries. The data show that in 1950, average GNP per capita in the developing nations was $3,446 lower than that of the developed ones, but by 1980, the absolute gap had reached $8,801.

Second, the per capita income of the developing countries as a proportion of that of their more developed counterparts (the relative income gap) remained at a fairly constant level (around 9–10 percent) between 1950–80. This is in part a reflection of the steady performance of the upper middle income developing countries. However, the relative gap between the poorest (low income) developing nations and the developed ones actually widened over this period. In 1950, the average income per capita in the low income developing nations was about 4.3 percent of that of the developed ones, but the gap had increased to 2.5 percent (a near doubling) 30 years later. Further, there is evidence to suggest that both the absolute and relative gaps will never be closed for the majority of developing nations. For example, a World Bank study has estimated that, if past trends continue, about eight of the fastest growing developing countries will be able to close the absolute gap within 100 years, and about 16 within 1,000 years. The gap will never be closed for the majority of developing nations (see Morawetz 1977).

Third, account should also be taken of the binary gaps, that is, the absolute and relative per capita income gaps between the low and middle income developing nations. As the data in Table 1.1 show, average per capita income in low income countries was about $461 less than in the middle income ones in 1950, but by 1980 this absolute gap nearly tripled to $1,276. A similar trend was noticeable for the relative binary gap. Average per capita income of the low income countries was about 26 percent of that

**TABLE 1.1**:  Absolute and relative gaps in GNP per capita between developed and developing countries, 1950-80

| Countries | Income levels[a] | | | Annual growth rates | |
|---|---|---|---|---|---|
| | 1950 | 1960 | 1980 | 1950-60 | 1960-80 |
| Developed countries[b] | 3,841 | 5,197 | 9,684 | 3.1 | 3.2 |
| Developing[c] | 395 | 488 | 883 | 1.6 | 2.5 |
| Middle income | 625 | 802 | 1,521 | 2.5 | 3.3 |
| Low income | 164 | 174 | 245 | 0.6 | 1.7 |
| | Absolute Gap | | | | |
| Developing | 3,446 | 4,709 | 8,801 | | |
| Middle income | 3,216 | 4,395 | 8,163 | | |
| Low income | 3,677 | 5,023 | 9,439 | | |
| | Relative Gap (Percentage) | | | | |
| Developing | 10.3 | 9.4 | 9.1 | | |
| Middle income | 16.3 | 15.4 | 15.7 | | |
| Low income | 4.3 | 3.3 | 2.5 | | |

[a]In 1980 U.S. dollars.

[b]The *Developed countries* are primarily the *industrial market economies*, which are members of the Organization of Economic Cooperation and Development (OECD), apart from Greece, Portugal, and Turkey, which are included among the middle income countries. A distinction is also made between these and the *Eastern European nonmarket economies* (developed and developing), including Albania, Bulgaria, Czechoslovakia, the German Democratic Republic, Hungary, Poland, Romania, and the USSR.

[c]The Developing countries comprise *low income countries*, with a 1982 GNP per person of less than $410, and *middle income countries*, with a 1982 GNP per person of $410 or more. Middle income countries are also divided into *lower* and *upper* strata, as well as *oil exporters* and *oil importers*. Middle income oil exporters include Algeria, Angola, Cameroon, Congo, Ecuador, Egypt, Gabon, Indonesia, Iran, Iraq, Malaysia, Mexico, Nigeria, Peru, Syria, Trinidad and Tobago, Tunisia, and Venezuela. Some middle income countries are also *major exporters of manufactures,* sometimes called *newly industrializing countries.* This subgroup includes Argentina, Brazil, Greece, Hong Kong, Israel, Republic of Korea, the Philippines, Portugal, Singapore, South Africa, Thailand, and Yugoslavia. A separate category comprises the *high income oil exporters:* Bahrain, Brunei, Kuwait, Libya, Oman, Qatar, Saudi Arabia, and the United Arab Emirates.

*Source:* Computed from World Bank Data Tapes; and World Development Reports: Sundry years.

of their middle income counterparts in 1950, but by 1980 the gap had widened, with the ratio declining to around 16 percent.

The absolute and relative gaps between the developed and developing nations also reflect the fact that the lion's share of the world's product of goods and services is produced and consumed by a relatively few people. About 80 percent of the world's total output of goods and services is produced in the developed countries, where only about 25 percent of the world's total population live. The remaining 20 percent of world output is shared by the 75 percent of the world's population living in the developing countries of Asia, Africa, Latin America, and the Caribbean. Further, only about 5 percent of global product is shared by the near 50 percent of the world's population living in African and Asian low income countries. The evidence also suggests that many of the dimensions of international inequality are replicated within the developing countries themselves and that the incidence of inequality in these countries may be more pronounced in comparison to the situation observed internationally or within more developed societies. The majority of people living in the developing world lack economic and social opportunity, and many now depend on remittances and other resource transfers from the developed world for mere economic survival.

The usual caveat must be added that comparisons based on the aggregate GNP measure should always be interpreted with extreme caution. This is because intercountry comparisons of GNP levels are based on a statistical procedure in which conversions are made into a common currency (U.S. dollars) using official currency exchange rates. However, these exchange rates do not always reflect income and price differentials among countries; the persistence of illegal, "underground," and other "nonprice" activities in some countries; and the lack of consistency among countries in calculating changes in real output over time. Some attempt has been made to overcome the limitations of procedures for exchange rate conversions in what is known as the International Comparison Project (see Kravis, Heston, and Summers 1982).

Another problem with the GNP indicator is related to the well-known fact that GNP is not a measure of overall societal welfare and therefore does not provide a good enough indication of the overall quality of life in society or other qualitative variables that are important to the study of development and underdevelopment. The latter include, among others, the distribution of income and wealth, employment and job security, the quality of the environment, infant mortality, literacy, longevity, and other indicators of basic human needs. Due to the complex statistical problems that normally accompany attempts to incorporate these conditions and variables into a more comprehensive indicator of general welfare or development, the usual practice is to complement the GNP measure by some of the qualitative indicators mentioned above. However, as shown elsewhere in the study, the differentials in these qualitative indicators tend to bear a close correlation with the income disparities highlighted earlier.

The absolute and relative disparities in overall well-being between the developed and the developing world, as well as between regions, sectors, and groups within the developing countries themselves, have provided an important motive force behind the contemporary quest for sustained economic progress. In this context, there is an urgent concern that the relative gaps in income and living standards (both domestic and international) have tended to widen over time and that this phenomenon continues to be associated with disparities in status, power, and influence in economic, political, and social spheres.

These discrepancies have resulted in an "aspiration gap," which represents a perceived divergence between actual and potential reality both within and across nations. This discrepancy is between standards of living and status that individuals, social groups, and nations now have and what they would like to have. The aspiration gap therefore refers to changes that these collectivities would like to experience relative to some reference groups, with the latter considered to be the advanced industrial nations and the individuals, social groups, and economic sectors that exist within them. Evidence of this aspiration gap can be found both nationally and internationally, and in both capitalist and socialist nations. From a development perspective, it is reflected in the fact that people in low and middle income developing countries now increasingly demand and treasure goods and life-styles to which people in high income developed countries are accustomed.

This "revolution of rising expectations" has been given momentum by the transnational process and the related spread of international communications. As a result, people in the developing countries are now much more aware of conditions obtaining in the reference group countries. The process has also been associated with an increasing mobility of people across national boundaries and the widespread imitation of reference group country life-styles and consumption patterns by people in the developing world. In general, the transnational process has been accompanied by a revolutionary shrinkage of international space and benefits resulting from the introduction of new modes of international communication. The shrinkage in space has also succeeded in narrowing the gap in consumer tastes among countries. McDonald hamburgers, Jordache jeans, Nike sneakers, and videocassette recorders are now available and, in some cases, eagerly sought after, in the remotest villages of the world.

The general point of emphasis is that factors accompanying the transnational process, for example, the spread of mass communications, international migration, and the international shrinkage of space, have sensitized the people of the developing world to the possibilities offered for human and material development. This realization has been translated into new aspiration levels and a rising development consciousness. On a related basis, there is now an urgency about the need to raise real incomes, living standards, and the overall quality of life in the developing countries that was not present during the early period of transformation in the now industrialized nations. Accordingly, many developing nations have shown a willingness to make deliberate choices as a means of accelerating the pace of economic change. They also experiment with policy options and transformation scenarios that are outside the historical experience of their more developed counterparts.

The quest for meaningful and sustained economic progress has also been endorsed by the United Nations in its successive "Development Decades," as well as in the call for the establishment of a New International Economic Order (see David 1977). These and other initiatives at the international level have helped to politicize the development problem and, to some extent, reflect the common desire of many leaders of developing nations to bring global attention to bear on development issues.

Given the urgency of the development problem, the past three decades have witnessed a spate of theories, empirical generalizations, and other analyses of economic development. As indicated earlier, this corpus of knowledge constitutes "Development Economics," or the "Economics of Developing Nations." However, this growth in knowledge has also been accompanied by what is perceived by many scholars to be a disjuncture between theory and praxis in the development field. As indicated earlier, the search for an explanation must to some extent go "beyond economics" and examine the cumulative interplay of ideas, ideologies, and development practice in the determination of truth.

## Paradigms and the Structure of Knowledge

A useful starting point is the sociology of knowledge or a consideration of those factors that determine what we come to accept as truth and knowledge in any form of scientific inquiry. The generation of knowledge and truth forms part of a more embracing intellectual system that shapes our thinking about social and economic reality. The intellectual system represents a mechanism or social process that is responsible for shaping people's images of the world and for inducing changes in these images. An individual's image of the world, or world view, is made up of diverse images about duties, obligations, expectations, relations to others in society, right and wrong, and so on. These images reinforce, and are reinforced by, behavior. This interaction between behavior responses and images becomes a crucial factor in our interpretation of the socioeconomic order and its potential for stability or change (Boulding 1968, 1968a).

Underlying the intellectual system is a process of social and organized learning that determines the possibilities for thought and action, and through which relevant cognitive structures are developed. The process, in its diverse operations, produces new cognitive structures that help to extend the boundaries of awareness, observation, and thought. The phenomenon of social learning emphasizes the fact that scientific and intellectual inquiry typically take place in a social setting and therefore tend to convey social meaning (Solo 1975). The generation of knowledge and related information flows tend to be embedded in some model or framework of thought through which ideas are interpreted. Society, social groups, and institutions form an integral part of the process through which this framework is generated. However, there is no consensus about the nature of the interactive process that develops between the larger society and its institutions on the one hand, and models of thought on the other. Some thinkers argue that the relationship is a deterministic one, while others view it as intercausal.

Thomas Kuhn's theory of scientific revolutions provides a useful point of departure and conceptual framework for our understanding of the social context of kowledge, and therefore the theory and practice of development. According to Kuhn (1962, 1970), most scientific inquiry tends to be based on a theory—implicit or explicit—of how the world operates and how investigations relating to its operation ought to proceed. The organizing concept is that of a "paradigm," which the dictionary defines as a "model or pattern," or as a practical illustration of an abstract principle. Thus, underlying the notion of a paradigm is some correspondence between the abstract and the applied, or between theory and praxis.

In Kuhn's formulation, emphasis is placed on a necessary connection between the generation of knowledge and group interests. This is explained in terms of a concept of "normal science," which he defines as "research firmly based on one or more past scientific achievements, achievements that some particular scientific community acknowledges for a time as supplying the foundations for its further practice" (Kuhn 1962, p. 10). In this context, it should be mentioned that Kuhn's primary concern was with the natural or physical sciences, since he considered the social sciences to be less well developed and therefore "preparadigmatic." However, from the perspective of the present study, his concept of "normal science" and his overall approach to the sociology of knowledge can be meaningfully applied to the theory and practice of the Economics of both Developed and Developing Nations.

Using the Kuhnian schema, intellectual activity in both disciplines can be viewed in terms of two types of realities. One is the "social system," which involves the scientific community of economists. From this has evolved various schools of thought, research programs, or paradigms that are "community based" in the sense that they tend to be propagated through institutional arrangements such as academic departments in major universities, peer review procedures, professional asociations, journals, and other forms of academic and intellectual communication. These institutional arrangements can be thought of as a "management control system" that reflects the social and professional values of the "community of economic scholars."

Even before Kuhn, Schumpeter (1949, 1978) had drawn attention to the fact that economists and other social scientists operate as "sociological groups," defined by similarities in social and cultural locations, resulting in similarities in intellectual perspectives, philosophies of life, and so on. Schumpeter's argument is that there is a cohesion or "corporate spirit" that tends to be associated with such group membership. His thesis is that while the cohesive spirit facilitates the accumulation of factual knowledge, it tends to produce a frame of mind that becomes increasingly conservative and resistant to change. He further posits that the social mechanism becomes a source of ideology that represents a pre- and extra-scientific "vision" of social and economic reality. It is this vision that loses the force of ideology once it is subjected to the rigors of scientific testing and analysis.

Second, and on a related basis, "normal science" in both conventional Economics and the Economics of Developing Nations represents particular systems of ideas that have unity and coherence. These ideational systems tend to be fully reflective of the cognitive apparatus of dominant groups of economists. This cognitive apparatus reflects certain metaphysical and ontological commitments, epistemological beliefs, shared values, and methodological principles to which the group subscribes. These are, in turn, passed on in the pages of standard textbooks, the more influential professional journals, and other vehicles of professional communication. An important part of this socialization process is the formal education and training of students who, over time, come to share the basic elements of a group commitment, including symbolic generalizations, beliefs in particular models, a value system, and exemplars or puzzles that reflect the empirical content of theories.

One important implication of this socialization process has been stated as follows:

> But "normal science" is in fact largely a set of practices in which members of a given scientific community *customarily* engage. Students

seeking to follow their professors in careers in which the latter will judge them and ultimately determine their fate are not encouraged to undertake projects which depart radically from those which their professors conceive for them. When suggestions for such projects arise, either from students or from competing members of the community, they are as often treated by sarcasm and ridicule as the subject of seasoned discourse and debate. In this process, what students acquire is less an abstract understanding of what they are doing than a set of habits, or instincts, about what constitutes a legitimate mode of inquiry or a plausible explanation (Piore 1983, p. 249).

These elements of group commitment help to explain why certain paradigms become dominant and are difficult to overthrow, even in the face of strong challenges from rival perspectives. During the course of its evolution, the conditions underlying a dominant paradigm tend to set limits on the types of questions that the analyst is willing to ask. This conservative attitude militates, in turn, against the analyst's ability to ask innovative and challenging questions, even when there are doubts about the explanatory power of existing theories. Where anomalies emerge in existing theories, the latter are never completely rejected but modified in various ways as a means of maintaining the community consensus.

One way of looking at a paradigm is in terms of clusters of interconnected theories or scientific research programs that have become dominant. Where such a set of theories or succession of theories exist, each successive theory arises from a reinterpretation of previous theories in order to accommodate some anomaly. During the course of testing predictions of particular research programs or theories, economists invariably encounter instances of anomaly, so that these research programs and theories have to be continuously amended in order to avoid their complete rejection.

The tenacity underlying dominant paradigms and their supporting clusters of theories and research programs can be explained in at least three ways. One such explanation is provided by Lakatos (1970), who drew a distinction between the "hard core" and the "protective belt" of any given scientific research program. The "hard core" consists of a set of purely metaphysical beliefs that define and inspire the program's research strategy. The "protective belt" refers to those assumptions that are combined with the hard core to produce specific testable theories. These are, in turn, responsible for providing specific research programs with their reputation. Lakatos therefore concludes that it is wrong to assume that we must stay with a research program until it has exhausted all its heuristic power, or that a rival program should not be introduced until everyone has agreed that a point of complete degeneration has probably been reached (see Blaug 1975).

Another explanation of the reason that old and dominant clusters of theories tend to coexist with newer and competing ones is provided by Bronfenbrenner (1971, 1976). He advocates a simple Hegelian dialectic of thesis-antithesis-synthesis as fitting the structure of revolutions in economic thought. In his formulation, the Hegelian dialectic is seen as representing a basic thesis or orthodoxy. This corresponds to Kuhn's use of the term "normal science" and includes a set of conventional theories and research programs. In this schema, the thesis or orthodox paradigm usually hardens from doctrine to dogma with the passage of time.

However, problems of anomalies arise for which the standard paradigm cannot provide any or suitable answers. As a result, an antithesis develops in juxtaposition to every thesis. This antithesis usually starts off in the form of objections to one or other conclusions or implications of the thesis. These are sometimes subsequently broadened to encompass a wide spectrum of analytic techniques, insights, and methodologies that support the basic thesis. Finally, a synthesis emerges out of the conflict between thesis and antithesis. Some of the elements of the preceding antithesis are absorbed in this process, while others are ignored. The result is a survival of the old thesis with very few modifications.The new thesis therefore usually has all the basic elements of the old thesis or standard paradigm.

A third explanation of paradigm tenacity is associated with the Marxian viewpoint that ideas, systems of thought, and intellectual systems tend to reflect the interests of the dominant economic classes in society, and are therefore used as weapons of social control.

In summary, the notion of a paradigm is used in a very general sense in this study to connote a set of shared intellectual commitments that help to shape our perceptions about social and economic reality. As such, a given paradigm provides an intellectual framework for the study of such reality, defines the class of problems considered worthy of investigation, and delineates the relevant criteria for judging the appropriateness of answers to such problems.

In this general sense, a paradigm reflects a "world view," "value system," or "ideology," which, in Schumpeterian terms, provides a "vision" of social and economic reality. Second, most well-developed paradigms usually draw their strength and support from research programs or clusters of theories that have emerged from well-respected research traditions and academic programs. Third, the research programs themselves tend to gain their respectability from clusters of theories, models, and empirical generalizations that have a distinct cognitive structure. As stated earlier, this means that they tend to reflect the shared values and intellectual commitments of the scientific community.

These factors help to explain why certain clusters of theories, schools of thought, and research programs become dominant and why few significant scientific revolutions occur within the social sciences. During the course of intellectual history, the testing of theories underlying a dominant paradigm may at times throw up important anomalies. However, the operation of social and ideological mechanisms helps to explain why the postulates underlying the dominant paradigm are not normally totally rejected but merely reinterpreted in order to accommodate the anomalies. Because of the various factors governing paradigm tenacity, what is typically encountered in "normal science" are old theories dressed up in new clothes. Under the circumstances, many strong rival theories and hypotheses hardly see the light of day.

From the perspective of this study, a large part of the accepted corpus of knowledge about development does not sufficiently address the specific historical realities of poverty and underdevelopment, but is more an extrapolation of the domain assumptions and analytical principles of the Economics of Developed Nations (mainstream economics) to the study of poor countries. However, as shown later, the Economics of Developing Nations encompasses much more than the "orthodox economics" of development, or, for that matter, the orthodox economics of developed countries.

In conventional Economics (the Economics of Developed Nations), as in major subdisciplines such as Development Economics (the Economics of Developing Nations), there exists one dominant orthodox paradigm that draws its support from research programs and clusters of theories that are acceptable to the scientific "community" of economists. Table 1.2 identifies seven research programs or schools of thought that define the Economics of Developed Nations. Four of these (the neoclassical, Keynesian, monetarist, and new classical) can be considered as forming the backbone of the dominant orthodox paradigm. Within this group, the neoclassical and Keynesian research programs continue to be the most influential. This remains the case even though important challenges to the theory and practice of orthodoxy have been continuously posed by various heterodox perspectives as articulated in the neo-Keynesian, neo-institutionalist, and Marxian research programs.

As shown in Table 1.3, these systems of thought also have their counterparts in the Economics of Developing Nations. In this context, a significant portion of the accepted corpus of knowledge consists of an application of neoclassical and Keynesian ideas, concepts, and patterns of reasoning to the study of developing countries. In a general sense, therefore, the orthodox paradigm of development is based on an adaptation of systems of thought that were originally formulated for Western industrialized nations to the developing ones.

This adaptation has moved in at least two methodological directions. In the extreme or neoconservative variant, it is argued that since the principles of economics are universal, there is but one Economics whose basic tenets are equally valid for both developed and developing nations. In other words, it is considered inappropriate to speak about two distinct Economics—one for the developed and the other for the developing nations. A more realistic or neoliberal variant is based on the recognition that there may be some differences between developed and developing countries. Even in this case, the view is that standard economic theory, properly modified and applied but not radically altered, can still provide a suitable framework for the analysis of development.

Both variants of orthodoxy have been challenged by the structuralist and Marxian (radical heterodox) approaches to economic development. These approaches consider orthodox theory to be thoroughly unrealistic, inadequate, and politically biased in its orientation and conclusions. Both perspectives emphasize the point that the reality of poverty and inequality in the developing world is not independent of the historical influence of developed "center" nations, and are therefore concerned with highlighting ways in which orthodox theory should be amended or otherwise totally rejected. Contextually, the concern is with developing a set of new propositions to explain the phenomena of development and underdevelopment. However, it must remain an open question whether this task has been successfully achieved.

The structuralist perspective is based on a recognition that there are certain historical and structural features of developing countries that make orthodox theory have only a limited applicability and relevance to the situation. The concern is therefore with identifying specific rigidities, lags, and other special institutional features that affect the development potential of these countries (see Chenery 1975).

Finally, the major challenge to orthodoxy continues to be posed by the Marxian or radical heterodox perspective. Both orthodoxy and radical heterodoxy have their origins in Western economics and share a universalist orientation. As is well known, the basic difference between orthodox (neoclassical) and Marxian development theory can be traced to the different underlying theories of value upon which each rests and from which each draws its logical framework and tools of analysis.

For example, in the neoclassical view of development, exchange relations are considered to be the primary determinants of production relations and form the basis of explanations of how society changes over time. By contrast, the Marxian perspective begins with a theory of value based on production relations considered to be historically determined. The production relations, in turn, determine or govern the relations of exchange. Within this analytical framework, poverty and underdevelopment are considered to be an endogenous part of capitalist accumulation on a world scale. The argument is that capitalism develops the "periphery"

**TABLE 1.2:** Paradigms and research programs in the Economics of the Developed Nations

| Paradigms and research programs | Ideology | Methology | Analytical base and assumptions | Income distribution | Employment | Policy thrust | Major theorist |
|---|---|---|---|---|---|---|---|
| New classical | Extreme right | Rationalism. Positivism. "Science as Science." Methodological individualism. | Perfect markets with all microunits price takers. All markets cleared. | Functional distribution of income explained by marginal productivity theory. | Full employment assumed. Natural rate of unemployment. Unemployment a voluntary phenomenon. | Nonintervention. Minimal state. Free enterprise Privatization. | Muth Lucas Sargent Wallace |
| Monetarist | Extreme right | Covering Law. | Price fundamentalism. Logical time and monetary equilibrium. | Distribution a matter of entitlements and not subject of scientific inquiry. | | Stresses the attainment of individual economic welfare. | Friedman Meltzer Brunner |
| Neoclassical | Right of center | | Rational choice and expectations. Perfect foresight. No uncertainty. | | Full employment assumed. Unemployment a disequilibrium phenomenon. | Emphasis on stable economic policies. | Samuelson Hicks Arrow |
| Keynesian | Center | | Irrational expectations. Disequilibrium a real possibility. | Not very important. | Full employment desirable, but underemployment equilibrium possible. | Activist fiscal and monetary policies by the state. | Harrod Weintraub Davidson |

Orthodox

| | | | | | | | |
|---|---|---|---|---|---|---|---|
| **Heterodox** | Neo-Keynesian | Left of center | Disequilibrium. Historical time. | Imperfect markets. Monopoly elements significant. Uncertainty. | Important, and based on differential savings between capitalist working classes. | Emphasis on growth with full employment. | Activist. Growth and full employment. | Kaldor Robinson Sraffa Harcourt |
| | Neo-Institutionalist | Left of center | Systems economics. Holism. | Monopoly power. Dual economy. Role of technology important. | Structural and institutional factors. | Broad set of national goals emphasized. Technological change. | Activist. Institutional change advocated. | Gruchy Myrdal Galbraith |
| | Marxian | Extreme left | Dialectical and historical materialism. | Monopoly capitalism. | Most important. Based on labor theory of value and exploitation. | Full employment creates crisis for capitalism. | State the arm of private capitalism. Socialism. | Marxist Dobb Baran Sweezy |

*Source:* Compiled by the author.

**TABLE 1.3:** Paradigms and research programs in the Economics of the Developing Nations

| Paradigms and research programs | Ideology | Analysis and method | Development goals and values | Development processes | Global structure | Policy thrust | Major protagonists |
|---|---|---|---|---|---|---|---|
| Neoclassical | Right of center | Rationalism. Positivism. Universalism. Macrohistorical stages. | Steady growth. Price stability. Balance-of-payment equilibrium | Incremental stages. Trickle down. Adaptation. | Harmonious. Interdependent. Factor and resource mobility. | Market-oriented. Marginalist. Free trade and investment. Supply-led. | Rostow Bauer |
| Keynesian | Center | | Growth with employment. | Savings, investment and resource mobilization. | No explicit assumptions. | Activist role of state. Demand-push. Monetary and fiscal policies. | Harrod Domar Chenery Kennedy Thirlwall |
| Structuralist | Left of center | Disequilibrium. Contextualist. Holist. Systems. | Broad-based. National economic and social goals. | Economic dualism. Structural and institutional rigidities. | Emphasis on unequal exchange between center and periphery. | Reformist. Structural change at all levels. | Prebisch Singer Lewis Myrdal Hirschman |
| Dependency | | Historical. | | Unbalanced. | Generates dependency—various forms and levels. | | Furtado Sunkel Cardoso |
| Marxian | Extreme left | Dialectical and historical. Universalist. | Socialist | Societal change through capitalist stages to socialism | Uneven development generated by capitalist expansion on a world scale. | Revolutionary transformation of society along socialist lines. | Frank Baran Amin Emmanuel |

*Source:* Compiled by the author

or "hinterland" by underdeveloping it. It does this by making producers in the developing world independent of domestic markets and by integrating them into the world market. Development and underdevelopment are therefore considered to be an integral part of the same dialectical and antithetical process.

## Overview of This Book

This book is divided into three parts and organized around eight chapters. The material in Part I (Chapters 1 and 2) sets the scene and presents a brief overview of models of thought that are typically encountered in the Economics of the Developed, that is, in standard or received economic theory. As emphasized earlier, there is a symbiotic relationship, in terms of philosophy and analytical thrust, between the Economics of the Developed and the Economics of the Developing. This is true for both its orthodox and radical heterodox variants. In the case of orthodoxy, the dominant interpretive model of thought is based on a "universalist" epistemology or "One World" ideology and "aesthetic," which assumes the existence of a continuous and homogenous world. Contextually, knowledge and society are viewed in terms of discrete individual elements that become the continuous and homogenous phenomena of economic and social life through a process of aggregation.

Chapter 2 presents a bird's eye view of the universalist epistemology and the way it has influenced patterns of reasoning in the Economics of the Developed. The emphasis is on the tenets of positivist methodology and rationalist modes of thought, as well as the heavy reliance placed on equilibrium price relations and market adjustments in explaining the fundamental economic problems of resource allocation, distribution, and economic growth. Some of the major areas of dissent from orthodoxy are also presented, with the relevant implications drawn for the Economics of the Developing.

The material in Part II (Chapters 3 through 5) covers well-trodden ground and highlights the main analytical thrust and philosophical underpinnings of the orthodox or traditional paradigm of economic development. The underlying world view sees economic growth in aggregate income and output and related adaptation in the social, political, and institutional structure of society as providing a necessary condition for sustained economic development. In the extreme case, material economic growth and development are also thought to be synonymous.

In this context, Chapter 3 presents some philosophical pillars on which orthodox perspectives of growth and change are based. These include the philosophies of polar ideal types, pattern variables, modernization, and the notion of continuous evolutionary change based on macrohistorical growth stages. Some reasons that economic growth is considered desirable are also highlighted.

A substantial portion of the Economics of the Developing consists of attempts to build growth models that purport to explain the factors and processes of change. Some of these models are abstract heuristic devices, while others are usually considered to reflect reality. Chapter 4 sets out the analytical framework and some of the major domain assumptions underlying conventional growth modeling. It should be pointed out that the concern is less with the features of specific models and more with broad dimensions of thought, philosophical assumptions, and analytical procedures.

First, the basic macroeconomic and national income relations that provide the analytical base for growth accounting are set out. Second, there is a discussion of Keynesian-type "savings-centered" perspectives. These variously stress the influence of demand-related factors such as savings, investment, and the balance of payments on the growth of aggregate income and output. Third, reference is made to classical-neoclassical supply-based perspectives that explain economic growth in terms of resource allocation and the expansion of factor supplies and productivity growth in national and international contexts.

The emphasis in Chapter 5 shifts to a consideration of perspectives that are based on analyses of "patterns of growth," that is, uniform structural changes that countries are supposed to experience as they move from low to high per capita income levels. These include sectoral transformation and a corresponding shift in production and employment from agriculture to industry and services; a demographic transition from low to high population growth rates, with an increasing occupational differentiation in the labor force; a transformation in the structure of trade from exports of primary staples to manufactured and sophisticated industrial products; and changes in the financial structure of the economy toward increasing monetization, intermediation, and financial deepening.

The exposition in Part III (Chapters 6 through 8) is more heterodox in orientation and presents some of the major anomalies that are thought to exist in the theory and practice of economic development. Chapter 6 examines the claim that the modern growth process has not resulted in the expected "trickle down" or "diffusion" of benefits to the masses of the population in the developing countries, but rather has been associated with increasing polarization and immiserization. Evidence of this is provided by the cumulative interplay of unemployment, poverty, the maldistribution of income and assets, and poor basic human needs fulfillment. The apparent persistence of these conditions of internal disequilibrium is traceable to a combination of factors, including the lack of emphasis on broad-based policies and strategies in the developing countries themselves; the rent-seeking nature of political bureaucracies; and, in general, the lack of a "development will" and commitment on the part of the ruling elite to pursue egalitarian forms of development.

In Chapter 7, the focus shifts to a consideration of international economic relations and their implications for the internal process of development and underdevelopment. Some of the factors that are considered responsible for what is perceived to be an unequal and asymmetrical pattern of international trade and exchange are highlighted. One part of the discussion deals with the evolution of trading relationships between the developed "center" and the developing "periphery" and why trade may no longer be viewed as an "engine of growth" but more as a "handmaiden." The related debate about trade optimism versus pessimism hinges on alternative perceptions about the influence of factors such as the persistently adverse terms of trade facing developing countries, their high partner and commodity concentration of trade, export earnings instability, rising protectionism in both developed and developing nations, and the use of trade as a weapon of foreign policy by the developed nations.

Chapter 7 is also concerned with aspects of the debate on the transnational process and direct foreign investment and their implications for development. Three interrelated dimensions of the debate are emphasized. The first, mainly theoretical, concerns the paradigmatic shift from a world view that traditionally analyzed the foreign investment process in terms of resource flows in a competitive international environment to one based on monopoly, oligopoly, and other forms of market imperfection. Second, some important changes in traditional patterns of foreign investment flows are highlighted. Third, the costs and benefits of the transnational process and direct foreign investment as seen through the eyes of the developing countries are discussed.

Chapter 8 presents four broad heterodox explanations of international inequality and unequal exchange and their links to domestic forms of underdevelopment in the developing world. Three of these are "structuralist" in orientation, while the other is Marxist. The most well-known structuralist perspective is the "center-periphery" thesis of Prebisch and Singer in which poverty, inequality, and underdevelopment in the developing world are explained in terms of the factors giving rise to unequal exchange in the international economy. The general argument is that the center has failed to sufficiently export its growth to the periphery through the diffusion of technological progress and related means. This, it is argued, has resulted in the creation and perpetuation of a dualistic economic structure (as explained by Lewis' dualistic model of development) and a generalized pattern of unbalanced development in the periphery. In a second variant of the structuralist thesis, this pattern of unbalanced development is explained in terms of the principle of cumulative causation (Myrdal), polarization effects (Hirschman), and the antithetical effects of spread and backwash effects.

In a third variant of structuralist thought, the center-periphery model has formed the point of departure for various perspectives of dependency and dependent development. These trace the underdevelopment of the periphery to the cumulative interaction between various external economic reliances (in the areas of trade, technology, finance, and class relations) and internal forms of structural deformity. Finally, there is a brief review of a fourth set of heterodox perspectives that rely on assumptions underlying Marxian value theory and related notions of dialectical change. Two aspects of Marxian heterodoxy are highlighted. One variant explains unequal exchange in terms of differentials in labor values (wage inequalities) and capital accumulation between the center and the periphery. A second and more thoroughgoing Marxian perspective views development in terms of the "development of the underdevelopment," or the antithetical or contradictory relations underlying capitalist expansion on a world scale.

# 2

# *Models of Thought in Orthodox Economics*

All societies (developed and developing, rich and poor, high, middle, or low income) are faced with decisions concerning production, consumption, resource allocation, distribution, and growth. How these decisions are made, as well as their outcomes, depends on the interplay of a variety of general and specific factors. The general factors are those over which countries have very little or no control, for example, natural resource endowments, economic size, and international economic forces. Specific factors include a given country's unique history, the sociocultural environment, and the government's political ideology as is normally reflected in specific programs and policies it is willing to pursue.

Given these factors, a pertinent question is whether the problems inherent in the economic decision-making process can be addressed by utilizing techniques of economic analysis that are universal, that is, invariant across countries and economic systems. This chapter outlines some basics of the orthodox world view of economics as well as areas of dissent raised under heterodox perspectives of thought and related research programs. Some relevant conclusions are also drawn for the study of the Economics of both Developed and Developing Nations.

## Some Methodological Considerations

The orthodox or mainstream economics (of developed nations) stands on universalist, rationalist, and positivist methodological pillars. The universalist foundations can be traced to aspects of classical Greek thought and the emphasis that was placed on innate ideas and the power of reason in deciding what was to be accepted as truth. A central proposition in classical Greek philosophy is that truth is universal and necessary, and therefore contradictory to the everyday world of accident and change. Since the primary concern was with establishing universally valid laws and concepts of change, truth and knowledge were considered to be logically prior to the mastery of nature and society.

This was the forerunner of a rationalist world view based on *a priori* reasoning as the mechanism for grasping eternal truths about the world. In the context of economics and other forms of intellectual inquiry, this theory of knowledge favors meditation and the acceptance of given truths as against laboratory experimentation, and mathematical as opposed to inductive procedures of investigation. The universalist-rationalist outlook was strongly influenced by the views of rationalist philosophers such as Descartes. He posited that, in the quest for knowledge and truth, we must accept only those ideas that are reasonable, clear,and distinct, that is, self-evident. Descartes saw the possibility of constructing the entire body of science just by making use of our own reason, and without recourse to experience.

The pure rationalist viewpoint was later challenged by nominalist theories of knowledge that deny the existence of innate ideas, except for those ideas that are connected with rules of reasoning. Such patterns of thought are primarily associated with the classical British empiricists— Locke, Berkeley, and Hume—who stressed the possibility of gaining knowledge through sense experience. This view came to influence the philosophy of logical positivism, which is based on a distinction between *matters of logic* and *matters of fact*, or *logical truth* as distinct from *factual truth*. Logical truths are true by definition, while factual truth takes the form of empirical statements that are concerned with the nature of evidence.

The rationalist-empiricist philosophy of knowledge has formed the basis of a positivist methodology that guides orthodox thinking in modern social science. This methodology is based on the notion that "science" is the only valid form of knowledge, and facts its only possible objects. It therefore denies the existence of substances or forces that go beyond facts or laws that are discoverable on a scientific basis, except, of course, for deductive rules of reasoning. Thus, the impact of positivism on the social sciences has been trasmitted primarily through the emphasis placed on the "scientific method" or the "scientific approach" in arriving at the truth, that is, in terms of a unity of methodology between the natural and the social sciences. This methodological approach is at the heart of neoclassical research programs in the Economics of both the Developed and the Developing countries. In general, it tends to be based on a conception of "science as science" as distinct from the moral, political, sociological, psychological, and other "noneconomic" aspects of scientific and intellectual inquiry.

The claim of a unity of methodology in all sciences is usually explained in terms of the hypothetico-deductive method underlying the logic of explanation. This can be illustrated by what is known as the *Covering Law Model of Explanation* (Hempel and Oppenheim, 1948; Hempel 1965). The law basically states that the occurrence of an event is explained when it is subsumed under, or covered by, a law of nature, that is, when it can be shown to have occurred in accordance with some general regularity of nature. However, since universal laws are rare in the social sciences, statistical, probabilistic, and historical laws are sometimes accepted as the basic laws of nature. Such laws may take the following forms: (1) deductive generalizations based on observation; (2) theoretical laws or principles from which empirical laws could be derived; or (3) a process of microreduction in which macro properties are explained in terms of micro properties, for example, where generalizations about society are explained by reference to, or by deductions from, the behavior of individuals (Brodbeck 1968).

Thus, the dominant methodological view is that the Covering Law Model provides the only scientific basis for explanation, and therefore should be strictly applied in the study of all human affairs. In applying the method suggested by this model, the scientist or economist is supposed to describe facts as minutely as possible, quantify what is quantifiable, and construct theoretical frameworks that are as elaborate as possible. The latter are supposed to help analysts to gain a better understanding of the problem being analyzed, thereby improving their ability to better explain, predict, or control the surrounding environment.

Besides the influence of positivism and other rationalist-empiricist patterns of reasoning, orthodox economic thinking also makes heavy use of the concept of mechanical equilibrium that has been borrowed from the physical sciences. In this context, the major influence has been provided by Newtonian physics and the evolutionary biology of Darwin and Spencer (Evolutionary Positivism). The main idea derived from evolutionary positivism is the concept of mechanical determinism, that is, a process of universal, necessary, and progressive evolution. This is, in turn, linked to mechanical equilibrium, which is explained by the self-regulating operation of equilibrating forces. Such forces, it is argued, not only tend to maintain equilibrium of the economic system but also to restore this equilibrium once it has been disturbed by external forces.

In its evolution, the concept of mechanical equilibrium has had to be based on some conception of the economic system. Accordingly, it was thought that the evolution of any logically consistent economic order required some institution of private property as well as a sharp conceptual distinction between the economic system and other aspects of social reality. This led to an emphasis on a capitalistic, free-enterprise ethic based on the principle of individualism. In this conceptual mode, individuals are considered to be at liberty to organize their social relationships in accordance with their own interests. Society therefore becomes no more than a collection of individuals, and individual behavior the goal and standard of moral behavior. As is well known, this utopianism was not only an offshoot of Newtonian mechanics but was also emphasized in the writings of Adam Smith, whose *Wealth of Nations* (1776) still provides one of the foremost statements of the individualistic and libertarian philosophy.

In modern economics, this pattern of thought has come to influence the ascendancy of *methodological individualism*. The philosophy postulates that the ultimate constituents of society are individual people who act appropriately in accordance with their own dispositions. In other words, the argument is that no social tendency exists and that theorizing about classes and other collectivities can only be represented by mental constructs, which are abstract models for interpreting certain relations among individuals. One implication is that it is impossible to have laws about society. Another is that the good of individuals is the primary objective of society (Hayek 1948, 1952; Friedman 1962).

The methodological principles stated above have come to have a lasting influence on contemporary economic thought. One such influence follows in the tradition of Cartesian mechanics alluded to earlier. The implication is that social scientists should be conservative, should not make daring or innovative assumptions in social thought, but rather should rely on self-evident and familiar material. This is the "curve-fitting" view of science, which posits that scientists should merely look for regularities in experience. Accordingly, economic models, theories, and conceptual systems should be considered devices that merely help the analysts to remember certain predictable regularities in observed phenomena.

A related implication follows from the widespread acceptance of the Covering Law model and the "science as science" methodology. These are based on the claim that the search for knowledge should be governed by scientific objectivity and the commitment to universal values that cut across national frontiers. Adherence to universal epistemological principles implies that there are common standards of scholarship and, as Streeten states, ". . . there cannot be African, Asian, and Latin American criteria for truth and validity. Mining companies can be nationalized, criteria for truth cannot" (Streeten 1974, p. 1293). As further emphasized below, the universalist thesis is also exemplified by the fact that economics is viewed as a positive science. As such, it is concerned with the logic of choice and related interactions among rational, homogeneous, and cooperative beings. As a result, economics is sometimes mistaken for a form of logic, truth for validity, and criteria for truth for its empirical content (Streeten ibid.).

## Price Fundamentalism
## and Economic Decisions

The universalist epistemology finds a foremost representation in the study of resource allocation. The underlying premise is that all societies must make decisions about the degree of sacrifice that must be borne if resources must be allocated efficiently. This is based on the assumption of a universal scarcity of resources relative to human wants and needs. Given scarce resources, it is impossible to satisfy all of society's goals simultaneously. Thus, if scarce resources are to be efficiently utilized, they must be properly allocated. The possibility of deriving meaningful benefits from the use of these resources is therefore predicated upon the nature of sacrifice.

The problem of economic decision making in conventional economics is therefore couched in terms of a "cost-benefit" calculus. This is related to the quest to derive maximum benefits from the scarce resources available. For example, it is assumed that consumers try to derive maximum benefits from the use of their incomes and thus have to make the choice of allocating their limited income between consumption expenditure and savings. In a similar vein, it is assumed that producers, in their quest for maximum returns, would try to allocate their productive resources (land, labor, capital, and so on) "efficiently" among alternative uses. These are examples of the general problem posed by scarcity, that is, the quest to obtain maximum benefits from given or fixed resources, or, alternatively, a given set of benefits from maximum means.

The orthodox approach to this problem emphasizes the need for rational choice in the use of scarce resources. The basis of this approach is that if the alternatives presented to us are not rationally chosen, resource scarcity is likely to increase with the passage of time, thereby impairing current standards of living and reducing the possibility for future economic growth. In this context, orthodox explanations of economic behavior tend to rely heavily on the neoclassical model of competitive equilibrium, which assumes that the behavior of free markets and prices provides the necessary conditions for individual economic agents to achieve maximum economic welfare and personal liberty. It is grounded on the methodological individualism mentioned earlier, the implication being that individual economic decision-making units (households, firms, national governments, and so on) are free and rational actors whose behavior is guided by harmonious equilibrating forces.

The overall economy is assumed to consist of a large number of interacting markets that have a tendency to clear, that is, reach equilibrium, with the latter defined in terms of equality between demand, supply, and price. These conditions are presumed to hold for individual markets, that is, partial equilibrium, or in other cases where there is a set of relative prices for all goods and services, resulting in a simultaneous clearing of all markets, that is, general equilibrium. Given the quantities of resources of all kinds available to economic agents, consumer tastes and preferences, and production technology, the problem of general equilibrium revolves around the determination of the relative quantities of goods of all kinds that will be produced and consumed, the prices at which they will be exchanged, and how the earnings derived from resource utilization will be distributed.

Income distribution is therefore treated as a special case of the general theory of price relations. The overall philosophy is that it is possible for self-interested individuals in a market-oriented economy to strive for, and receive, their fair share of income and wealth created by the competitive process. In this context, the orthodox model posits that marginal productivity forms the basis for payments to all factors of production. The assumption is that individuals have at their disposal a set of factor endowments and that income merely represents the sum of the product of these factors and their marginal products. The evolution of factor shares and incomes over time thus depends on factor prices and quantities, the elasticity of substitution among factors, changes in demand patterns, and the capital or labor-saving bias of technological change.

It is therefore assumed that, given competitive conditions and perfect information, resources will be efficiently allocated, and there is thus no need to tamper in any way with the manner in which the economic system gives out economic prizes. In other words, given the assumptions made above, adjustments in factor prices are expected to bring about equality in factor shares, with each factor receiving its "just" or equitable reward. Under the circumstances, any attempt to enforce equality in the prevailing pattern of income distribution is considered inimical to economic growth and efficiency. To the extent that inequalities exist, they should be considered necessary for guaranteeing productivity levels.

The implications of the marginal productivity theory of income distribution can be further explained by considering the distribution of labor and capital incomes. In the case of returns to the human factor (wages and salaries), the theory suggests that differences in marginal products can be explained by differences in both innate and acquired abilities. These differences tend to be particularly acute in those societies, for example, developing countries, where highly skilled people are in short supply relative to the large supply of unskilled labor. The argument therefore is that individuals with relatively scarce skills would receive quasi-rents. These rents and other payment differentials would disappear as more people acquire skills through education and training.

One clear implication of the theory is that any attempt to equalize wages and salaries would prove to be inefficient. The implicit assumption is that pay differentials not only reward those with superior natural abilities but also serve as an incentive to those not so blessed to acquire skills and to increase their productivity and efficiency.

Second, marginal productivity theory explains the distribution of income from physical assets such as land (property income) in terms of differences in the marginal time preference between consumption and savings, and thus in terms of differences in risk aversion (Meade 1964). The general proposition is that people who accumulate assets tend to have a low rate of time discount, save and invest more, and generally have a low risk aversion, that is, they are willing to take extra risks in order to earn higher returns on accumulated assets. Differential rates of return on physical assets are therefore rationalized on the grounds that they are an incentive to people to accumulate such assets. For a fuller discussion of marginal productivity theory and its ramifications, see Frank and Webb (1977).

Returning to the general case of the orthodox model, the overall philosophy is that, given competitive conditions, and assuming that a system of prices exists in the economy, each individual economic agent will behave in a manner as to derive maximum economic benefits from their economic actions. Individual owners of productive resources will sell their services at a price, with the income earned seen as representing the sacrifice they have to bear. A part of this income is spent on consumer goods, with the rest saved and invested in the creation of capital and intermediate goods required for the continuation of the productive process. Entrepreneurs buy the various productive services and utilize them to produce goods and services at maximum profits or minimum costs. Thus, given a set of competitive prices, the actions and reactions of individual economic agents will determine the quantities of goods and services demanded, and these will be matched by the quantities supplied in the various markets of the economy.

The achievement of such an overall equilibrium requires two sets of conditions. First, there is a subjective one in which the individual pursues the goal of maximum income and satisfaction. The second is an objective one in which the market provides for these incomes and wants based on the maximum profit goals of business people. Thus, through the equilibrium between demand and supply, with all markets cleared, the optimum economic position reached by each individual economic agent becomes compatible with that attained by others.

General equilibrium theory essentially postulates that, in principle, the set of equilibrium prices tends to provide all the information that each individual economic agent needs to have in order to be able to coordinate its activities with those of all other economic agents in the economic system. It is therefore based on the assumption of perfect knowledge and foresight, and the absence of uncertainty. This ensures that the requisite adjustments would take place if a disequilibrium situation were to arise. Where prices diverge from their equilibrium values, inconsistencies will arise in the plans of economic agents, and they would be forced to adjust to an equilibrium situation. The underlying assumption is that the operation of the market is based on a negative feedback mechanism that reduces discrepancies to zero through a process of iterative price adjustments. The market adjustment process is also assumed to be stable. This means that once the system diverges from its equilibrium path, a process of automatic readjustment would take place. Full employment is also implicitly assumed. With the demand for goods and services equal to their supply, labor markets will also clear.

Finally, orthodoxy considers this equilibrium to be the most efficient one, and thus the standard against which particular sectors of the economy as a whole should be appraised. The reasoning is that when overall economic equilibrium is achieved, each individual economic agent will have reached an "optimum" position, that is, one that it cannot possibly improve by altering its behavior. This is the utopian or ideal state described by Pareto. It is considered to be the most efficient state and implies that any attempt made to improve a given economic agent's position would have to be at someone else's expense.

Pareto optimality represents a zero sum society, with the ideal or optimum configurations of the economy defined in terms of a situation in which no one could be made better off without making someone worse off. Conversely, the state of the economy is considered to be improvable if someone could be made better off without making anyone worse off, even if some people have to compensate others to achieve this result. A configuration is therefore considered optimal when all other possible configurations are either inferior to the one in question or are not comparable to it.

## Free Trade, Efficiency Prices, and Social Profitability

The general framework outlined above is also replicated in the analysis of international economic relationships. In this case, trade and exchange are considered to be two of the most effective weapons for promoting resource allocation, distribution, and growth. This follows from assumptions of harmony of interests among nation states, patterns of trade based on comparative advantage, an equitable distribution of the gains from trade, and the free international flow of resources. The same normative forces are assumed to operate both nationally and internationally, with the private market considered to be the most effective mechanism for allocating and distributing resources in all spheres.

The model of trade based on comparative advantage can be summarized in terms of three basic propositions. First, in a no-trade situation in which two countries produce two commodities with different relative prices, both can profit by exchanging such commodities at an intermediate price ratio. In other words, both countries can gain from trade even if one of them produces the traded goods more efficiently than the other. The above proposition can be considered a generalization of the static model of international trade, which is based on very limited assumptions.

The model can be explained as follows. Assuming two countries with identical production functions, two factors of production, full employment, and perfect competition in domestic and international markets, it can be shown that both countries would be better off with free trade, or at least one country would be better off without any deterioration in the position of the other. In other words, the assumption is that by applying the principles of Pareto optimality and utilitarianism to international trading and exchange relationships, the likely result would be an improvement of world economic welfare as well as that of individual trading nations.

The second proposition is that countries should specialize in the production and export of those commodities that require relatively large injections of those factors of production in which they are relatively well endowed. Accordingly, a nation that is relatively well endowed with labor would specialize in labor-intensive products, while a capital-rich country would specialize in capital-intensive production. As further explained below, the gains that are likely to emanate from the process of specialization are both static and dynamic in nature.

The argument is that, given the conditions of international exchange, specialization according to comparative advantage and factor endowments would lead to increases in real incomes due to the beneficial effects on production. The static argument is that, given factor availabilities and

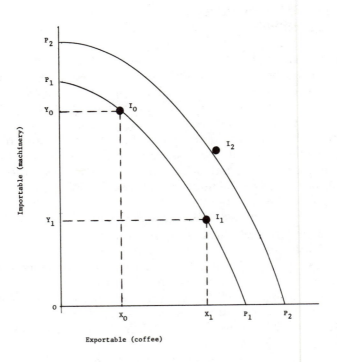

**Figure 2.1.** Comparative advantage and the gains from international trade.

production techniques, trade tends to inject more efficiency into the pattern of resource allocation. This is tantamount to a movement along a given country's production possibility frontier (see Figure 2.1).

In a more general sense, however, the beneficial effects of increased specialization are assumed to result from the increased domestic production and export of goods and services based on the exploitation of relatively abundant domestic resources, and the importation of those goods and services that cannot be produced domestically, either because it is too costly or impossible to do so. The dynamic benefits from trade stem from the exploitation of economies of scale, horizontal specialization (increases in product variety), vertical specialization (increased production of goods and services at various levels of sophistication, e.g., spare parts and accessories), and technological change.

These gains depend, in part, on the competitive nature of international markets and their size, with the latter setting a constraint on the division of labor. The size of the market is considered important for at least two reasons. First, during the early phases of development, countries tend to gain by importing those goods that can be produced more cheaply, and on a larger scale, in other countries. Under such circumstances, trade is considered to improve the supply of goods and services, for example, the intermediate and capital goods, necessary for development. The idea is that this helps to reduce domestic shortages and enables countries to overcome diseconomies stemming from the small size of their domestic markets. Second, while these markets exist initially for imports, they are expected to form the basis for import substitution and industrial development based on domestic market expansion during later stages of development.

The static and dynamic benefits of trade are illustrated in Figure 2.1. In the diagram, the commodity requiring relatively large amounts of the abundant factor (in this case, coffee, which is considered an exportable item) is shown on the horizontal axis, while the commodity requiring scarce inputs (machinery requiring scarce capital) is shown on the vertical axis. $P_1P_1$ is the original production possibility frontier or transformation curve, which shows the various combinations of the two commodities that can be produced, given the economy's resource endowments and available technology. First, suppose that the economy is at an initial equilibrium point $I_0$, with a combination of $X_0$ (coffee) and $Y_0$ (machinery) produced and utilized domestically. Second, as the country begins to trade, it specializes in the production of that commodity in which it is relatively more efficient (in this case, coffee) and reduces its production of that commodity whose production cost is relatively higher (machinery). Thus, with trade, the country moves to a point $I_1$ on the production possibility frontier, with the additional amount of coffee produced ($X_0X_1$) exchanged for machinery whose production has been reduced by an amount equal to $Y_0Y_1$.

The argument is that, in this new position, the economy is better off (measured in terms of a net gain) compared to the original situation. These primary or static gains can be attributed to net increases in real incomes stemming from the improved allocation of resources and, as mentioned earlier, constitute a movement along the production possibility frontier (from $I_0$ to $I_1$). However, over time, there will also be some dynamic gains that can be measured in terms of an outward shift in the production possibility curve. One such set of gains is predicated on increased productivity due to (1) increased market size, economies of scale, and increasing returns; (2) learning and related benefits resulting from increased access to new production technologies and managerial skills; and (3) benefits stemming from opening up the economy to competition and a wide range of international resource flows. A second set of dynamic benefits is associated with the vent for surplus, that is, the benefits accruing from the fuller utilization of resources that were formerly unemployed or underemployed, thereby allowing the country concerned to generally expand its production potential.

A third proposition is that commodity trade reduces, and may eventually eliminate, international differences in returns to factors (for example, interest rates, wages, and so on). The model postulates that, under certain assumptions, trade in factors of production could serve as a perfect substitute for commodity trade. The general idea is that, in a competitive world, maximum efficiency could be achieved either by a perfect mobility of goods across international boundaries or by a movement of factors of production. In other words, free trade in factors can become a perfect substitute for commodity movements, with trade in the latter leading to an indirect exchange of factors of production embodied in them. The overall implication is that, with free trade, there will be a tendency toward equalization of product and factor prices, and therefore real incomes, throughout the world.

Against the above background, a major concern in both mainstream Economics and the Economics of Developing Nations is with "getting prices right." In this context, the "right" prices are those that induce what are generally considered to be "appropriate" responses from producers, consumers, laborers, and other economic agents. As emphasized above, "appropriateness" connotes some idea of "efficiency," and prices are considered to be efficient when they induce efficient patterns of resource use. Three interdependent notions of efficiency are usually encountered in the neoclassical framework. The first is technical or engineering efficiency that involves the choice of combinations of factors of production or inputs that guarantee the highest production possibility, given available technologies. Second, there is the notion of economic efficiency that involves the attainment of maximum output from a given set of inputs or factors of production. A third concept is that of social efficiency (Pareto optimality). As explained earlier, this refers to the impossibility of rearranging patterns of production, consumption, and trade so that some people become better off without making others worse off.

These considerations have given rise to the use of "efficiency" or "border" prices as benchmarks for judging the optimality of resource use. Contextually, the real value of any resource to the economy as a whole is thought to depend on the alternative opportunities for its use. In cases where such resources can be traded (exported or imported), foreign trade is seen as offering the relevent opportunities. On this basis, the real value of importable commodities to the economy as a whole is given by its domestic price at the national border, that is, the c.i.f. price (the price inclusive of cost, insurance, and freight). On a similar basis, the real value of an exportable commodity to the economy as a whole is given by its domestic price at the point of export, that is, the f.o.b. (free-on-board) price covering all charges, including delivery at the designated point of shipment.

Importable and exportable goods are usually referred to as "tradeables," as distinct from items such as land, which are called "nontradeables." For tradeable commodities, "border prices" are considered to be the efficiency or accounting prices for the economy as a whole. For example, in the case of importables, the c.i.f. price represents the cost to the economy of acquiring an additional unit of imports; and for exportables, the f.o.b. price represents the real value to the economy of producing an additional unit of the exports. These prices are therefore considered to reflect the relevant opportunities the economy faces in the production and consumption of tradeables.

In the case of nontradeables, the relevant opportunities are analyzed in relation to the domestic market, and the efficiency values are given in terms of contributions made by considering the next best alternative uses. These efficiency values are usually termed "domestic shadow prices." Such shadow prices are equivalent to market prices in cases where markets are perfectly competitive. In other cases, the shadow prices of nontradeables are conceptualized in terms of some approximation to the accounting prices of tradeables. Thus, in the case of both tradeables and nontradeables, the concept of efficiency prices involves some notion of opportunity cost, that is, what has to be given up in order to pursue some course of action. Because of scarcity, the cost or value of utilizing any resource in a particular venture is the benefit foregone by not using it in the next best alternative use, and therefore implies a trade-off between opportunities.

For any given commodity or set of commodities produced in an economy, the decision rule for optimal efficiency of resource use is one of profit maximization or private market profitability. This represents the difference between the market value of output and the private cost of all inputs. These private costs and returns include the effects of all taxes, subsidies, government policies, and other market interventions. The concept can be defined as follows:

$$\text{NPP}_i = \sum_{i=1}^{N} a_{ji} P_i^d - \sum_{k=1}^{M} f_{ki} P_k^d \tag{2.1}$$

where $\text{NPP}_i$ is the net private profitability of the $i$th production activity, $a_{ji}$ is the quantity of the $i$th output produced or intermediate input used by the producing activity, $P_i^d$ is the domestic market price of the $i$th output, $f_i^k$ is the quantity of the $k$th primary factor of production or input used in the production activity, and $P_k^d$ is the domestic market price of the $k$th primary factor of production. The number of production activities is represented by

$i (= 1, 2, 3, \ldots N)$, and the number of factors of production by $k (= 1, 2, 3, \ldots M)$.

However, policies based on the private profitability criterion are unlikely to result in a nation's best or optimal use of its resources when monopoly elements or the presence of labor market segmentation gives price signals to producers that cause them to misallocate resources. Further, price distortions induced by government policies may cause the prevailing set of prices to diverge from the true opportunity costs of inputs and outputs. Four broad sets of such policies are usually encountered in practice: (1) foreign trade policies, including duties and other quantitative restrictions, subsidies on imports, and taxes/subsidies on exports that may cause domestic prices to diverge from international prices; (2) domestic pricing and institutional policies, for example, minimum wage legislation, maximum interest ceilings, and overvalued exchange rates; (3) input taxes/subsidies that cause the returns to producers to be different from what they would be if producers were to pay full costs; and (4) investment policies involving the long-term subsidization of capital creation, for example, through low and at times negative real interest rates (for a fuller discussion, see David 1985).

These institutional barriers and price distortions are thought to create a misallocation of resources and a divergence between private profitability and social profitability. The latter reflects the net national comparative advantage associated with production activities. In this case, a given country's resource endowments and the technical efficiency of production are all evaluated by using a set of international or "efficiency" prices. Contextually, a technique for producing an extra (marginal) quantity of a commodity is considered efficient if the value to the national economy of producing this extra output is greater than the social opportunity costs of the other commodities and factors of production used in producing it (see Pearson, Stryker, and Humphreys 1981; Timmer, Falcon, and Pearson 1984).

This social profitability is measured in terms of the difference between the value-added in world prices and the opportunity cost to the economy of obtaining this value-added. This value-added at world prices represents the net addition to national income evaluated at its social opportunity cost. It is defined as follows:

$$\text{NSP}_i = \sum_{i=1}^{N} a_{ji} P_i^b - \sum_{k=1}^{M} f_{ki} P_k^b \tag{2.2}$$

where $\text{NSP}_i$ is the net social profitability of the $i$th production activity ($i = 1, 2, 3, \ldots N$), $a_{ji}$ is the quantity of the $i$th output produced or intermediate input used by the production activity (as before), $P_i^b$ is the international, "border," or "efficiency" price of the $i$th intermediate input or output, $f_i^k$ is the quantity of the $k$th primary factor of production used in the production activity ($k = 1, 2, 3, \ldots M$, as before), and $P_k^b$ is the international price for the $k$th primary factor of production.

Thus, the measure of net social profitability involves at least two types of adjustments to the net private profitability criterion. First, inputs and outputs that are traded in international markets are valued at world prices to eliminate any transfer effects caused by government and other institutional policies. Output is valued at the price a country must pay for imports of a commodity (or which it can receive for its exports) instead of the actual market price that prevails domestically. Similarly, an input that can be purchased or sold abroad is valued at its international cost rather than at its subsidized or taxed domestic market price. The underlying rationale is that international prices measure the opportunity costs of producing various commodities because countries have the option of selling or buying goods abroad, irrespective of the degree of competition existing in these international markets.

Second, domestic resources of land, labor, and capital are valued to reflect their social opportunity costs within the country, that is, at the value of output foregone from not using these resources in their next best use. The first term on the right-hand side of equation 2.2 measures the level of value-added at world prices per unit of output generated by the production activity. The second term measures the opportunity cost of primary factor inputs evaluated at accounting or border prices. When the opportunity cost of these inputs exceeds the net addition to national income, net social productivity (NSP) is negative, and the domestic factors of production could be employed more profitably in the best alternative uses. A negative NSP implies a lack of comparative advantage and/or a loss of efficiency in the neoclassical sense. By contrast, production activities are considered efficient from the national perspective if the respective NSPs are positive, and the larger the NSPs the more efficient the production activities.

## The Dissent from Orthodoxy

Before turning to a consideration of development issues per se, it is necessary to draw attention to some general and specific criticisms that have been advanced against orthodox economic analysis. Economists of varying ideological hues contend that the analytical procedures of orthodox economics may be inappropriate and that much of the subject matter of orthodox economics has become irrelevant to real-world problems. Some of the general criticisms encountered in the literature include (1) the inadequacy of the theoretical constructs of orthodox economics, and the "thralldom of technique" (Heilbroner 1970); (2) the tendency for orthodox economics to concentrate on a narrowly defined set of problems; (3) its lack of predictive force; (4) the nonholistic nature of orthodox theory and its treatment of the abstractions of economics without paying attention to their inextricably linked noneconomic causes and consequences; and (5) the fact that much of economics is a "temperate zone" subject, and therefore may be "culture bound" (see, for example, Heilbroner 1970; Boulding 1970; Leontief 1971; Kaldor 1972, 1975; Myrdal 1973; Eichner and Kregel 1975; Gordon 1976; Robinson 1981; Balogh 1982; and Bauer and Walters 1975).

A pertinent question for both rich and poor countries is whether economic behavior should be interpreted from the much wider political, social, cultural, and institutional relations in society. In other words, the problem is whether there is not a need for a more comprehensive economics that would be concerned not only with market-related decisions but, more importantly, with the dynamic interactive processes in society. One strand of thought, emphasized in neo-institutionalist and Marxian research programs, advocates a "systems economics" rather than the dominant "market economics" as being more relevant to the study of economic and social life.

Such a systems economics would be based on holism and interdisciplinary modes of analysis. Related to the holistic method are principles of totality and interdependence. It is based on the premise that individual economic behavior cannot be defined outside the wider context of functional relationships among integrated wholes and their constituent parts. Such integrated wholes represent societal systems or organisms in which the behavior of some members tends to adjust mutually to situations created by others. At the philosophical level, the principle of totality is based on the premise that no unrelated ideas exist, but only as members of wholes. Therefore, in the study of social and economic phenomena, one should be prepared to provide exhaustive accounts and analyses of their relationship to some whole. The principle of interdependence forces the analyst to recognize the contextual nature of things and events, and to see the world as consisting of more than an aggregation of unrelated individuals, activities, and processes, in a purposeless environment.

During the process of interaction, individual economic agents tend to encounter obstacles stemming from the external constraints imposed by the larger society, both nationally and internationally. At both levels, the requisite socioeconomic order is not necessarily a harmonious one, but is replete with conflicts and tensions stemming from the interaction of individuals, social and economic classes, international economic actors, and nations. In this context, most heterodox thinkers argue that conflict is a ubiquitous feature of all social systems. One subgroup (Marxians) see this as resulting from one or more opposing forces within the system. It is therefore argued that we can only discover truth about the world by strenuously coming to grips with the systemic distortions and contradictory relations that define the behavior of society.

One implication of the systems or holist perspective is that free competition cannot be adopted as a logically consistent method for organizing economic life since there is no inherent tendency toward equilibrium. This is explained by the fact that social systems tend to be complex and open; the requisite actors are not only economic agents but political, cultural, and social beings as well. Their diverse action possibilities tend to be constrained by the distribution of resources of all kinds, by institutions in different spheres, and so on.

This issue can be interpreted from the perspective of the economic, political, and social rights that are supposed to exist in a civilized and democratic society. The foundations of modern social thought can be traced to early liberal concerns for economic justice and the principles considered conducive to equity and freedom. From this has emerged a view of the good society based on two fundamental principles. The first concerns the nature of economic rights. These are supposed to be arbitrated by market institutions, which, it is assumed, tend to guarantee equal incomes. The second is concerned with political and social rights that are supposed to be guaranteed by the principles of political democracy and democratic government. These political and social rights are supposed to be "given," and therefore not arbitrable in the marketplace. Thus the general philosophy follows from the assumption that the economic and political institutions of capitalism would guarantee equality in the distribution of rights, that is, equal rights and privileges for all members of society.

However, as Okun (1975) has pointed out, a society that is both democratic and capitalistic in orientation usually faces a basic conflict between economic rights on the one hand, and political and social rights on the other. He terms this a conflict between "rights" and "dollars." At one level, this conflict reflects the unequal distribution of economic rights due to differential patterns of ownership and control over resources. At another level, it reflects the split-level structure of capitalist society, which rewards those who succeed and penalizes those who fail in the system of market relations. The general point of emphasis is that tensions tend to arise in several spheres, for example, between the economic principles underlying competition on the one hand, and the political and social principles of democracy and equality, respectively, on the other.

It is evident therefore that economic relations cannot be meaningfully wrenched from their larger societal context. As a further illustration, orthodox economists usually view the problems of production (what is produced), allocation (how it is produced), and distribution (who will benefit), primarily as *economic* decisions to be arbitrated in the marketplace. However, in both rich and poor countries, many of these decisions essentially represent problems of political choice.

In most societies, a critical institutional linkage in the overall economic decision-making process is provided by the government. For example, it usually has a tremendous impact on the distribution of economic prizes through a wider process of interest representation and patron-client relationships. In this context, a primary role is normally assigned to the budgetary process. In an ideal sense, the government budget and the related patterns of expenditure and revenue allocations should reflect the manner in which society intends to allocate and distribute resources to various groups and sectors in society. Both efficiency and equity criteria should be used in this process. In practice, however, the budgetary process has increasingly come to reflect the outcomes of political struggles. Thus, there are conflicts among various political groups and other segments of the population over whose preferences shall prevail in determining the parameters of national policy and the selection of specific programs.

We now turn to some specific problems in the area of orthodox economic analysis. The first concerns the centrality of place held by notions of scarcity and allocation. There can be no denial of the fact that in both rich and poor countries, economic agents always have to face the allocation problem. However, the intensity of this problem depends on the nature of the situation and ultimately on whether there is a genuine scarcity of resources. There are many situations in which resources of various kinds appear to be scarce, but are not actually so. In some cases, even moderate changes in ways of doing things can help to resolve the apparent scarcity of resources. In other situations where resources or means are scarce in relation to specific ends, the human agent can find ways of removing this obstacle. Of course, this would depend on the extent to which human agents are given the freedom and opportunity to make those adaptive responses considered desirable. This, in turn, depends on the nature of institutions and the manner in which they function.

A second problem concerns maximizing behavior and the rationality of choice. In general, it can be argued that maximizing of economic gains represents only one type of behavior, and it is possible for people to use several alternative approaches in attaining their economic and other goals. What may be rational in one society or culture may not be so in others. Different societies subscribe to different value systems, and these, in turn, determine what is ultimately desirable. Even within the same society, a person may not necessarily maximize utility or real income (in terms of the requirements of the cost-benefit calculus), but may be more concerned with "satisficing" or searching for satisfactory alternatives. The basic idea is that whenever individuals find alternatives that are satisfactory, they tend to reduce the search for additional alternatives. The underlying assumption is that a satisfactory alternative is always better than the level of aspiration.

Neo-institutionalists argue that levels of aspiration tend to be closely related to achievement goals and also change over time, depending on the degree and level of achievement. Both achievement and aspiration levels can be assumed to move in the same direction, with aspiration levels adjusting better upward than downward. Further, the discovery of satisfactory alternatives tends to set limits to aspiration levels (Gordon 1973).

This situation can be further explained in terms of the perceived role of human motivation in the economic decision-making process. As a general proposition, it can be argued that, besides his basic biological needs, man does not start off with a structured set of wants and needs. These evolve as he develops. This phenomenon is explained by theories of motivational psychology that attempt to identify and explain higher order states associated with the achievement of various values of freedom, for example, self-expression, self-actualization, and self-determination. Two alternative types of explanation are given for the source of these qualities. Some theorists stress instinct, while others place greater emphasis on environmental influences. Whatever their true source, the general presupposition is that barriers to the attainment of these forms of freedom may be major contributory factors to social unrest, aggression, and ultimately the lack of economic progress.

The basic premise is that the satisfaction of the psychological needs of mature individuals requires the development of a human personality that is predisposed toward the various goals of freedom and development. The achievement of this requires, among other things, a movement from passivity to activity, dependence to independence, subordination to equality, and awareness to self-control (Argyris 1957). Maslow (1957) looks at the same issue from the perspective of a needs hierarchy. Within this hierarchy, there are certain basic needs that are transcultural, while "higher order" ones such as self-actualization and its correlates are culturally determined.

Maslow first identifies the basic physiological needs for food, clothing, shelter, and reproduction, followed by the need for love, affection, and the sense of belonging. Once these basic needs are satisfied, others come into the picture, for example, self-esteem (achievement, adequacy, mastery, competence, independence, and confidence) and self-actualization. The achievement of self-esteem, self-actualization, and other higher order motives depends on the prior satisfaction of the other needs in the hierarchy. In general, the satisfaction of all these needs is considered a necessary prerequisite for the development of a mentally healthy personality.

One conclusion emerging from motivational psychology is that economic agents cannot be considered goal-less entities whose behavior is governed by immutable forces beyond their control. This can be contrasted with orthodox assumptions of dependable behaviorial functions from which all future configurations of the economic system can be derived. However, things that people value change with the passage of time, as conditions and technology change, and as they become better able to adapt to changing situations. This instrumentalist view does not deny that man is capable of rational behavior, but places much more emphasis on the fact that behavior patterns are usually determined by the nature of institutions in society. Economics therefore becomes a goal-oriented discipline.

A third set of issues concerns the factors determining the distribution of income. In both rich and poor nations, there is reason to believe that differentials in wages and salaries, and therefore returns to the human factor, cannot be adequately explained by differentials in marginal products, especially where market imperfections and structural rigidities exist. In both types of societies, the wages and salaries of large numbers of people are not determined by competitive market forces, but by the manner in which institutions function. In general, wages and salaries tend to diverge from the competitive norm because of labor market segmentation.

There are many explanations of labor market segmentation (for a review, see Cain 1976). In the typical case, the economy can be divided into two sectors—one primary and high wage, and the other secondary or low wage. There are two distinct types of jobs and occupations in the two sectors and a substantial divergence in the behavior of firms and individuals between them. Jobs in the primary or internal labor market are usually marked by the following characteristics: relatively high wages, favorable working conditions, employment stability, and good chances of advancement. The reverse is true of the secondary labor market. Not only do wage and employment mechanisms differ sharply in the two sectors, but economic mobility from one to the other tends to be institutionally restricted. This is explained by the fact that labor markets are usually characterized by various mechanisms that protect employers and employees alike, with both groups having an incentive to maintain past and present forms of segmentation.

Factors other than efficiency play a crucial role in the primary or internal market. The system is not an open one, with jobs and earnings in this market determined more by forces of custom than by productivity considerations. In the case of the secondary market, workers tend to remain trapped in dead-end jobs that offer very little scope for advancement, with employers having very little or no incentive to promote stable employment relationships. Further, several structural and institutional mechanisms, for example, discrimination by race, class, ethnicity, and sex, tend to restrict movement from the secondary to the primary market, giving rise to various forms of unemployment and underemployment. What makes this dual labor market theory more credible than the competitive theory of wage determination is its emphasis on the various discontinuities and structural rigidities that define real-world labor markets.

Besides the influence of labor market segmentation, wages and salaries tend to diverge from the competitive norm because of the fragmentation of capital markets. This implies that there is not equal access to education and training as a means of acquiring requisite skills. Capital market fragmentation restricts the borrowing power of poor families who may be desirous of financing the education and training of their children, and only the very rich can forego income during the periods required for such education and training.

There are also difficulties with orthodox explanations of the distribution of income from assets. As mentioned earlier, differential rates of return on physical assets are explained in terms of marginal productivity theory. These returns are supposed to provide incentives for people to accumulate such assets, for example, buying and improving land, investment in buildings, equipment, machinery, and other capital assets. The returns to such investments may take several alternative forms, for example, pure rent, interest income, and so on. There are both theoretical and practical limitations to this approach.

At the conceptual level, this approach has been criticized, especially by neo-Keynesians (Cambridge capital theorists), on the grounds that it is based on some heroic assumptions that do not hold in practice. One such assumption is that the rate of interest be equal to the marginal productivity of capital or that of capital goods in general. For this assumption to hold, however, capital must be conceived of as a homogeneous product. In practice, capital is heterogeneous. Neither can it be measured as a factor of production, nor is its value as a means of production uniquely determined (see Robinson 1956; and the collection by Sen 1971).

A related problem concerns the possibility of "reswitching" (Kaldor 1955; Sraffa 1960; Harcourt 1972; Sen 1971). While the debate on reswitching is a complex one, the basic problem can be explained as follows. In the neoclassical (marginal productivity) model, the conditions for producing a given commodity are usually described in terms of a pseudo-production function that describes an infinite range of production or transformation possibilities based on alternative factor combinations. Each point on the production curve is supposed to represent a distinct method of production or "technique" that depicts the equality between the ratios of marginal productivities and the corresponding ratios of factor prices. Each production technique is therefore supposed to reflect a unique set of factor prices (wages, profits, rents, interest rates). A further implication is that under competitive conditions, and given the state of technology, changes in relative factor prices would effect corresponding changes in production methods and techniques. For example, if wage rates were to increase relative to profits, there will be a shift to more capital-intensive techniques of production, and vice versa.

In this context, reswitching essentially concerns the possibility of ordering production techniques according to various ranges of profits and wages associated with them. Cambridge capital theorists argue that it is perfectly normal for the same production technique to be eligible at several discrete rates of profits and wages. In other words, there can be reswitching between capital- and labor-intensive techniques. In neoclassical analysis, lower wages tend to be associated with a more labor-intensive technique. However, the argument is that, over certain ranges of the production function, the technique that becomes eligible at a higher rate of profit, with a correspondingly lower wage rate, may be less labor-intensive than that chosen at a higher wage rate, that is, it may have a higher output per person employed.

A basic difficulty facing marginal productivity theory stems from the fact that it is an equilibrium theory that is based on an assumption of a tendency toward equalization of returns to assets and factors. In practice, however, what is typically encountered is a disequilibrium situation marked by substantial divergences in returns to factors among owners and sectors of the economy. Some of the causal factors were mentioned earlier. Some further elaboration is provided below.

One set of rival theories is based on the phenomenon of a dual class structure stressed in classical political economy, with (1) workers whose income is derived solely from wages and salaries, which represent payment for their labor services, and with the larger proportion of this income spent on personal consumption and (2) capitalists whose income consists solely of profits derived from their ownership of the means of production. These two classes are distinguished by differences in their respective marginal propensities to consume or save, with the marginal savings of wage and salary earners relatively small compared to that of capitalists.

The differential savings hypothesis has formed the basis for the neo-Keynesian theory of income distribution. As further explained in Chapter 4, the basic idea is that profits provide the major source of finance for capital expenditure so that capitalists tend to control the level and rate of investment. One implication for income distribution has been articulated in the "predator-prey" model of cyclical growth (Goodwin 1967). The model's emphasis is on the relationship between labor's share in national income and the employment rate in a growing economy. It posits that equilibrium between the appropriate income distribution and a balanced rate of employment can almost never be simultaneously attained. As a consequence, there tends to be a perpetual class conflict. This follows an assumption of a symbiotic relationship between wages and profits in a growing noncommunist economy.

The reasoning is as follows. When the share of workers' earnings in national income is at its highest, there is a concomitant reduction in profitability and a rapid increase in the reserve army of the unemployed. This, in turn, causes a reduction in the bargaining strength of workers and a shift in the income distribution against wages and salaries and in favor of profits. The depression comes to a halt when the unemployment level reaches its highest point. At this stage, there is a very rapid increase in the return to capital, and a turning point toward recovery sets in. The boom sets in when profitability is at its lowest point and employment expands rapidly. Recession sets in when employment becomes too high to be profitable. At the end of the recession, a new cycle of conflict begins again. This perpetual cycle of class conflict highlights the contradictions of capitalism. The livelihood of each class in society depends on the livelihood of the other, with workers and capitalists fighting for their share in national income.

This type of conflict theory is in the same vein as those that explain distribution in the context of differential power wielded by groups in society. At a fundamental level, distributional outcomes tend to be determined by the resources that groups in society have at their disposal, that is, by economic power. As articulated by Sen (1981), a person's command over resources in a market-oriented economy based on private ownership of resources depends on the nature of ownership rights and exchange entitlements, that is, what can be obtained in exchange for what is owned. This is usually achieved through relations of production and trade. However, large numbers of people may face severe limitations on income, basic needs support, and other resources they can command because of poor ownership rights and exchange entitlements. As emphasized earlier, this may occur because of market imperfections, government policies, and factors underlying the prevailing political and social structure.

Ownership bundles and exchange entitlements may collapse where land distribution patterns are highly skewed, or where there is a lack of equal access to capital and other resource markets. Many people lose command over the resources they own because of unemployment. Under such circumstances, they are not able to sell their labor power, or otherwise face a deterioration in their terms of trade. This is particularly true in cases where there are unequal or limited opportunities for acquiring education and skill.

The issues raised about income distribution partly reflect some of the drawbacks of competitive analysis and related assumptions about the nature of equilibrium adjustments. Present and future decisions are assumed to take place within a single point in time within the neoclassical schema, that ·is, instantaneous adjustments in the movements toward equilibrium. Needless to say, everything does not happen all at once in the real world. Despite its tremendous heuristic power, the idea of a competitive equilibrium must remain an unattainable ideal. The real world is defined by various forms of price inflexibility, uncertainty, market failure, and monopoly power. This casts doubts on the entire notion about Pareto optimality. In actuality, society is never at this ideal point, and it is arguable whether it is ever achievable. In general, since wants, tastes, resources, and technology are constantly changing, the optimal state also undergoes constant change. Further, it is not possible to define the ideal state independently of the path through which it is approached.

The Theory of Second Best has been developed by orthodox economists as a means of overcoming these difficulties. As indicated earlier, the utopian Paretian world is considered to be "The Best" or "The First Best," euphemistically speaking. The underlying assumption is that it is the most efficient and that there are no obstacles to the operation of freely competitive market forces. By contrast, "second best" situations are thought to represent certain behavioral and environmental constraints that stand in the way of achieving optimal efficiency. Examples of behavioral constraints can be found in situations where business people have goals other than pure profit maximization, where consumer behavior is influenced by nonmarket forces, or where workers have goals other than maximizing wages. Examples of environmental constraints include taxes, subsidies, monopoly, and various externalities related to production, consumption, and trade.

In the orthodox model, the presence of one or more of these constraints is considered to represent "distortions" in the optimal resource allocation process, that is, second-best situations. This has given rise to questions whether the optimal state is really the "best" one and whether the "second best" may not actually represent the "best" in some situations. In this context, it is now part of the conventional wisdom of orthodoxy that the achievement of optimal efficiency· may be impossible since it is predicated upon the removal of all forms of market distortions.

The case of tariffs on trade can be used as an example. A long time ago, Meade (1951) demonstrated that if a set of countries imposes tariff restrictions on trade among themselves, but two of them decide to remove tariffs on trade with one another, this will not necessarily result in a net welfare gain. The reason is that the removal of import restrictions from one trading partner is likely to cause the diversion of imports from third countries (against whose products the tariff still applies) to the country in which trade is now freer. If the latter country is a relatively high cost producer, and the country that previously supplied the exports a relatively low cost one, the net effect of freer trade might well be a diversion of output from low to high cost sources. Thus, the removal of one market distortion while others are still in force may result in a net reduction in economic welfare.

The general problem arises because orthodoxy sets up free competition and free trade as ideal or optimum situations, while the real world is replete with distortions. "Second best" situations seem to be the rule rather than the exception. The typical orthodox response is that there is an analytical advantage in setting up free trade and free competition as ideals. The argument is that it is easier to build a simple model based on these assumptions and note the deviations from it than to list a number of cases where the free competition/trade model is not applicable and generalize from these diverse situations.

In the case of both developed and developing countries, and especially in the latter case, there are several instances where trade and market intervention can produce a net gain in overall economic welfare. Given the wide range of development goals and objectives that countries variously pursue, intervention may be justified, for the following reasons, inter alia: (1) employment creation; (2) the promotion of forms of domestic self-reliance, especially in food production; (3) as a means of improving the internal and external terms of trade; (4) in order to provide infant industry protection and reap the benefits that are likely to accrue from learning-by-doing, economies of scale, and technological change; and (5) the need for some countries to insulate themselves against the effects of foreign trade barriers. A point of emphasis is that all countries, rich and poor, tend to attach independent weights to these goals, irrespective of the requirements of Pareto optimality or efficient resource allocation in the short run.

As discussed elsewhere (David 1985), this is germane to the more specific issue surrounding the applicability of neoclassical price analysis to the developing countries. In general, the problem arises because these countries face a large number of structural and institutional rigidities and supply bottlenecks. These are exemplified by resource immobility, market fragmentation, and disequilibria between sectoral demands and supplies. These, in turn, cause bottlenecks in the supply of foreign exchange, savings, intermediate inputs, and in production. Many of these rigidities are endogenous and reflect the overall lack of development. Others are traceable to factors operating in the wider international economic system (see Chapter 7). A large number have been induced by the economic policies followed by several developing countries, with many economic sectors administered in the pursuit of goals other than efficient resource allocation.

The policy instruments used have included various forms of price fixing through trade monopolies, exchange controls, quantititive restrictions on trade, as well as the usual decisions on taxes, subsidies, and investments. As a result, many price, cost, and other "distortions" have emerged, with correspondingly wide divergencies between price incentives and social goals. Under these circumstances, the structural and institutional rigidities cannot be expected to move resources in the desired direction of short-run allocative efficiency.

# II

# THE ORTHODOX ECONOMICS
# OF DEVELOPING NATIONS

# 3

# *The Development Quest and the Economic Growth Solution*

Orthodox thinking about development and underdevelopment is rooted, explicitly or implicitly, in several related currents of intellectual history. The meeting point is the universalist epistemology alluded to in the previous chapter. The underlying intellectual model views development as a rational process of modernization based on certain universal factors of growth and change. The process is considered to be an evolutionary one, defined in terms of the increasingly adaptive capacities of countries, structural differentiation, and functional specialization. Related to the evolutionary process is a kind of homogenization whereby developing countries come to acquire polar ideal characteristics found in the Western economic model.

## The Philosophy of Modernization and Ideal Types

The modernization ethic is based on the implicit assumption that developing countries are "deviant" examples of the Western growth and modernization experience and that all human history should move inexorably toward the same destiny and value system adopted by Western man. This value system, and the related process of adaptation, emphasizes the need for developing countries to embrace certain "modernization ideals," including the achievement of high levels and rates of growth in aggregate income and output; a high degree of urbanization, commercialization, and industrialization; extensive social and geographical mobility; an extensive and penetrative system of mass communications; and the widespread involvement of members of the society in modern economic and social processes.

Social scientists who view development from a modernization perspective differ in terms of the emphasis that is placed on one or more of these ideals. However, there is consensus on the importance of increased income and output as a necessary condition for achieving the broader dimensions of social change. As one modernization theorist states: "Modernization produces the societal environment in which rising output per head is effectively incorporated. For effective incorporation, the heads that produce (and consume) rising output must understand and accept the rules of the game deeply enough to improve their own production behavior and to diffuse it throughout the society" (Lerner 1968, p. 387).

Given the income or output ideal, some writers emphasize the importance of industrialization in the transition from "traditional" or "pre-modern" to "modern" society. This involves "the extensive use of inanimate sources of power for economic production, and all that that entails by way of organization, transportation, communications, and so on" (Moore 1963, p. 92). In this context, emphasis is usually placed on the importance of energy use and technology as integral parts of the cultural change and socioeconomic reorganizations that are supposed to accompany increases in income and output.

Industrialization is also considered to be linked to urban growth, with "primate cities" evolving as "growth poles" around which a set of manufacturing, service, and political activities cluster. The reasoning is that such locations normally build up several strategic externalities and net benefits that provide the momentum for future economic growth. This forms part of a much more embracing philosophical perspective that sees urbanization as a motive force in national economic growth, due to the externalities and agglomeration economies that have been associated historically with the growth of large cities and their pivotal role in the industrialization process.

From the perspective of intellectual history, the view of development in terms of modernization can be traced to the philosophy of "ideal types." The sociologist Max Weber is credited with the development of this philosophy as a means of explaining polar types of social action. In the Weberian schema, the ideal type represents a model of what actors in a situation would do if their behavior were completely rational. This is articulated in terms of a contrast between two polar action possibilities: "traditionality" vis-à-vis "rationality" or "modernity." His view was that the ideal type tends to facilitate *Verstehen* (understanding) by providing a vocabulary or grammar for the clear description of reality and by aiding in the construction of causal hypotheses that purport to explain behavior that deviates from the norm (Weber 1930, 1947).

Related to the notion of the ideal type is the extent to which every social system attempts to establish and cultivate a belief in its own legitimacy, that is, the extent to which the existing social order is accepted as a natural order. This, according to Weber, involves a legitimization process based on "power," "imperative control," and "discipline." The existence of "power" connotes the probability that actors in a social relationship will be able to carry out their own will regardless of forms of resistance. "Imperative control" refers to the probability that specific commands will be obeyed, and "discipline" refers to the probability that commands will receive automatic obedience in stereotyped forms. These notions are also related to Weber's three examples of ideal types. One is his distinction between three "pure types" of authority—traditional, legal, and charismatic. Another is the theory of competitive markets in economics. However, his most celebrated application of the concept was in his idea of a "Protestant ethic." As is well known, he used this notion to argue that the development of European capitalism could not be explained in purely economic or technological terms, but more in terms of the emergence of an ascetic and secular morality.

From the perspective of intellectual history, Weber's ideas could be interpreted in the much wider context of classical social thought. One distinct strand posits an interdependence between overall economic growth and the growth of individualism. This variant stresses certain processes that have been historically associated with economic growth, for example, occupational differentiation, the growth of urban occupations, the demystification of religion, and the erosion of social systems that emphasize group loyalties. A related strand of thought posits the necessity to recognize the existence of an authority that demands a forfeiture of certain rights. Weber views this authority in terms of a benevolent dictatorship that has no peer with respect to its structure and efficiency.

In general, the influence of the above pattern of reasoning on modern social thought can be explained in terms of its emphasis on a dualistic approach to the study of economic and social phenomena. In the development context, it is exemplified by a world view that dichotomizes countries in the world into two basic polar ideal types. In this intellectual model, the typical features of a "developed" or "modern" society are abstracted as a polar ideal type, and these are then contrasted with what are considered to be the ideal-typical features of countries at the other extreme of the pole. These countries are variously called "underdeveloped," "developing," "less developed," and "Third World." The various connotations attached to each of these labels form part of a

"Diplomacy in Terminology" discussed by Myrdal (1970). We do not pursue that aspect here.

Problems of semantics and linguistic diplomacy aside, the process of development is then conceptualized as a historical transition or evolution from the latter ideal-typical situation to the former, with a prototype of a developed country considered to be the typical Western industrialized nation. A related conceptualization places emphasis on certain perceived "development gaps" between the two polar types of countries. In this "gap approach," the typical features of a developing country are subtracted from those of a typically developed one, and the difference represents the gaps that must be closed during the transition process (Kindleberger 1958).

At one level of analysis, these gaps are thought to include pivotal economic scarcities with respect to savings, skilled manpower, and strategic goods and services (capital goods, essential materials, power, transportation, and the like). In this context, the most critical problem facing the majority of developing nations is considered to be their inability to raise the currently low investment levels. The consequence is a slow pace of economic growth. This implies a necessity to increase the supply of real resources available for investment by removing the domestic savings gap.

The philosophy underlying the gap approach has also formed the basis for the conventional approach to development planning. In conventional development planning, alternative macroeconomic growth targets are usually set, and these are considered achievable through the supply of certain key inputs (e.g., capital, labor, and foreign exchange) required to satisfy these targets. In the case of these inputs, the estimated requirements are first compared with projections of anticipated supply availability as a means of ascertaining shortfalls or gaps between supply and demand for these scarce resources. This also provides an indication of the direction and magnitude of efforts that will be required to fill these gaps if the relevant growth targets are to be achieved.

This pattern of reasoning is also replicated in the analysis of the social structure and its adaptation. A good illustration is provided by the Parsonian notion of "pattern variables" (Parsons 1951). In line with Weber's philosophy of "ideal types," Parsons used the notion of "pattern variables" as a means of explaining the dilemmas of orientation that are likely to confront an actor in a social situation. His view is that any social system or social action can be exhaustively analyzed in terms of five contrasting pairs of pattern variables, which are supposed to characterize all possible forms of social action. These include (1) affectivity versus affective neutrality, (2) collective versus self-orientation, (3) particularism versus universalism, (4) ascription versus achievement, and (5) diffuseness versus specificity. The process of economic development is then conceptualized in terms of shifts in prevailing choices in the pattern variables:

from affectivity to affective neutrality, from collective to self-orientation, from particularism to universalism, from ascription to achievement, and from diffuseness to specificity.

First, affective neutrality is demonstrated when an actor postpones or renounces immediate gratification in favor of future satisfaction. A common example is the decision to save and invest rather than the reliance on present-oriented benefits to be derived from current consumption and expenditure. This orientation toward the future and the related motivation toward increasing capital accumulation are considered important vehicles for the future expansion of economic resources, and therefore economic growth. Affective neutrality is therefore based on the Weberian Protestant ethic and reflects social relations that are contractual, legalistic, impersonal, and calculating in nature. Such relationships define behavior in more developed, capitalist-oriented, societies. By contrast, affectivity connotes an orientation toward the present, a lack of will to save, and a dislike for hard work and ascetic forms of existence.

Second, collective orientation refers to an attachment to communal forms of organization, for example, the extended family as distinct from individualistic and competitive forms of orientation.

Third, particularism connotes modes of behavior that are based on dimensions of the specific situation in which one finds oneself, or where a choice is made by reference to some particular quality in the individual at whom the action is directed ("who the individual is"). By contrast, universalistic patterns of behavior tend to be based on universally accepted precepts and rules. The general presupposition is that particularistic modes of action tend to be subjective and inefficient, thereby resulting in an underutilization of resources. In terms of polar contrasts, the presumption is that universalistic patterns of behavior tend to prevail in most highly developed societies, while particularistic exclusiveness tends to predominate in lesser developed ones.

Fourth, and in the case of ascription versus achievement, the choice possibility is between the achieved aspects of other persons, for example, their professional qualifications, levels of educational attainment, and so on, as distinct from ascribed characteristics such as sex, age, social class, and ethnicity. Achievement therefore implies a downgrading of the role of kinship systems and programs of "affirmative action," with more emphasis placed on recruitment based on "merit" and other "universal" attributes.

In the case of the fifth action possibility, the actor in a situation has to choose between limited and specific factors (specificity) and diffuse obligations (diffuseness), for example, between contractual obligations, on the one hand, and family loyalty, on the other. The point of emphasis is that more developed societies tend to exhibit greater organizational complexity, with an increasing importance of division of labor and specialization. Accordingly, development is construed in terms of a shift from social relations that are wide and all-embracing in scope to others in which actors confine their concerns to specific or specialized spheres of activity.

The dualistic pattern of reasoning underlying the notion of "pattern variables" is also exemplified in Hoselitz's "Index Method" (Hoselitz 1960). He used this method to interpret the behavior of individuals during the course of economic development and found the pattern variables to be highly intercorrelated. He concluded that in more developed societies there tends to be a correspondence between the functional specificity of economic roles and a greater emphasis on universalistic characteristics, as well as on achievement motivation. By contrast, economic roles in less developed societies tend to be more diffuse, there is a greater reliance on particularistic criteria, and a greater importance is attached to ascribed status.

First, more developed societies, it is argued, tend to allocate economic prizes on the basis of individual achievement, whereas their developing counterparts do so on the basis of ascribed status, for example, race, sex, kinship, or caste. In the former case, Hoselitz contends, the rewards to be derived from participation in economic activity are largely dependent on what individuals are able to achieve for themselves. It is facilitated by the fact that such societies typically have well-developed education systems that provide members of the population with the requisite skills needed for participation in diverse forms of economic activity. By contrast, the view is that economic roles in less developed societies are more or less defined by the criteria mentioned earlier. For example, men are hunters, while women perform specific roles on the farm in certain African societies. In a similar vein, members of certain castes in East Indian society tend to be priests, warriors, money lenders, bankers, and so on.

Further, Hoselitz posits that economic tasks in developing countries tend to be more diffuse due to the low levels of productivity and specialization. In the typical case, the individual performs several tasks, for example, as farmer, carpenter, and blacksmith. These multiple roles normally form part of the obligations imposed by family, village, or other kinship relations. By contrast, and as mentioned earlier, economic roles become more functionally specific, more highly specialized, and more economically complex as countries develop. Accordingly, they call for more specialized forms of training, and the process of job allocation and employment is increasingly based on factors such as educational attainment, training, and experience.

While no full-scale critique of the ideal-typical framework is attempted here, it can be commented that there are some developed societies in which particularistic criteria take precedence over universalistic ones. This has by no means proved inimical to the development quest in countries such as Japan.

Second, the model assumes that many of the rewards accompanying ascription are undesirable. In many societies, developed as well as developing, the institution of the extended family continues to make a positive contribution to the development process. In many respects, it is an important mechanism for resource mobilization, self-help, and other positive development attributes, for example, the case of ethnic minorities in the United States. Further, it plays a positive role in building family cohesion and in blunting the edges of the kinds of alienation that accompany industrial growth and urban life.

The pattern variables of development, that is, specificity, universalism, and achievement, tend to be associated with a middle-class ethic. The implication therefore is that development will be enhanced through the promotion of the middle class. While no attempt is made here to test the empirical validity of this proposition, the more recent experience of developing countries has revealed that the rise of the middle class, especially in urban settings, has not necessarily resulted in visible improvements in the living conditions of the masses of the population. In this context, it can be commented that development does not depend on fixed parameters. It is true that in many developing countries, the propulsive development influence is provided by modernizing elites who hold the reins of political and economic power. Even in this case, however, there is a predominance of particularistic tendencies that help to perpetuate the old socioeconomic order.

The general conclusion is that the conditions of underdevelopment would not simply disappear with a shift from one set of pattern variables to another, that is, from the diffuseness/particularistic/ascriptive modality of underdevelopment to the polar opposite of specificity/universalism/achievement. As further emphasized in Part III of this study, the abstract model based on polar ideal types neglects a consideration of the historical and structural factors in the international economy that help to perpetuate underdevelopment. To the extent that these factors help to explain the unequal and uneven development of nations, the latter condition cannot be totally ascribed to what are considered to be the "original" polar characteristics of underdevelopment, for example, traditional relationships such as low productivity, backward technology, and primitive agrarian conditions.

## Evolutionary Change and Growth Stages

The process of adaptation and transformation is also viewed as a gradual and continuous one based on sequential and inevitable macrohistorical growth stages. This philosophy is an outgrowth of the Newtonian notion of change mentioned in the previous chapter. It views development in terms of a gradual, evolutionary, mechanical, and unilinear process of adjustment in a world of perfect equilibrium. The price and market mechanism are considered to provide the requisite system of incentives for the establishment of a supporting institutional structure and for improving the capacity of people to make rational decisions geared toward the promotion of individual growth and achievement. The rationale is that such mechanisms tend to minimize conflict, thereby ensuring that development benefits all groups.

This pattern of reasoning has been eloquently articulated as follows:

> The ruling paradigm of the economics of development rests on the classical-neoclassical view of the world in which change is gradual, marginalist, non-disruptive, equilibrating, and largely painless. Incentives are the bedrock of economic growth. Once initiated, the growth process becomes automatic and all-pervasive, spreading among nations and trickling down among classes so that everybody benefits from the process. This view is analogous to the communicating vessels of elementary hydraulics; the pressure of the vessels with higher initial endowments leads to raising the water level in the other vessels. The mechanism that trips off change and restores equilibrium is the pressure created by non-identical endowments. The impulse is transmitted through the pipeline that connects the vessels. Analagously, development is initiated by incentives arising from inequality and is promoted by the market mechanisms that connect the rich and the poor. According to this paradigm, therefore, what is required for development is to create the proper incentives, to perfect the market mechanisms, and thereby to initiate the changes that lead to self-propelled take-offs. The incurably optimistic payoff is the general spread of development and the homogenization of the rich and the poor to the extent that they become indistinguishable (Nugent and Yotopolous 1979, p. 542).

The process of natural economic evolution is emphasized in various macrohistorical growth models that first indentify the economic, political, and social factors that have been traditionally associated with the historical growth process in developed nations and then extrapolating from these to the situation facing contemporary developing countries. The most well-known of these is Rostow's "Stages of Growth" or "Non-Communist Manifesto" (Rostow 1960, 1963, 1971). This model has been extensively discussed in the development literature, and its salient features are repeated here for emphasis and in order to maintain analytical continuity in the exposition. As is well known, Rostow identifies five such stages and contends that all societies belong to one stage or another. These are (1) traditional society, (2) the preconditions of take-off, (3) the take-off, (4) the drive to maturity, and (5) the age of high mass consumption.

The first stage, or traditional society, is primarily agricultural and is defined by low levels of production and productivity, a backward technology, and low levels of income. Such societies usually exhibit a feudal social structure, with political power centralized in the hands of a land-owning class. Historical examples are the dynasties of China, the civilizations of the Middle East and the Mediterranean, and the world of medieval Europe.

The second stage, or preconditions of take-off, refers to those societies in the process of transition from traditionalism to modernity. According to Rostow, this stage arises from some "external intrusion from more advanced Societies," and the modernization process is thereby set in motion. This stage is also marked by a diverse set of ideas concerning national consciousness, private profit, education, entrepreneurship, resource mobilization, and institutional change. However, he stresses that the new ideas and methods encountered at this stage result in only limited gains since most of the characteristics of the traditional society still remain. These include low productivity methods, old social structures and values, and regionally based political institutions.

Before the period of transition from the traditional to the take-off stage, the economy and society may go through some other basic changes. In Rostow's view, however, the motive force tends to be political in nature. A necessary condition for the third stage, or "take-off," lies in the emergence of an effective and centralized nation-state in opposition to the traditional landed interests and colonizers. Rostow gives as an example Western Europe during the late seventeenth and early eighteenth centuries when a series of forces led to the breakup of the Middle Ages. The take-off stage finally appears when resistances to change are overcome. This stage is characterized by (1) a rise in the rate of investment from around 5 percent of national income to 10 percent or more; (2) the emergence of one or more substantial manufacturing sectors with a high growth rate; and (3) the existence or quick emergence of a political, social, and institutional framework that exploits the impulses to expansion in the modern sector.

Further, the stimulating effects of new technology and the spread of social and economic overhead capital result in an expansion in new industries with relatively high rates of return. These, in turn, lead to the development of growth and employment potentials in secondary and tertiary activities, primarily in urban areas. The expansion of industrial activity in these modern "leading" sectors increases both savings and investment and stimulates entrepreneurial development. The techniques also spread to agriculture, which becomes increasingly commercialized. The associated revolutionary changes in agricultural productivity are considered an essential condition for successful take-off. Examples of the take-off, according to Rostow, include Britain two decades after 1783,

France and the United States several decades preceding 1860, Germany during the third quarter of the nineteenth century, Russia and Canada during the quarter century or so preceding 1914, and India and China during the 1950s.

The fourth stage, or the drive to maturity, depicts a regularly growing economy in which modern technology permeates the entire economic fabric of society. As the rate of technological innovation spreads throughout the economy, there is also an expansion of export and import propensities. This is accompanied by a new set of political and social values that are generally supportive of the growth momentum. In Rostow's schema, the maturity is generally attained about 60 years after the take-off. During this phase, the economy has the technological capacity and entrepreneurial skills to produce anything it deems economically feasible.

The fifth stage, or the age of high mass consumption, is one in which the leading sectors shift toward the production of durable consumer goods and related services. Standards of living have risen well above the necessary minimum, and there is a change in the structure of employment, with more blue-collar, white-collar, and urban cadres. It is the age of gadgetry, consumerism, and the predominance of the welfare state. This stage is supposed to have been pressed to its logical conclusion in the United States during the 1920s and again during the post-World War II era. Western Europe and Japan are supposed to have entered this stage during the 1950s. It is also thought that the Soviet Union is technically ready for this stage, though, as Rostow argues, communist leaders are likely to face difficult political and social problems of adjustment when this phase is launched.

In the contemporary development context, the stages are considered to have given characteristics that are supposedly alterable with concerted aid and the expected trickle down from the developed to the developing countries. This is thought to require transfers of capital, skills, education, the culture of savings and investment, and the capacity to create new sectors and institutions.

While the author is in no position to comment on details of historiography, the ideological bias underlying the Rostovian perspective is quite evident. Reference must also be made to the differences in the historical experiences of contemporary developing societies compared to that of the more developed countries during their transition. More generally, the view that development should follow certain uniform patterns that are applicable to all countries tends to abstract from certain unique dimensions of the historical, cultural, and political experience of developing countries. Further, Rostow's approach does not have any specific mechanisms of evolution that link the various stages or that can be used to justify the movement from one stage to another (see Baran and

Hobsbawm 1961; Frank 1967; Foster-Carter 1976; and the collection in Rostow et al. 1963).

From one perspective, it can be argued that the search for uniform and universal patterns of change is a fruitless exercise and that the concern should be more with "historical variations," that is, with the diversity in the historical patterns of growth (Gerschenkron 1968). The latter approach places less emphasis on the universal and uniform factors underlying growth stages and points to the relatively greater difficulty faced by contemporary developing countries in reaching the presumed "take-off." In this context, Gerschenkron has highlighted the fact that the industrialization process of developing countries differs considerably from that of their more developed counterparts, both in terms of the speed of development as well as in the productive and organizational structures that have been established. More specifically, his argument is that the more underdeveloped or "backward" a country is, the more likely it is that the subsequent patterns of development will be characterized by the following: a de-emphasis of agriculture, a high growth rate in manufactures, greater emphasis on large-scale and capital-goods industries, and greater centralization in entrepreneurial activity and financial institutions.

In conclusion, the significance of the "historical variations" approach lies in the fact that it allows the analyst to take into account the particular histories of developing countries and to formulate empirically relevant generalizations. In this context, Gerschenkron's view is that the historian's contribution to the understanding of the development process consists in pointing to potentially relevant factors as well as to potentially significant combinations of these that could be easily perceived within a more limited sphere of experience. A general implication is that decisions should be made on the basis of what history has taught us. Nevertheless, the primary policy determinants should be the material conditions and circumstances facing individual countries.

## The Desirability of Economic Growth

Within the overall context of modernization, the dominant analytical thrust in the Economics of Developing Nations is concerned with the phenomenon of economic growth. In the eyes of many economists, this "growth fetishism" stems in part from the world view that considers growth in aggregate income and output to be the most important proximate end of, and a necessary condition for, sustained economic development, modernization, and progress. In this context, the quest for human happiness and the "good life" becomes coterminous with the search for abundance of material goods and services that are considered necessary for human existence. There are differences of opinion about the optimal mix of such goods and services. However, the common practice is to specify some minimum bundle, with an emphasis on opportunities and rights relating to this bundle.

Contextually, a developed society is construed to be a materially wealthy one, and one in which the concomitant values of development are of a wealth-seeking nature. By contrast, less developed or developing societies are considered to be on this wealth-seeking path. In a broad sense, this wealth consists of all material goods and services that people use to satisfy their various wants and needs. It also includes the means of producing them, for example, land, labor, and capital. The latter represent claims over resources. These claims vary in direct proportion to the complexity of society and tend to increase in sophistication as society becomes more developed. Society's stock of wealth is considered to produce, in varying degrees, a flow of income, and there is a direct and cumulative relationship between the two. This is the familiar "circular flow of income." The larger the stock of wealth, the larger the resulting income flow is likely to be. This enlarged flow of income can then be used via the savings mechanism to increase the stock of wealth, and this conduces to a larger income flow in the future.

Economists usually distinguish between private (personal, corporate) and public wealth, depending on the ownership of, or claims over, material goods and services. The standard paradigm stresses private claims so that the quest for abundance or the "good life" becomes synonymous with a strife after personal wealth and individual achievement. In some accounts, this strife after personal wealth is given a moral connotation, that is, it is considered to be "good" or desirable. Others contend that while the pursuit of private wealth is not necessarily "bad," it must be accompanied by equality of opportunity for individuals and institutions in a wealth-seeking society.

It is in the above context that growth in the stock of wealth, and therefore in aggregate income and output, is considered a *sine qua non* for sustained economic progress. Rapid growth is considered desirable or preferable to no growth, or to growth that is too slow to meet material necessities. Lewis (1955) has identified the following benefits of economic growth: (1) it expands the range of human choice because it enables people to better control their environment, thereby increasing their freedom; (2) it affords people greater freedom to pursue leisure; (3) where political aspirations run ahead of the economy's ability to provide them because of resource constraints, growth may forestall unbearable political and social upheavals; and (4) it enables people to escape from unbearable starvation and servitude since it offers possibilities for the satisfaction of basic human needs.

To elaborate, while no one is likely to choose poverty and retardation over plenty and abundance, there are some situations in which the benefits of economic growth have to be weighed against the need to establish and maintain a sustainable society by protecting the human environment and enhancing human relationships. Nevertheless, people may prefer to tolerate a considerable amount of environmental degradation and social disruption in the quest for higher incomes and a more modern way of life. Conservationists and advocates of "limits to growth" emphasize the need to conserve both exhaustible and renewable resources on account of factors such as soil erosion, forest degradation, and the adverse effects of ecological disturbance (Brown 1981). While these concerns are important, they may be less pressing at low levels of development. In any event, Lewis' reply to the conservationists who call for the preservation of resources for future generations is an interesting one. He asks: "Why should we stay poor so that the life of the human race may in some centuries to come be extended for a future century or so?"

One important consideration is that the competition for survival, and therefore social tensions, tends to be much more marked at low levels of development compared to higher levels. This is because the majority of people are involved in a basic strife to escape from starvation, servitude, and other forms of dependency. The situation tends to be aggravated in those societies not governed by a plural majority, but otherwise defined by tribal, racial, ethnic, and similar social divisions. As the experience shows, the mere struggle for survival that takes place at low levels of development usually results not only in social divisiveness but also in various forms of militarism and political dissension.

It is also recognized that the quest for material gain and economic growth depends on the extent to which a competitive ethos is allowed to develop, that is, the extent to which people can seek out the seize opportunities for material gain. This requires an understanding and acceptance of new "rules of the game" that may run counter to traditional social and economic obligations. In this context, rapid material progress may be associated with undesirable economic, political, and social consequences. This is because the new rules of the game require the promotion of self-interests rather than the wider set of social obligations.

Some economists believe that the ability of countries to move on to the growth and development path is intimately bound up with the opportunities that are offered to a few innovative individuals to break out of the shackles and traditions of a static society. Members of this dynamic class include not only entrepreneurs but also capitalists, since the latter are considered to be the primary savers and investors in society. A further claim is that people's ability to maintain the growth momentum depends on the extent to which they are willing to work hard, steadily, and persistently, and, in general, subscribe to the Protestant ethic (Lewis 1955, p. 39).

At least three conditions must be satisfied if the above requirements are to be met. First, opportunities must be provided for those who are thrifty, industrious, and innovative to rise to the top. This requires that there should be a reasonably high degree of social mobility. Second, there should be a differentiated incentive structure that encourages hard and conscientious work and encourages people to seek relatively scarce skills, and therefore forms of employment for which there is a high demand. Such an incentive system would compensate people according to "hard work, conscientious work, for skill, for responsibility, and initiative" (Lewis 1955, p. 39). A third condition is the availability of a stream of goods and services to meet the basic and higher order wants of these cadres. This suggests a need for technological progress as a means of maintaining the pace of investment and to secure an adequate labor supply and quality.

Even if the above conditions for material progress are accepted, it can be commented, first, that the vertical mobility associated with such progress is never attainable without bias and malevolence. With economic growth, and the corresponding increase in the ability to transform resources, there may be a displacement of skills and jobs by machines, with an exacerbation of class conflicts between capitalists and workers. To the extent that this occurs, people will remain quiet only if government authorities are able to suppress conflict through the use of force, or otherwise introduce social and economic programs designed to reduce the negative impacts of the growth process.

Second, the requirements of economic progress outlined above are based on the implicit assumption that a certain amount of inequality is a necessary condition for moving the economy on a development path. It can also be assumed that some of this inequality will be preserved as the growth process gathers momentum. As mentioned earlier, the reasoning is that development requires an incentive structure that favors certain groups in society, and is therefore associated with income and other forms of inequality. In this context, one viewpoint is that it is better to have an unequal society in which no one is poor, even though some are rich, than an egalitarian society in which everyone is poor. This idea is forcefully articulated by Boulding as follows:

> It may very well be that in the long view of history inequality must be viewed as a protracted process of transition from the primitive society of

equal poverty to the ultimate goal of equal riches. In the long climb from the slough of equal poverty to the plateau of equal riches, certain individuals and groups lead the way, leaving others behind, and inequality develops. But because we are all roped together in the means of economic and social relations, the climbers cannot help pulling others after them and the whole level rises. Those who insist that we must all rise together or not at all may be actually condemning us forever in the slough of poverty (Boulding 1973, p. 81).

While not denying that a certain amount of inequality may be a necessary prerequisite for development, an important question concerns people's tolerance threshold for inequality. During the early phases of economic development, people can be expected to tolerate a certain degree of inequality, on the expectation that this will be reduced or eliminated as material conditions change. If this does not occur, the frustration and discontent that result may ultimately lead to tensions and open conflict. As one noted student of the subject states: "This tolerance is like a credit that falls due at a certain date. It is extended in the expectation that eventually the disparities will narrow. If this does not occur, there is bound to be trouble and, perhaps, disaster" (Hirschman 1973, p. 545). The process of transition from low to high levels of income and standards of living is not necessarily an orderly or harmonious one and typically involves various forms of adjustment and, at times, even revolutionary changes in institutions and ways of doing things. It may be associated with various costs inherent in the painful dislocations in traditional attitudes, beliefs, and institutions, as society moves from one way of life to another. Some of these changes may have to be forced, resulting in a curtailment of liberty. This poses a basic dilemma for the growth quest.

On the one hand, economic growth and progress are supposed to bring about expanded opportunities and freedoms. The latter involves freedom from want, poverty, starvation, joblessness, and so on; as well as the more "positive" freedoms to choose, and so on. On the other hand, where change has to be forced, it may be associated with reduced freedoms stemming from people's reluctance to change old ways and to accept new ways of thought and discipline. One aspect of this basic paradox revolves around the extent to which people are willing to make certain sacrifices and accept reduced freedoms in the short run in the expectation that they would achieve expanded opportunities and wider freedoms in the longer run.

Finally, it should be mentioned that maximum economic growth is considered a necessary prerequisite for the attainment of other proximate economic and social goals, including employment creation, the attainment of balance-of-payments equilibrium, and a satisfactory distribution of economic prizes. These proximate ends are considered to be by-products of the general process of economic growth and achieved through a diffusion of "trickle down" of the benefits of the growth process to all segments of the population. One implicit assumption about this diffusion process is that the social and political institutions will adapt readily to changes taking place in the economic sphere, that is, there is an automaticity in the nature of the responses of the noneconomic conditions to the economic ones.

# 4

# *The Philosophy and Analytics of Economic Growth*

The "growth fetishism" alluded to in the previous chapter is exemplified by the tremendous amount of intellectual capital that has been devoted to the generation of models and theories of economic growth. This chapter presents a panoramic view of the main orthodox approaches to the modeling of economic growth. At the outset, it should be stated that the objective is to highlight some of the major domain assumptions, analytical underpinnings, and broad philosophical thrusts that undergird the alternative theoretical perspectives. There is therefore less concern with the details of specific growth models, and the latter aspect is only touched upon for point of emphasis.

## Basic Macroeconomic Relations and Social Accounting

Most theoretical perspectives of economic growth are based, explicitly or implicitly, on some conception of how the economy, or its constitutent parts, function. A convenient point of departure therefore lies in considering how aggregate income or output is determined in an average economy, abstracting from country variations with respect to size, resource endowments, specific histories, development strategies, and so on. The general picture could be gleaned from Table 4.1, which is based on the United Nations System of National Accounts—called the SNA (see United Nations 1968). For ease of reference, some of the broad relationships are further summarized in Table 4.2.

**TABLE 4.1**: The consolidated accounts of the nation

*A. Domestic Product (value-added) and Expenditure*

| | Outgoings | | | | Incomings | |
|---|---|---|---|---|---|---|
| 1. | Income to labor (17) | 152 | 5. | | General government consumption expenditure (12) | 42 |
| 2. | Income to capital (19) | 55 | | | | |
| 3. | Depreciation (26) | 19 | | | | |
| 4. | Indirect taxes, net (20) | 29 | 6. | | *Less* direct purchases abroad by government services (−39) | −1 |
| | | | 7. | | Household consumption expenditure in domestic market (13) | 168 |
| | | | 8. | | Increase in stocks (23) | 6 |
| | | | 9. | | Investment (24) | 41 |
| | | | 10. | | Exports of commodities (32) | 50 |
| | | | 11. | | *Less* imports of commodities (−38) | −51 |
| | Gross Domestic Product (value-added) at purchasers' values | 255 | | | Gross Domestic Expenditure at purchasers' values | 255 |

*B. National Disposable Income and Outlay*

| | Outgoings | | | | Incomings | |
|---|---|---|---|---|---|---|
| 12. | General government consumption expenditure (5) | 42 | 17. | | Income to labor from domestic employment (1) | 152 |
| 13. | Household consumption expenditure in domestic market (7) | 168 | 18. | | Labor income received from the rest of the world, net (34–41) | 0 |
| 14. | Direct expenditure abroad by resident households (40) | 2 | 19. | | Income to capital (2) | 55 |
| 15. | *Less* direct expenditure in domestic market by nonresident households | −2 | 20. | | Indirect taxes, net (4) | 29 |
| 16. | Savings (27) | 27 | 21. | | Property income from the rest of the world, net (35–42) | 5 |
| | | | 22. | | Direct taxes on income and other current transfers from the rest of the world, net (36–43) | −4 |
| | National Outlay | 237 | | | National Disposable Income | 237 |

## C. Capital Account

| | Outgoings | | | Incomings | |
|---|---|---|---|---|---|
| 23. | Increase in stocks (8) | 6 | 26. | Depreciation (3) | 19 |
| 24. | Investment (9) | 41 | 27. | Savings (16) | 27 |
| 25. | Net lending to rest of the world (30) | –1 | 28. | Capital transfers from the rest of the world, net (–46) | 0 |
| | Gross Accumulation | 46 | | Finance of gross accumulation | 46 |
| 29. | Net acquisition of financial assets (47) | 17 | 30. | Net lending to the rest of the world (25) | –1 |
| | | | 31. | Net issue of liabilities (44) | 18 |
| | Capital Outgoings | 17 | | Capital Incomings | 17 |

## D. The Rest of the World

| | Outgoings | | | Incomings | |
|---|---|---|---|---|---|
| 32. | Exports of commodities (10) | 50 | 38. | Imports of commodities (–11) | 51 |
| 33. | Direct expenditure in the domestic market by nonresident households (–15) | 2 | 39. | Direct expenditure abroad, general government services (–6) | 1 |
| 34. | Income to labor (18 + 41) | 0 | 40. | Direct expenditure abroad by resident households (14) | 2 |
| 35. | Property income (21 + 42) | 11 | | | |
| 36. | Direct taxes on income and other current transfers (22 + 43) | 2 | 41. | Income to labor (34–18) | 0 |
| | | | 42. | Property income (35–21) | 6 |
| 37. | Surplus on current transactions (45) | 1 | 43. | Direct taxes on income and other current transfers (36–22) | 6 |
| | Current Outgoings | 66 | | Current Incomings | 66 |
| 44. | Net acquisition of financial assets (31) | 18 | 45. | Surplus on current transactions (37) | 1 |
| | | | 46. | Capital transfers, net (–28) | 0 |
| | | | 47. | Net issue of liabilities (29) | 17 |
| | Capital Outgoings | 18 | | Capital Incomings | 18 |

*Source:* United Nations (1968).

First, the SNA table (4.1) shows that, for any given economy, macroeconomic balance is achieved through an equilibrium between the total supply of goods and services (aggregate supply) and the total expenditure on these goods and services (aggregate or final demand). From Table 4.2 it can be gleaned that aggregate supply includes the total value of goods and services produced by resident production units (GDP at market prices) plus imports, while aggregate demand consists of all final demands, that is, private and public purchases of goods and services not used directly as inputs into the production of other goods and services. The latter include private and government consumption, investment (gross capital formation), exports, and changes in stocks. In symbolic terms:

$$GDP + M = C + I + G + X + \Delta S \qquad (4.1)$$

where GDP is gross domestic product at market prices, $M$ is the value of imports, $C$ is private consumption expenditure, $G$ is government consumption expenditure, $I$ is gross capital formation or investment, $X$ is the value of exports, and $\Delta S$ represents changes in stocks. The latter variable has been included for completeness but is not further used in the exposition.

The basic principle underlying the above macroeconomic relationship can be explained in the following terms. The various institutions in society (households, private corporate and incorporated enterprises, and the government) usually express a demand for certain goods and services. These demands are, in turn, fulfilled by the production of various combinations of commodities, for example, rice, flour, bread, cloth, dresses, steel, automobiles, and so on. Each production unit therefore generates a demand (derived) for various factors or inputs to be used in the production of the needed goods and services. The value of output of each production unit less the value of its inputs is referred to as value-added, with gross domestic product representing the total value-added in all resident-producing units. It is called "gross" because no deduction is made for consumption (depreciation) of fixed capital used in the production process.

The stream of value-added, or the balance between inputs and outputs, provides earnings to the various factors of production. Thus, the total value-added, or GDP, is usually paid out to the various factors in the form of wages and salaries, various types of property income, payments to capital, and payments to government (indirect taxes less government subsidies). These payments are shown on the left-hand side of both Table 4.1 (items 1 to 4) and Table 4.2. The balance between payments to inputs and total value-added can be expressed as follows:

$$GDP = wL + rK + zN + T \qquad (4.2)$$

**TABLE 4.2:** The consolidated production accounts of the nation

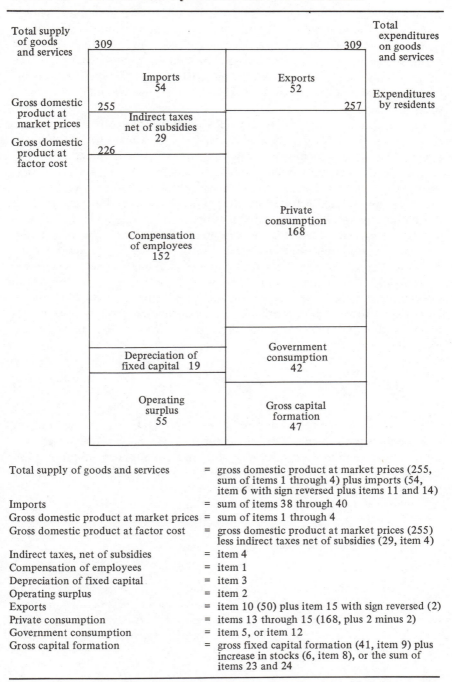

| Total supply of goods and services | = | gross domestic product at market prices (255, sum of items 1 through 4) plus imports (54, item 6 with sign reversed plus items 11 and 14) |
| Imports | = | sum of items 38 through 40 |
| Gross domestic product at market prices | = | sum of items 1 through 4 |
| Gross domestic product at factor cost | = | gross domestic product at market prices (255) less indirect taxes net of subsidies (29, item 4) |
| Indirect taxes, net of subsidies | = | item 4 |
| Compensation of employees | = | item 1 |
| Depreciation of fixed capital | = | item 3 |
| Operating surplus | = | item 2 |
| Exports | = | item 10 (50) plus item 15 with sign reversed (2) |
| Private consumption | = | items 13 through 15 (168, plus 2 minus 2) |
| Government consumption | = | item 5, or item 12 |
| Gross capital formation | = | gross fixed capital formation (41, item 9) plus increase in stocks (6, item 8), or the sum of items 23 and 24 |

*Source:* The entries are derived from SNA tables, pp. 29–30, reproduced in Table 4.1 in the text. There are some minor departures from the U.N. terminology.

where $wL$ is total labor income, broken down into some average wage/salary ($w$) and the total employment ($L$) of wage and salary earners; $rK$ is payments (rent, interest, dividends, royalties, and so on) and retained earnings of incorporated enterprises, broken down into some average return ($r$) and the total capital stock employed ($K$); $zN$ is the total returns to unincorporated enterprises, broken down as above; and $T$ is indirect taxes less subsidies.

As indicated above, the total value-added for the economy as a whole depends on the nature of the industries and production units that are responsible for producing the various commodities demanded. In other words, the relationships expressed in equations 4.1 and 4.2 have their analogues at the regional, sectoral, industrial, plant, and activity levels, as the case may be. To illustrate this, the supply of goods and services by each production sector can be separated into two basic components. First, there are deliveries to production sectors as intermediate inputs. The production process involves intermediate sales from one sector to another, for example, the sale of raw sugar to the food-processing industry, where it is used as an input in the manufacture of breakfast cereals. Second, these intermediate inputs should be distinguished from the final demands mentioned earlier, that is, private and government consumption, investment, and exports. These two components can be expressed in the following form:

$$\text{GDP}_i = \sum_{j=1}^{N} \text{GDP}_{ij} + C_i + G_i + I_i + X_i - M_i \qquad (4.3)$$

where $\text{GDP}_i$ is the total output of sector $i$; $\text{GDP}_{ij}$ is the volume of intermediate sales from sector $i$ to sector $j$; $C_i$, $G_i$, $I_i$, $X_i$, $M_i$ represent the set of final demands of sector $i$, that is, private consumption ($C_i$), government consumption ($G_I$), investment ($I_i$), exports ($X_i$), and imports ($M_i$); and $i$ and $j$ are production sectors, with $i = 1, 2, 3, \ldots N$. Alternatively, equation 4.3 can be stated in a shorter form as:

$$\text{GDP}_i = \sum_{j=1}^{N} \text{GDP}_{ij} + F_i \qquad (4.3a)$$

where $F_i$ is the sum of sector $i$'s final demands ($= C_i + G_i + I_i + X_i - M_i$).

Equations 4.3 and 4.3a provide a breakdown of the intermediate sales and final demands of sector $i$. In a similar vein, a breakdown of the sector's cost of production can be shown by using the macro-input equation 4.2, as follows:

$$\text{GDP}_i = \sum_{j=1}^{N} \text{GDP}_{ji} + w_i L_i + r_i K_i + z_i N_i + T_i \qquad (4.4)$$

where $\text{GDP}_{ji}$ is the sum of intermediate purchases of sector $i$ from all other domestic sectors $j$, with the other variables defined as before.

The disaggregated picture presented above usually forms part of input-output analysis, which is an analytical method used to estimate the economy-wide or macroeconomic effects of an expansion of a given sector's output. Its meaningful application requires a fully articulated set of tables showing interindustry transactions for the economy. The typical input-output table for an economy usually summarizes the transactions of goods and services by origin and by destination. The summary of transactions by origin separates the value of output by each industry or sector by three categories: the value of intermediate inputs purchased from various industries, payments to primary factors of production, and payments to government. The summary of transactions by destination separates the supply of goods and services by each industry into deliveries to industries as intermediate inputs (the intermediate demands) and deliveries to private and public consumption, investment, and net exports (final demands). A fuller discussion of the ramifications of input-output analysis can be found in Chenery and Clark (1964), Miernyk (1965), Leontief et al. (1977), and Stern and Lewis (1980).

The exposition so far has concentrated on the use of gross domestic product and its cost. However, it is necessary to show what the various economic agents who receive payments for selling their factor services do in order to determine the uses to which gross domestic product are put. This determination of expenditure from income (and vice versa) usually mirrors another crucial aspect of macroeconomic equilibrium, that is, the relationship between aggregate savings and aggregate investment. This is shown in sections (B) and (C) of Table 4.1. A summary is also provided in Table 4.3 for easy reference. The implications for growth analysis are discussed in the next section of this chapter.

Finally, there is the account for the rest of the world [section (D) in Table 4.1]. In explaining this, we depart slightly from the United Nations accounting convention and try to capture the basic features of the balance of payments of two distinct groups of countries: (1) the majority of developing nations that do not have any oil resources and (2) the developed industrial nations. Following the double-entry bookkeeping system used for the national accounts, the balance-of-payments identity can be written for the group of nonoil exporting developing nations, as follows:

$$X_{ldc} - M_{ldc} - P_{ldc} + AID_{ldc} + \Delta K_{ldc} - \Delta R_{ldc} = 0 \qquad (4.5)$$

**TABLE 4.3:** National disposable income and its uses

| | | | |
|---|---|---:|---:|
| 1. | Gross Domestic Product | | 255 |
| 2. | Depreciation | | 19 |
| 3. | Net domestic product (1–2) | | 236 |
| 4. | Net factor income from abroad | | 5 |
| 5. | Net national product (3 + 4) | | 241 |
| 6. | Depreciation | | 19 |
| 7. | Gross National Product | | 260 |
| 8. | Net current transfers from abroad (−) | | −4 |
| 9. | National disposable income (5 + 8) | | 237 |
| 10. | Consumption (−) | | −210 |
| | Private | −168 | |
| | Government | −42 | |
| 11. | Saving, net (9 + 10) | | 27 |
| 12. | Depreciation | | 19 |
| 13. | Saving, gross (11 + 12) | | 46 |
| 14. | Investment (−) | | −47 |
| | Fixed capital | −41 | |
| | Change in stocks | −6 | |
| 15. | Net international capital transfers | | 0 |
| 16. | Surplus or deficit on nonfinancial transactions (13 + 14 + 15) | | −1 |

*Source:* Computed from Table 4.1.

where $X$ is total value of exports, $M$ is total value of imports, $P$ is net income payments to the rest of the world (including debt service, outflow of foreign investment income, and so on), $AID$ is all forms of official development assistance received from the rest of the world, $K$ is the net value of all private capital inflows (portfolio and direct foreign investment), $R$ is official international reserves, and $\Delta$ the change from one time period to another.

The basic balance-of-payments identity can then be decomposed into its current and capital account components. The current account balance ($CAB$) is:

$$CAB_{ldc} = X_{ldc} - M_{ldc} - P_{ldc} \tag{4.6}$$

and the capital account balance ($KAB$) is:

$$KAB_{ldc} = AID_{ldc} + \Delta K_{ldc} - \Delta R_{ldc} \tag{4.7}$$

Since the overall balance of payments must always balance in an accounting sense, the balance on capital account is the negative of the balance on current account. The term on the right-hand side of the equation 4.7 is usually termed the "net resource balance." It provides an indication of the resources that have to be transferred from abroad and the extent to which a country's external reserves will have to be drawn down as a means of offsetting any deficit in the current account, as well as to effect an overall balance in the balance of payments in an accounting sense.

The deficit on current account can be expressed as:

$$CAB_{ldc} = X_{ldc} - M_{ldc} - P_{ldc} \leqslant 0 \tag{4.8}$$

This describes the situation facing the majority of developing countries and arises from a combination of sluggish export growth, substantial expenditure leakages for imports, large debt service payments, and, in some cases, outflows of investment income. The negative or deficit situation is financed by a combination of private capital inflows ($\Delta K$), injections of bilateral and multilateral loans and grants ($AID$), and/or a drawing down of reserves ($-\Delta R$).

The opposite situation would seem to apply to the majority of developed nations. In this case, the current account balance can be written as:

$$CAB_{mdc} = X_{mdc} - M_{mdc} + P_{mdc} = 0 \tag{4.9}$$

The combined surplus on current account can be explained by a positive trade balance ($X_{mdc} - M_{mdc} > 0$) and net inflows of investment income. The implication is that there is less strain on the "net resource balance" as a means of achieving overall balance-of-payments equilibrium. This is the case even though there may be some outflows on the capital account to finance official aid and direct foreign investment.

The national income and social accounting frameworks presented above, though not exhaustive, do provide some alternative pictures of the macroeconomy and its constituent parts. They also provide at least four interrelated mirrors for viewing the problems and possibilities of economic growth. One general picture mirrors the behavior of factors influencing aggregate demand. First, this forms the basis of Keynesian-type growth models that variously stress the role of savings, investment, trade, and related demand influences on the growth process. Second, and as a subclass of the general Keynesian perspective, some analysts view the balance-of-payments equilibrium growth rate as posing a major constraint to the overall development process.

A third aspect is concerned with the generation of value-added in the economy, and therefore with input-output relations and the economy's cost structure. This provides one of the main intellectual pillars of classical and neoclassical growth models, which generally analyze economic growth in terms of increases in supply capacity and total factor productivity augmentation, both nationally and internationally. In the latter context, primary emphasis is usually placed on trade as an "engine of growth" through the beneficial effects to be derived from exploiting comparative advantage.

A fourth broad picture focuses on the differential contribution various production sectors are supposed to make to the overall growth process. This is reflected in historical changes in the sectoral composition of output, demand, trade, and the labor force. These structural changes are usually emphasized in models of "patterns of growth." These growth patterns are supposed to represent uniform changes in the economic structure of countries as they move from low to high per capita income levels.

In conclusion, it should be reiterated that the various pictures of the macroeconomy presented above are drawn from images derived from the United Nations national income accounting system and related dimensions of Keynesian-type macroeconomic theory. These analytical frameworks are appropriate when the concern of economic analysis and policy is with the maximization of aggregate growth rates and the removal of savings and investment gaps. However, they cannot adequately model policies that focus on objectives such as employment creation, income redistribution, and basic needs fulfillment.

For example, the Keynesian and United Nations national income framework is primarily concerned with the functional as distinct from the personal distribution of income, and therefore tells us very little about the sources of such incomes. The latter requires an accounting and conceptual schema that substantially disaggregates the relevant economic aggregates and link these to the income and expenditure sources. Such a procedure, or consistency planning framework, can be considered a prerequisite not only for modeling a broad range of development objectives but also for evaluating the effects of developmental change on regions, individual economic sectors, activities within and across sectors, as well as on the institutions in society.

Such a consistency planning framework is suggested by the Social Accounting Matrix or SAM methodology (see Pyatt and Thorbecke 1976; Pyatt and Round 1977; and King 1981). The conceptual framework underlying the SAM can be looked at from two interdependent angles. In general, it can be thought of as a modular planning and analytical framework that specifies for the economy a set of interrelated subsystems and the major relationships among variables both within and between these subsystems. From a policy perspective, the framework is designed so as to incorporate those policy instruments that can be manipulated so as to move the entire economic system or parts of it in alternative directions.

The latter reflect policy choices with respect to economic growth, employment, income distribution, basic needs fulfillment, and so on.

From a narrower perspective, the SAM is really a data classification system that, for any given point in time, provides a disaggregated view of crucial links among policy variables, for example, the interrelationships among (1) the structure of production; (2) distribution of value-added generated by production activities; (3) final demand—consumption, savings, investment; (4) wants, that is, household expenditure on basic needs for food, clothing, education, shelter, and so on; and (5) the external sector, that is, the balance of payments. These interrelationships are illustrated in Table 4.4. They are similar to those normally shown in an input-output table. However, in the SAM format, they are arranged in matrix form, with receipts and incomings shown along the rows and payments or outgoings along the columns.

Thus, the SAM format provides certain features that are not normally encountered in the conventional planning and national income framework. In particular, it incorporates mechanisms that translate the generation of value-added into different forms of institutional income, by means of linkages with factors of production. The level and structure of different production activities generate the aggregate demand for different types of labor, capital, and natural resources. This provides some indication of employment creation. The stream of value-added from the production activities provide returns to the various factors of production in the form of wages (labor), profits (capital), and rent (land). The functional distribution of income is thereby derived from the value-added generated by the various production activities. The functional distribution can then be translated into an institutional income distribution, that is, the income received by household, businesses, and the government.

## Neo-Keynesian Demand-Oriented Perspectives

A starting point for most demand-based perspectives of economic growth is the Keynesian dichotomy between consumption and savings and his general thesis, developed during the Great Depression, that production and employment could be regulated through a well-coordinated set of government policies (Keynes 1936). The general idea was that, if production and employment increase, consumption would rise and savings fall as a proportion of income. As a result, an amount of investment sufficient to fill the savings gap at high levels of economic activity (that is, the amount by which consumption would fall short of income at full employment) would not be realized automatically. Therefore, supporting

**TABLE 4.4:** A simplified social accounting matrix

|  |  | Expenditures | | | Other Accounts | | |
|  |  | 1 | 2 | 3 | 4 | | Totals |
|  |  | Factors | Institutions, including households | Production activities | Combined capital | Rest of world |  |
| Receipts | 1 Factors |  |  | Factorial income distribution. |  |  | Income of factors. |
|  | 2 Institutions. Households. Companies. Government. | Income distribution to households and other institutions. | Transfers, taxes, and subsidies. |  | Government receipts from combined capital account. | Institutions (government). Receipts from rest of the world. | Income of institutions. |
|  | 3 Production activities. |  | Institutional demand (households and others) for goods and services. | Interindustry demand. | Gross capital formation. | Exports. | Gross demand– gross output. |
|  | 4 Combined capital. |  | Savings by institutions. |  |  | Balance of payments current account deficit. | Aggregate savings. |
|  | Rest of world |  | Imports of competitive goods. | Imports of non-competitive goods. |  |  | Total foreign exchange outflow. |
|  | Totals | Outlay (= income of factors) | Expenditures of institutions. | Gross output. | Aggregate investment. | Total foreign exchange inflow. |  |

Source: Pyatt and Thorbecke (1976).

78

monetary and fiscal policies were needed to ensure an equilibrium between total consumption and investment demand on the one hand, and production at the full employment level on the other.

These ideas have come to have a profound influence on macroeconomic thinking about developing economies. In a sense, they can be considered "depressed economies." The underlying assumption is that the investment process tends to be inadequate because these countries are unable to save enough. In passing, it should be mentioned that the Keynesian perspective was in many respects different from the traditional classical and neoclassical views about the impact of savings on economic activity. The latter perspectives view the impact of savings primarily in terms of the rate of return on investment, with a positive association assumed between the rate of interest and the supply of savings. The assumption is that, with positive interest rates, the greater will be the volume of savings, and therefore the capacity to invest in the economy.

By contrast, Keynesian-type models are based on the Keynesian absolute income hypothesis, which posits that absolute income rather than the interest rate is the major determinant of savings. As is well known, the Keynesian position has been challenged over the years by several rival savings-income hypotheses, including Friedman's "permanent income" (Friedman 1957), Duesenberry's "relative income" (Duesenberry 1949), and Modigliani and Ando's "life-cycle" hypothesis (Modigliani and Ando 1963). These rival hypotheses were developed primarily to explain savings behavior in the U.S. economy. In general terms, however, they do emphasize the fact that the propensity to save is an increasing function of income due to the diminishing marginal productivity from consumption over time (see Mikesell and Zinser 1973).

In a Keynesian context, the most famous class of models is the Harrod-Domar growth model (Harrod 1939; Domar 1946). As explained in detail elsewhere (David 1985), the model postulates that savings and investment not only create capital capacity but also generate output, incomes, and employment. In this model, the entire growth of output, income, and employment is attributed to investment or the past growth of capital, with the relationship between output/income growth and investment determined by the capital/output ratio, that is, the amount of capital required per unit of output. The relationship is viewed as a technological one, with the rate of growth of output determined by the proportion of past output that has been used for capital formation. This has led to the generalization that the main obstacle to the development of poor countries lies in the pervasive lack of capital formation to meet investment needs.

The relationship between capital capacity creation and output growth can be explained in the following terms. To begin with, we state the well-known condition for macroeconomic equilibrium implied in the

Keynesian final demand equation for a closed economy, with national income (GDP) dichotomized into consumption (*C*), savings (*S*), or investment (*I*). Thus:

$$GDP = C + S \qquad (4.10)$$

$$GDP = C + I \qquad (4.11)$$

$$S = I \qquad (4.12)$$

If we assume a constant ratio of savings to income (*s*), and a constant capital to output ratio (*k*), output and income will increase by *s/k* (GDP). In other words, income and output growth are made to depend on the increase in capital capacity as follows:

$$\Delta GDP = s/k \, (GDP) \qquad (4.13)$$

and

$$\Delta GDP/GDP = s/k \qquad (4.13a)$$

The implication of equation 4.13a is that aggregate income or output must grow at a constant rate ($g = s/k$) if full employment of resources is to be assured. This is Harrod's "warranted rate of growth." However, in a capitalist-oriented economy, this warranted rate of growth may not materialize because of the nature of institutional responses. For example, one possible source of stagnation may occur if investors underspend. If this occurs, the capital growth rate will be lower than the warranted rate of growth, and the overall rate of growth of output and income will be even less due to the decumulative effects of reduced investment expenditures. The reverse is likely to take place if investors overspend. Overspending and underspending are therefore considered to be major causes of instability in capitalist economies. In general terms, however, what equation 4.13a suggests is that high savings rates and low capital/output ratios are major growth-promoting factors.

An interesting variant of the "savings-centered" approach is provided by the Cambridge (England) growth models (Kalecki 1939; Kaldor 1955, 1957; Robinson 1956). The bare bones of the model can be stated as follows. First, based on a differential savings hypothesis, the recipients of national income in a capitalist-type economy are dichotomized into two groups—capitalists and workers. The income of capitalists (profits) can be represented by $GDP_p$ and that of workers (wages and salaries) by $GDP_w$.

Therefore:

$$GDP = GDP_p + GDP_w \qquad (4.14)$$

Second, we can divide total savings into capitalists' and workers' components, based on the assumption that each group saves a proportion of its income. Thus:

$$S = S_p + S_w \qquad (4.15)$$

with

$$S_w = s_w \, GDP_w \qquad (4.15a)$$

and

$$S_p = s_p \, GDP_p \qquad (4.15b)$$

where $S_w$ is total savings of workers, $s_w$ is the proportion of workers' income that is saved, $S_p$ is the total savings of capitalists, and $s_p$ the proportion of capitalists' income that is saved. A further assumption is that capitalists tend to save more than workers. In the extreme, total savings is made up entirely of capitalists' savings so that $S_p = 1$ and $S_w = 0$.

Using the relationships defined earlier, we can then obtain an equation in which savings sum to investment, as follows:

$$S = I = s_p \, GDP_p + s_w \, GDP_w \qquad (4.16)$$

Combining equations 4.15 and 4.16, we obtain

$$S/GDP = I/GDP = s_w + (s_p - s_w) \, GDP_p/GDP \qquad (4.17)$$

Using equation 4.13, that is, assuming that the economy is growing at a constant rate, yields:

$$g = I/GDP = s_w + (s_p - s_w) \, GDP_p/GDP \qquad (4.18)$$

Given the differential savings rate assumption, equation 4.18 implies that the rate of growth of aggregate income or output tends to vary directly with the share of profits in national income ($GDP_p/GDP$). Second, for any given rate of economic growth, this share of profits will vary inversely with the propensity of capitalists to save. One implication is that lower savings by capitalists tend to enhance their share of national income. The paradoxical conclusion is that the more conspicuous consumption on the part of capitalists tends to raise their total profits (Kaldor's "Widow's Curse" parable of income distribution). An alternative statement of the same proposition is that capitalists tend to earn what they spend, and workers spend what they earn! (Kalecki's theory of profit).

Be that as it may, the Cambridge savings-centered approach bears a close similarity to those theories of development that identify the capacity to save as the major factor limiting the rate of investment in reproducible capital, and therefore economic growth. One variation on this theme is that steps should be taken to increase the capacity to save of those who can save, that is, an encouragement of savings by the capitalist class whose members are considered to be the primary savers in society. It is therefore advocated that the income distribution should be shifted in favor of the savings/capitalist class who are the profit earners and have the largest incomes in the economy. On this basis, Lewis (1954) has posited that the growth of the capitalist class, that is, people who think of investing capital productively, constitutes a necessary condition for sustained economic growth.

These assumptions are at the heart of Lewis' well-known model of dualistic development. In this model, the economy is divided into two sectors. One is the modern sector controlled by capitalists who provide employment, obtain profits by using reproducible capital in production, and augment both capital and national economic growth by reinvesting these profits. The other is the tranditional or subsistence sector in which reproducible capital is not used and workers subsist at minimum consumption levels. Capitalists have an interest in holding consumption levels at a minimum since they determine the wages paid to hired labor and therefore profit levels. The general idea is that, with the reinvestment of profits and the growth in capital, the demand for labor would increase, unemployment would disappear, and the economy is therefore likely to develop out of its dualistic condition.

The model therefore emphasizes the role of increasing profit shares in pushing up the aggregate savings/income ratio. On the assumption that capitalists have a high propensity to invest, increasing profits will automatically lead to a transformation of savings into additional productive capacity. A further expectation is that the growth in reproducible capital will also lead to an accumulation of human capital. The argument is that, if capital is available for development, capitalists or their government will soon provide the facilities for training more skilled people, and other complementary growth-promoting factors such as technological change will also develop.

Besides the ability or capacity to save, emphasis is also sometimes placed on the willingness or opportunity to save. The ability or capacity, willingness, or opportunity to save can be considered interdependent. The ability to save can be considered the primary variable and is related to income through the propensity to consume. Given the ability, the willingness to save depends on the relative balance between present and future consumption. This balance, in turn, bears a close relationship to long-term income prospects and incentives provided savers. The opportunity to save depends on the availability of appropriate assets in which savings can be held, and therefore on the nature of the financial system and its efficiency.

In general, the savings-centered or threshold theories stress the inability of poor masses to save due to insufficient margins above subsistence income, or consumption habits in which the available income tends to be used up in conspicuous consumption. The resultant low level of savings, when invested, proves insufficient to maintain per capita output so that developing countries are caught in a "vicious circle of poverty" (Nurske 1953) or "low level equilibrium trap" (Nelson 1956; Leibenstein 1957).

The vicious circle of poverty and low level equilibrium trap are caused by a combination of rapid population growth, low incomes, low savings, and inadequate investment. The general proposition is that, with population growing at about the same rate as national income, per capita income stagnates and results in severe restrictions on the propensity to save and the ability to finance productive forms of investment vis-à-vis "demographic investment." Further, where investment levels are low, both production and employment levels are depressed, giving rise to low incomes and savings. The vicious circle is thereby completed. On the other hand, low savings result in low levels of capital accumulation and investment, thereby perpetuating the low income trap.

Table 4.5 provides some indication of consumption, savings, and investment levels in developing countries. Consumption expenditure averages about 77 percent of GDP for all developing countries and ranges between 72 percent for middle income oil exporters to as much as 94 percent for low income Africa. The data also indicate that the correspondingly low levels of domestic savings have proved insufficient to finance investment needs, especially in the low income countries. While there is no consensus as to what constitutes optimal levels of savings and consumption, the opinion has been advanced that "at the resource level, a country may be judged to have reached self-sustaining growth when it is more or less self-sufficient in savings . . . its net capital inflow is less than 2 percent of national income, [and] private consumption is down to 60 percent of GDP" (Lewis 1984, p. 9).

**TABLE 4.5:** Consumption, savings, and investment indicators, selected years, 1965–83 (percent of GDP)

| Country group and indicator | 1965 | 1973 | 1980 | 1981 | 1982 | 1983[a] |
|---|---|---|---|---|---|---|
| **Developing countries** | | | | | | |
| Consumption | 79.8 | 76.7 | 75.6 | 77.2 | 77.9 | 76.0 |
| Investment | 21.1 | 24.3 | 26.7 | 26.0 | 24.6 | 24.7 |
| Savings | 20.2 | 23.3 | 24.4 | 22.8 | 22.1 | 24.0 |
| **Low-income Asia** | | | | | | |
| Consumption | 79.8 | 75.1 | 75.5 | 76.3 | 75.8 | 74.7 |
| Investment | 21.5 | 25.4 | 27.6 | 25.7 | 25.7 | 26.5 |
| Savings | 20.2 | 24.9 | 24.5 | 23.7 | 24.2 | 25.3 |
| **Low-income Africa** | | | | | | |
| Consumption | 88.6 | 85.7 | 90.4 | 92.7 | 94.1 | 94.6 |
| Investment | 14.2 | 16.8 | 18.7 | 17.3 | 16.2 | 14.7 |
| Savings | 11.4 | 14.3 | 9.6 | 7.3 | 5.9 | 5.4 |
| **Middle-income oil importers** | | | | | | |
| Consumption | 79.1 | 77.0 | 77.5 | 78.7 | 79.1 | 77.0 |
| Investment | 22.0 | 24.9 | 26.6 | 25.7 | 24.0 | 24.0 |
| Savings | 20.9 | 23.0 | 22.5 | 21.3 | 20.9 | 23.0 |
| **Middle-income oil exporters** | | | | | | |
| Consumption | 79.9 | 76.8 | 71.0 | 74.2 | 76.0 | 71.2 |
| Investment | 19.8 | 22.3 | 26.7 | 27.6 | 25.7 | 26.2 |
| Savings | 20.1 | 23.2 | 29.0 | 25.8 | 24.0 | 28.8 |
| **Industrial market economies** | | | | | | |
| Consumption | 76.7 | 75.0 | 78.4 | 78.4 | 80.1 | 80.0 |
| Investment | 22.9 | 24.7 | 22.5 | 21.9 | 20.1 | 20.0 |
| Savings | 23.3 | 25.0 | 21.6 | 21.6 | 19.9 | 20.0 |

[a]Estimated.
*Source:* World Bank (1985).

The general problem is that the domestic savings rate is barely sufficient to enable investment to keep pace with the rapid population increase facing many developing countries so that there are problems of maintaining current standards of living at the very low per capita income levels. As indicated earlier, this constitutes an important dimension of the low level equilibrium trap. However, as long as per capita income and productivity levels remain low, attempts to force increases in domestic savings can cause considerable hardships and undesirable economic, political, and social consequences. This leads to a question about the potential role of capital imports (foreign savings) and the external sector in general in helping developing countries to overcome the domestic savings impasse.

## Foreign Capital and the Balance-of-Payments Constraint

While the literature contains several alternative explanations of the interaction between domestic savings and foreign capital imports in the growth process, one of the most well-known is provided by the "two-gap" models (see Chenery and Bruno 1962; McKinnon 1964; and Chenery 1979). In general, these models highlight the dual role of foreign capital in augmenting national savings and in providing foreign exchange to cover part of a country's import requirements (for a discussion, see Newlyn 1977). The general issues raised by these models can be looked at from two interrelated angles. The first can be illustrated by incorporating the foreign exchange counterpart of savings into the original growth equation (4.13) above. The second is concerned with the balance-of-payments equilibrium growth rate.

Given the level of domestic savings, the foreign account counterpart of national savings represents the supplementary amount of foreign exchange needed to meet domestic investment requirements and to preserve the growth momentum. It can be expressed in terms of the relationship between the GDP growth rate and the deficit on current account, as follows:

$$\Delta GDP/GDP = [s + (X - M - P)]/k \tag{4.19}$$

or, in terms of financial flows, by:

$$\Delta GDP/GDP = [s + (AID + \Delta K - \Delta R)]/k \tag{4.20}$$

Given the savings rate ($s$) and the capital/output ratio ($k$), a current account surplus tends to augment national savings, and therefore the GDP growth rate. By contrast, a current account deficit tends to reduce it, and an inflow of official and/or private capital is required to maintain desired investment levels and output growth.

It is evident, therefore, that the economic performance of most countries (depending on the degree of openness of the economy) tends to bear a close relationship to the behavior of the trade sector and the overall balance of payments. Economic growth tends to be constrained by the balance of payments since such growth is approximated by the rate of growth of exports divided by the income elasticity of demand for imports. This is termed "the balance-of-payments equilibrium growth rate." As a general proposition, no country can grow faster than its balance-of-payments equilibrium growth rate unless it can obtain resources (usually from foreign sources) to finance the deficit created by an import growth rate in excess of that of exports.

The above proposition has formed the basis of demand-oriented models of Thirlwall (1979, 1980) and Kennedy and Thirlwall (1979). The exposition that follows draws heavily on their statment of the model. It is based on an extension of the Keynesian income/savings identity to an open economy and explains the balance-of-payments equilibrium growth rate in terms of the operation of Harrod's foreign trade multiplier. Harrod's idea (Harrod 1933) is that, in an open economy, a country's output is explained by the operation of the foreign trade multiplier, which is the mechanism for keeping the balance of payments in equilibrium. This is explained by the fact that the gap between exports and full employment imports in such an economy may prove much more difficult to eliminate than the savings/investment gap.

In the simplest case, it is assumed that income is generated by two types of output: production of home consumption goods and exports. All income is disposed of by purchasing home-produced goods and imports. Given these assumptions, we may write:

$$Y = C + X \tag{4.21}$$

$$Y = C + M \tag{4.22}$$

$$X = M \tag{4.23}$$

where $Y$ is income, $X$ exports, $M$ imports, and $C$ home-produced goods. Equation 4.23 ($X = M$) defines the equilibrium condition under which Harrod's foreign trade multiplier works. When exports are expressed in terms of income, the equation becomes

$$X = mY \tag{4.24}$$

or

$$Y = X/m \tag{4.24a}$$

where $m$ is the marginal propensity to import $= \Delta M/\Delta Y$. Therefore:

$$\Delta Y/\Delta X = 1/m \qquad (4.25)$$

The same result obtains if an autonomous term is added to the import function. In such a case, we may write:

$$M = \bar{M} + mY \qquad (4.26)$$

$$X = \bar{M} + mY \qquad (4.26a)$$

$$Y = (X - \bar{M})/m \qquad (4.26b)$$

Therefore:

$$\Delta Y/\Delta X = \Delta Y/(-\Delta M) = 1/m \qquad (4.27)$$

or

$$\Delta Y/\Delta \bar{M} = -1/m \qquad (4.27a)$$

The following general conclusions can be drawn. First, given the marginal propensity to import, any change in exports will induce a high enough change in income that, in turn, will bring about changes in imports to match the new level of exports. Second, changes in autonomous imports will change income sufficiently so that import changes adjust to the level of exports. The point of emphasis is that income adjusts to preserve the balance of trade so that any plans to import in excess of exports will depress income, and vice versa. (Thirlwall 1980).

More realism can be introduced into the above analysis by taking into account income leakages and induced expenditures. In the real world, there are income leakages in the form of savings and taxation and induced expenditures in the form of government transfers and investment. When these factors are taken into account, equations 4.21–4.23 can be written as:

$$Y = C + X + I + G \qquad (4.28)$$

$$Y = C + M + S + T \qquad (4.29)$$

$$X + I + G = M + S + T \qquad (4.30)$$

where $I$ is investment, $G$ is government expenditure, $S$ is savings, and $T$ is taxation. Further, assume that these variables partly depend on income and are partly autonomous. The point is that, irrespective of income levels, there may be certain autonomous elements of consumption, investment, savings, government expenditure, and so on. We may therefore write:

$$I = \bar{I} + aY \tag{4.31}$$

$$G = \bar{G} + gY \tag{4.31a}$$

$$S = \bar{S} + sY \tag{4.31b}$$

$$T = \bar{T} + tY \tag{4.31c}$$

By collapsing all the autonomous elements into one catchall autonomous variable ($\bar{E} = \bar{I} + \bar{G} + \bar{S} + \bar{T}$), and by substituting into equation 4.30, we obtain

$$Y = (X - \bar{M} + \bar{E})/(m + s + t - a - g) \tag{4.32}$$

Comparing this equation with 4.23, it is evident that if the conditions underlying the Harrod foreign trade multiplier are to hold, autonomous expenditure must be zero ($\bar{E} = 0$), and induced expenditures must equal induced leakages ($a + g = s + t$). A balance-of-payments deficit occurs when autonomous expenditure is positive ($E > 0$), and/or induced expenditures exceed induced leakages ($a + g > s + t$).

The conclusion emerges that in open economies, export demand plays a critical role in overall economic growth, especially where the propensity to import is large. However, this depends on the extent to which any shortfalls can be made up by other compensating expenditures, such as autonomous expenditures and various income transfers designed to maintain consumption and investment levels. This conclusion is synergistic with the export-led growth perspective. The latter stresses that it is only through export expansion that the growth rate can be raised without a simultaneous deterioration in the balance of payments. However, the impact of such export expansion will ultimately depend on the extent to which it induces further increases in import expenditure. This conclusion also helps to explain why orthodox economic stabilization programs emphasize the need for a combination of both export expansion and import restraint.

In conclusion, without doing injustice to the analytical strengths of the balance-of-payments equilibrium growth model, it is evident that the model stands or falls on assumptions that are made about the behavior of the foreign trade multiplier. In this regard, the model basically assumes a given structure of international demand and does not identify important structural factors underlying international trading relationships, and in particular those that have traditionally determined patterns of exchange between developed and developing countries. Some of these considerations are addressed in Chapters 7 and 8.

## Classical-Neoclassical Supply-Oriented Perspectives

Finally, we turn to a brief consideration of supply-side analyses of changes in aggregate income and output. The general analytical framework has its origins in classical economics in which the growth in material production was thought to depend on various inputs or factors of production, including the abundance of natural resources (primarily land), capital, skilled labor, and good organization. These ideas have come to influence modern neoclassical growth theory, which links economic growth to the possibilities offered for improved resource allocation and mobilization, increased factor supplies, and the growth in total factor productivity.

In the latter context, aggregate economic growth is analyzed by utilizing the concept of a production function that, for any given economy, shows the relationship between aggregate income or output at any given point in time and the quantitities of factors of production utilized in the production process. Under certain assumptions, for example, if the state of technology and society's social and political structure remain unchanged, the production function concept can be used to show the maximum output or income that is attainable by using alternative combinations of factors of production or inputs. This approach mirrors the production and input-output relations referred to in the first section of this chapter.

Further, the growth relationships are predicated on the free flow of factors of production between countries, regions, sectors; and individual economic activities. It is also assumed that this free flow of resources will act as a mechanism to effect equilibrium and to equalize growth, income, and employment rates across the different spheres mentioned above. The perspective is therefore based on some notion of equilibrium growth, that is, one that proceeds slowly, continuously, and on a stable path, with minimum disturbances from exogenous forces. Implicit in this is a "natural" or "biological" theory of economic growth, with progress assumed to depend on the "evolutionary possibilities" facing an economy.

The analytical thrust can be illustrated by considering a generalized production function of the following form:

$$Y = f(x_1, x_2, x_3, \ldots, x_n) \tag{4.33}$$

where $Y$ is income or output and the $x$s represent various inputs or production factors. In the standard neoclassical formulation, the production function is assumed to be linear and homogeneous, that is, doubling the quantity of factors would lead to an unambiguous doubling of output. From equation 4.33, we may derive a growth equation, as follows:

$$r_y = f_1 q_1 r_1 + f_2 q_2 r_2 + f_3 q_3 r_3 + \cdots + f_n q_n r_n \tag{4.34}$$

First, the $r$s are growth rates for aggregate income and the various factors, with $r_y = \Delta Y/Y$, and $r_i = \Delta x_i/x_i$. Second, the $q$s are input coefficients, so that $q_i = x_i/Y$. The $f$s are marginal productivities so that $f_i = \Delta Y/\Delta x_i \cdot \Delta x_i/t = \partial Y/\partial x_i$. As explained in Chapter 2, the marginal products are assumed to be proportional to factor prices.

The general relationship shown in equation 4.34 can then be expressed in terms of a conventional three-factor model, as follows:

$$Y = F(K, L, U) \tag{4.35}$$

where $K$ is capital, $L$ is labor, and $U$ is a term for other unspecified factors. From equation 4.35, we may derive a special case of equation 4.34, so that

$$r_y = ar_k + br_l + cr_u \tag{4.36}$$

where $a$, $b$, and $c$ are the elasticity coefficients, and $r_y$, $r_k$, $r_l$, and $r_u$ are the growth rates of the variables denoted by the subscripts. In the neoclassical model, the growth elasticities with respect to the various factors are assumed to be constant throughout time, that is, the elasticity of substitution is unity. Relative factor shares are also used as weights on the rates of growth of the factor inputs.

The number of neoclassical growth models based on the above analytical format are legion. Some of the most celebrated are those of Denison (1967) and Solow (1956, 1957). In both the theoretical and empirical analyses, these models are usually referred to as "sources of growth" models. This is because the variables on the right-hand side of equation 4.36 are considered to be "sources" or "causes" of income or output growth. The general approach apportions the growth of total output between the growth of capital, the growth of labor, and the growth in total factor productivity, with the latter obtained in empirical analyses as a residual. This residual explains the influence of factors such as education and technological change on the overall growth process.

The neoclassical approach has been criticized both in general and in terms of its relevance to developing countries. The general criticisms are in the spirit of the objections raised in Chapter 2. In addition, the conditions of economic growth are almost invariably interpreted in purely quantitative terms. This overlooks the possibility that the quantitative dimensions of economic growth may in fact reflect qualitative changes in the structural relations that underlie the growth process. In other words, the analysis fails to take into account the changes in economic and other institutions that tend to be associated with extensive growth in the economy.

The assumptions of neoclassical growth theory are far less relevant to developing countries. One set of criticisms stems from the assumptions underlying marginal productivity theory, for example, the assumption of proportionality between marginal products and factor prices. While this may approximate conditions existing in developed countries, price disequilibria are a much more common feature in developing countries. Another problem concerns the assumption of constant growth elasticities with respect to the various factors. There is reason to believe that factor proportions tend to change over time and that the perfect factor substitution assumption breaks down in the case of developing countries.

Another broad set of issues concerns the relative importance that should be attached to specific factors in the growth process and how their influence should be analyzed. These factors include natural resources, reproducible capital, human capital and education, and technology. They are briefly discussed below for illustrative purposes. We begin by considering the role of natural resource endowments in the growth process. Such resource endowments may take a variety of forms, including climate, fresh water, fertile soil, useful minerals and raw materials, and a geographical topography that facilitates transportation. The role of natural resources in the growth process therefore becomes a very complex one. One reason is that natural resource availability may be a matter of sheer luck. Another is that the value of a particular natural resource usually depends on its usefulness. This usefulness, in turn, tends to undergo constant change due to changes in tastes, prices, technology, aspirations, and so on.

In this context, traditional thinking on the role of natural resources in the process of economic growth has followed two basic paths. One approach is the environmental determinism of geographers and historians, for example, Toynbee (1947, 1966) and Huntington, (1915, 1962), who stress the impact of climatic efficiency on civilization, cultural development, and productivity levels. However, the more influential strand of thought follows in the tradition of Malthusian and Ricardian models. In these models, land is viewed as a fixed factor, and economic growth is therefore thought to be limited by the overall scarcity of natural resources.

One generalization emerging from these models is that the low level of production and productivity experienced by the developing countries is primarily the result of rapid population growth combined with relatively poor natural resource endowments. A second generalization starts off from the premise of natural resource scarcity, but emphasizes the need to conserve both exhaustible and renewable resources on account of factors such as soil erosion, forest degradation, and the disturbance of ecological systems (see Brown 1981).

In terms of the link with population growth, the argument is that while natural resources may have been plentiful in the past, there is now a scarcity on account of population growth. One aspect of the debate centers around the world's ability to feed its ever-increasing numbers. The "doomsday prophets" as well as "triage" and "lifeboat" theorists have therefore posited that it would be necessary to achieve a zero or negative population growth in the near future to bring demand and supply into balance. A variant of this argument is that large numbers may have to be allowed to starve to death in order to ensure greater benefits for survivors.

In general, it can be commented that the abundance or scarcity of natural resources is not an absolute but a relative phenomenon. The experience of countries like Japan, Switzerland, and Great Britain suggests that natural resource scarcity can be changed through technical progress, increasing returns, and by the extent to which countries are able to draw on the resources of others through trade and other resource transfers. In other words, the theoretical possibility exists that countries can make up for their resource scarcity by substituting capital, labor skills, and other socioeconomic improvements. The lack of capital, skills, technology and other factors that can be used in the substitution process or to augment the usefulness of existing natural resources is a major factor explaining contemporary forms of underdevelopment.

Another set of issues revolves around the role of reproducible capital in the growth process. Orthodox and heterodox economists alike agree that capital should be considered an important dimension of mankind's stock of wealth, and therefore a resource to be used in improving the general productive capacity of the economy and the further generation of income and wealth. The empirical evidence also suggests that countries with high growth rates also show high rates of capital accumulation, and vice versa (see Sen 1983). However, there is no unique one-to-one correspondence between capital expansion and economic growth. One set of problems is concerned with the specific interpretation that should be given to the capital-output ratio concept (see Myrdal 1968 and Streeten 1972). This is related to the issue, alluded to in Chapter 2, that the capital factor is by no means homogeneous. Further, its contribution depends on the nature of the cooperant factors of production with which it is combined. Finally, as stressed in Cambridge, Ricardian, and Marxian-type growth models, rapid capital accumulation tends to promote various forms of inequality.

From the perspective of modern neoclassical theory, it is now recognized that the contribution of reproducible capital to the growth process depends on the interplay with other factors such as technology and human capital. In general, this is because economic growth is accompanied by an increasing complementarity and substitution among various factors of production. Some factors complement the use of others that are relatively plentiful or, alternatively, are substituted for those factors that are relatively scarce.

In the above context, the technology factor makes a positive contribution to income and output growth because the introduction of new methods associated with its injection helps to expand the resources employed in the economy, or enables it to use existing resources more efficiently. It helps in the exploitation of new resources through the introduction of previously unknown methods of production. Alternatively, it can contribute to the growth process in terms of the possibilities offered for effecting changes in the structure of output, that is, by differential expansion in the volume and quality of traditional products.

Contextually, technological change leads to increases in efficiency, that is, improvements in total factor productivity. The latter is usually defined as the ratio of total output to all factor inputs taken together. The increase in total factor productivity can lead to increases in income and therefore provide the basis for further growth, assuming that the increased resource use does not lead to widespread unemployment. This is likely to result, for example, when such resource use is accompanied by increased substitution of capital for labor.

Within the standard neoclassical framework, the study of the technological factor usually forms part of the *economic analysis* of price and resource use patterns, with technological change viewed as a random variable in the technical parameters of production. This follows from the assumptions underlying the behavior of linear homogeneous production functions based on various quantities of capital and labor in perfectly competitive markets. Accordingly, technological change is analyzed in terms of purely quantitative adjustments of homogeneous capital and labor inputs in the production process.

On a related basis, technological change is viewed as "disembodied," that is, as a function of time. This implies that its effects are entirely separate from the impact on the growth process of other resources employed. In reality, technology is "embodied" in the factor inputs that are used. In real-life situations, technological change is brought into the production process through investments in new machines, the use of higher

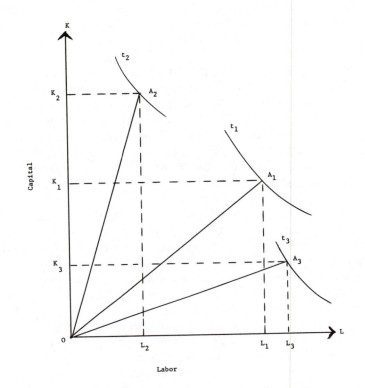

**Figure 4.1.** Capital/labor ratios under alternative production techniques.

quality factor inputs, the employment of more skilled labor, and so on. The type of technology chosen determines not only the nature of production but also the structure of employment and income distribution. It has implications for the types of commodities that are produced as well as the regions and sectors of the economy that will be given priority.

Economists sometimes analyze the problem in terms of the "factor proportions" issue, that is, the nature and appropriateness of alternative capital/labor ratios associated with given production techniques, or the degree of capital/labor intensity in the production process. This is illustrated in Figure 4.1, which depicts three alternative production techniques and the related capital/labor ratios. The average for the economy as a whole, or for any given production activity, is shown by the curve $t_1$ and the capital/labor ratio $A_1L_1/OL_1$. In this case, there is no discernible bias toward either the capital or the labor factor. This can be contrasted with a second case represented by curve $t_2$ and the respective capital/labor ratio $A_2L_2/OL_2$. This is a situation of relatively high capital or low labor intensity. The reverse situation of relatively low capital of high labor intensity is shown by curve $t_3$ and the capital/labor ratio $A_3L_3/OL_3$. The three alternatives given above are mainly illustrative, and several other alternative combinations of capital and labor are possible.

Under the circumstances, one would expect that countries (especially developing ones) are in a position to choose several alternative types of technology and factor proportions, depending, of course, on the production activities in which they are engaged. However, the neoclassical view is that the decision should always be based on the need for injecting "technical" and "engineering" efficiency into the growth process, and to minimize financial and economic costs. Underlying this pattern of reasoning is a belief in fixed factor proportions vis-à-vis the possibilities for factor substitutability. One rationale is that fixed factor proportions have proved most efficient in the growth process of the now developed countries, especially in terms of the requirements of financial cost minimization. This has led to the generalization that capital-intensive techniques of production tend to be much more efficient than labor-intensive alternatives and, for that matter, intermediate ones.

It is therefore believed that the introduction of modern technology (synonymous with capital-intensive methods of production) is a necessary requirement for sustained economic growth. The reasoning is that labor-intensive techniques geared toward employment creation may actually inhibit the pace of technological change and therefore limit a given country's ability to compete in export markets. A related argument is that in cases where the introduction of modern technology results in labor displacement, the surplus labor could be absorbed in the growing services sector that accompanies economic expansion. However, as shown in Chapter 5, this has not been borne out in the experience of the majority of developing countries.

Underlying the fixed factor proportions thesis is the idea of fixed capital/labor ratios and the implication that the choice of technology is given for all time. Questions of technological appropriateness are therefore thrown out of court. While it may be true that production processes that are most efficient or least costly should be given high priority in the growth process, it cannot be readily assumed that modern capital-intensive technologies fit this bill neatly or that they are necessarily the most efficient. In any event, this may represent an overly narrow view of technical efficiency, especially in the case of developing countries where employment creation is an important national developmental objective.

In this context, the introduction of modern technology would have to be balanced against the resource and other costs that are normally associated with labor underutilization. One such resource cost is associated to the output foregone relative to some full employment situation. There may also be significant welfare costs stemming from the demoralization and physical deprivation that tend to accompany joblessness. Related to the employment question are the potentially adverse distributional impacts of technical change. The effects of labor-saving technical change are by no means unambiguous. However, while such technical change can foster rapid capital accumulation and generate a surplus of output over wages, it may also create a bias against labor income and its share in the overall income distribution (see Taylor 1979).

Issues of technological appropriateness aside, it is now agreed that the quality of the labor force is an important factor in technological diffusion. This quality is improved through education, training, and other forms of investment in "human capital," with the latter considered to be as important as investment in reproducible capital. Such investments in human capital can take a variety of forms, including investments in schooling (primary, secondary, and higher education); health: on-the-job and vocational training; job search; preschool investment in child care; and other investments in the family (Becker 1964, 1976; Schultz 1975, 1980).

In the above context, all types of investments in humans that help to enhance their future earnings capacity are therefore considered important to the overall capital formation and growth process. This process itself raises the demand for educated manpower, and therefore leads directly to the rapid accumulation of human capital. Further, human capital theorists argue that increases in the level of education tend to raise both the private and social rates of return on education significantly, leading to higher levels of both human and reproducible capital in the future.

Most studies show that there is a positive effect on income and output growth stemming primarily from the improved skills and knowledge created, with the resultant higher productivity rewarded in the form of higher incomes. The employment (derived demand for educated manpower) and income benefits are also related to an allocative effect, with the latter referring to the ability of educated individuals to evaluate and take advantage of new opportunities. Schultz (1980) terms this "the ability to deal with disequilibria" and gives as an example the rational response of farmers to prices and other incentives.

The above discussion takes a very limited and technocratic view of the labor factor. At least two qualifications need to be added. First, as further discussed in the next chapter, account needs to be taken of the adverse effects of rapid population and labor force growth on the labor allocation process in contemporary developing countries. Second, as argued in Chapter 6, there is a need for a broader focus on human resource development not only as an input into the production process but, more important, in terms of basic human needs fulfillment and the role of human beings in the overall development process. In this context, human beings are both a means and an end of authentic development.

# 5

# *Patterns of Growth and Structural Change*

As indicated in the previous chapter, an important dimension of growth analysis is concerned with the identification and measurement of changes in resource allocation and mobilization patterns that accompany the historical transition from low to high per capita income levels. This chapter focuses briefly on the following aspects of such structural changes: (1) the transformation of production structures, demand, and trade; (2) sectoral labor allocation patterns and demographic change; and (3) generalizations about changes in the monetary and financial sectors.

## The Transformation of Demand, Production, and Trade

The most general model of structural changes that are supposed to take place during the transition from low to high levels of development posits a decline in the agricultural sector and a concomitant increase in the role of industry and services. This expectation is based on an extrapolation of the historical growth experience of both developed capitalist and socialist nations. In the former case, the patterns of structural changes observed in the past, and especially the increasing imbalance between the agricultural and nonagricultural sectors, are usually traced to changes in the structure of domestic and foreign demand. In the latter case, the generalization grew out of the Soviet industrialization debate between 1924 and 1928 and the philosophy of rapid industrialization underlying the New Economic Policy (1921–28). The emphasis was on the development of heavy industry and the collectivization of agriculture, which severely constrained the decision of peasant farmers with respect to the marketing of agricultural surpluses. This resulted from a deliberate policy in which the agricultural sector was made to subsidize industry in the Soviet Union through a monopolistic pricing policy for industrial goods.

Returning to the general case of sectoral changes in production sectors, one basic explanation is that goods and services with a higher income elasticity of demand become increasingly more important in final demand and consumption as per capita income rises. In this context, Engel's Law is considered to be the most pervasive force in a growing economy. It states that the proportion of income spent on basic food items tends to decline as per capita income increases, that is, that the income elasticity of demand for food is less than unity. On a related basis, increases in per capita income are also accompanied by changes in the composition of food items consumed, with basic grains, roots, and tubers being increasingly replaced by fruits, vegetables, meat products, and high-quality processed foods. This shift in demand patterns, it is argued, is related to a decline in agriculture, with a gradual transition in the mix of commodities produced and a concomitant growth in processing, marketing and distribution activities by the nonfarm sector.

From this has emerged the well-established generalization that, for every region of the world, living standards tend to be higher when the relative importance of the agricultural sector in the generation of output, employment, and income is reduced (Kuznets 1966). The relative decline in the agricultural sector is predicated on the assumption of differences in sector growth rates resulting from uneven increases in sectoral productivity as new techniques and processes are adopted, as well as by the uneven expansion of factor inputs among sectors. Since new techniques are typically embodied in capital, a combination of increases in factor inputs and new technology provide the mechanism for differential sector growth rates (Johnston and Kilby 1975).

In elaboration, a study by Chenery and Syrquin (1975), using a sample of 93 countries for the 1950–70 period, found that as per capita income rises from $100 to $1,500 there is a major change in the composition of demand, with a decline in food consumption from 36 to 15 percent of GDP. Primary industry (comprising agriculture, fishing, forestry, mining, and quarrying) makes up about 45 percent of a country's value-added at the $100 per capita income level and declines to about 14 percent as per capita income increases to $1,000. Over the same income range, primary industry's share in employment falls from 68 to 25 percent. Industry (comprising manufacturing and construction) has sector shares in value-added and employment increasing from about 15 to 35 percent and from 9

**TABLE 5.1:** Normal variation in economic structure with level of development

| Sector[a] | Per capita GNP levels (U.S.$ 1964) | | | | | | |
|---|---|---|---|---|---|---|---|
| | 100 | 200 | 300 | 400 | 500 | 800 | 1,000 |
| Value Added Shares | | | | | | | |
| Primary | 0.452 | 0.327 | 0.266 | 0.228 | 0.202 | 0.156 | 0.138 |
| Industry | 0.149 | 0.215 | 0.251 | 0.276 | 0.294 | 0.331 | 0.347 |
| Utilities | 0.061 | 0.072 | 0.079 | 0.086 | 0.089 | 0.098 | 0.102 |
| Services | 0.338 | 0.385 | 0.403 | 0.411 | 0.415 | 0.416 | 0.413 |
| Employment Shares | | | | | | | |
| Primary | 0.658 | 0.557 | 0.489 | 0.438 | 0.395 | 0.300 | 0.252 |
| Industry | 0.091 | 0.164 | 0.206 | 0.235 | 0.258 | 0.303 | 0.325 |
| Services | 0.251 | 0.279 | 0.304 | 0.327 | 0.347 | 0.396 | 0.423 |
| Structure of Domestic Demand[b] | | | | | | | |
| Private | 0.700 | 0.686 | 0.667 | 0.654 | 0.645 | 0.625 | 0.617 |
| Government | 0.137 | 0.134 | 0.135 | 0.136 | 0.138 | 0.144 | 0.148 |
| Food | 0.392 | 0.315 | 0.275 | 0.248 | 0.229 | 0.191 | 0.175 |

[a]Sectoral definitions are as follows: Primary production comprises agriculture, forestry, fishing, mining, and quarrying; Industry comprises manufacturing and construction; Utilities comprises electricity, gas, water, transport, and communication; and Services comprises most everything else.

[b]As percentages of GDP.

*Source:* Chenery and Syrquin, Table 3, p. 20.

to 32 percent, respectively, over the same income range. These and related patterns are shown in Table 5.1.

Further, the effects of these changes on the structural composition of the economy can be deciphered by sorting out countries by size and export orientation. The same study found that large countries transform their economic structures at an earlier point in their development. In the $200 to $800 per capita income range, the share of industry is 5 to 6 percent higher in large countries compared to small countries. This difference is also concentrated in industries that have important economies of scale, for example, basic metals and chemicals. The exports of large countries are also more biased toward industrial rather than primary products. Chenery and Taylor (1968) also analyzed large and small country effects and disaggregated small countries into those that primarily export manufactures vis-à-vis those that primarily export agricultural products and raw materials. They found that in the case of small country-primary exporters, the GNP share of primary production exceeds that of industry up to an income level of nearly $800 GNP per capita, whereas for large countries and small country exporters of manufactures, industrial production exceeds primary production at income levels of about $275 GNP per capita.

It can be commented that the level of aggregation in this type of analysis tends to conceal the changes that occur because of increased specialization in agriculture as development proceeds. In the early stages of development, agriculture tends to be self-sufficient, uses few modern inputs, and processes most of its own products (e.g., butter making and milling on the farm). As development proceeds, there is a growing reliance on purchased inputs (chemicals, machinery, and so on) and a downstream transfer of many of the processing, marketing, and transport functions to the nonfarm sector. Expressed differently, an agro-industrial complex begins to emerge that, while dependent on agriculture, is nevertheless classified under the industry and service sectors in aggregate statistics. This gives a false impression of the speed at which countries industrialize. For example, Denmark and New Zealand are relatively developed countries that are still very dependent on agriculture, yet the aggregate statistics show the share of agriculture in their GNP to be only about 12 percent. Even in Iowa in the United States, agriculture accounts for only 11 percent of total state output.

A crucial issue in the debate on sectoral transformation concerns the specific role that agriculture should play in the growth process and, on a related basis, the appropriate kinds of intersectoral linkages that should be developed over time so that the requisite "balance" is maintained between the agricultural and nonagricultural sectors. In other words, the concern is whether agricultural growth and development can be made commensurate with that experienced by other sectors of the economy. In this context, three broad sets of roles have been traditionally envisaged for the agricultural sector. The first concerns the necessity to raise agricultural production and productivity as a means of meeting essential domestic food requirements and as a source of foreign exchange earnings through agricultural exports. However, the experience of developing countries suggests that these two objectives may conflict, especially where there is dualism in the agricultural sector, for example, where food is produced by subsistence farmers and the export crops by a modernized and progressive subsector. We return to this subject in Chapters 6 and 7.

Second, agriculture can help to increase the size of the domestic market. The rationale is that agricultural transformation is usually accompanied by an increasing share of output that enters the market, that is, the marketed surplus. Related requirements are that (1) there should be an efficient, price-responsive agricultural sector; (2) that all agricultural output should pass through commercial marketing channels; (3) that there should be a price for all agricultural commodities; and (4) reliable information on production and market performance is instantly and freely available.

The market contribution is also predicated on increases in farmers' incomes, and therefore their spending power and capacity to save. The general argument is that rises in agricultural productivity would bring about increases in the domestic market for industrial goods on account of a rise in domestic food production relative to exports and an increase in the income and spending power of farmers. It is further assumed that increased food production would benefit poor farmers primarily. This, in turn, would lead to a more equal distribution of income and, given the increase in total incomes, expenditures on industrial goods would increase. However, the development experience suggests that there is no unambiguous relationship between increased farm incomes and spending on the one hand, and the creation of a larger domestic market for industrial goods on the other. The result depends on farmers' spending propensities for domestically produced goods relative to imports and the extent to which the former are allowed to compete with the latter.

A third set of roles for the agricultural sector is related to the links that are forged between it and the industrial sector. In this context, the agricultural sector is required to provide raw materials for industrial production, domestic savings for industrial expansion, and surplus labor for the more rapidly growing industrial and services sectors. In the latter case, the expectation is that the abundant supplies of labor that are released from the agricultural sector would permit a rapid expansion in agricultural output. The higher productivity in the industrial sector would concurrently raise wages of those employed in the modern sector, and these higher wages would draw labor from agriculture. A further assumption is that if the increase in industrial growth exceeds that of population, output per head in agriculture would also increase, even if there are no changes in land tenure arrangements, cropping patterns, or production techniques.

The nature of the intersectoral linkages is related to the more general question whether agriculture has the "ability to lead" or "needs to follow" other sectors during the process of economic transformation. There are at least three alternative perspectives of thought on this issue: the "pro-industrial," the "pro-agricultural," and the "balanced growth" perspective. The pro-industrialization alternative is based on the argument that industry raises incomes by providing employment at higher levels of productivity compared to agriculture. Further, industry is thought to provide the potential for self-sustaining growth through the reinvestment of profits and through linkages to other sectors that use industrial outputs as inputs. In this context, the stimulation of industry is sometimes considered a necessary condition for agricultural improvement since incomes generated in the industrial sector may help to reduce input constraints on agricultural sector expansion. Some supporters of the pro-industrial argument also point to (1) the difficulty encountered in introducing modern agricultural technology into traditional agriculture; (2) the fact that the low price elasticity of demand for agricultural products in both domestic and international markets tends to frustrate the leadership potential of the agricultural sector; and (3) the possibility that the capital cost (for water, fertilizer, pesticides, machinery, and so on) may be higher in agriculture than in industry.

By contrast, supporters of the pro-agricultural perspective question the efficacy of the industrial sector as a vehicle for creating income and employment and point to the sector's inability to absorb surplus labor. Accordingly, it is argued that the agricultural sector should receive primary attention on the grounds that the per unit cost of increasing output and employment in agriculture is much lower than that in industry. According to two noted students of the subject, "Apart from the question whether a program that leaves the bulk of the nation's population out of account can properly be called national development, industrialization itself moves on its stomach; it must be supported by an adequate food supply" (South-worth and Johnston 1967, p. 11).

In the final analysis, therefore, there is a need to recognize that the development of manufacturing industries does not necessarily preclude the expansion of agriculture. The problem of intersectoral transformation may not be so much one of choosing between agriculture and nonagriculture, but rather one of ensuring a balanced expansion of all appropriate sectors of the economy. This should not be interpreted to mean that the best development path is necessarily one in which every sector or activity expands perfectly in step with each other. In some cases, countries will have to select those activities and sectors where progress will induce further progress elsewhere. As Hirschman (1958, 1977) argues, the process of transformation should not be viewed merely in terms of a set of alternatives (agriculture versus industry) but more in terms of the potential linkages that can be created over time. The related policy prescription is that activities with a high degree of interdependence (measured by the proportion of output purchased from other sectors) should be established early in the transformation process because of the growth stimulus provided by output-using and input-supplying sectors and industries.

Finally, another link in the pattern of resource allocation is provided by the nature of foreign demand, with trade perceived to play a pivotal role as an engine of growth. The theoretical explanation is provided by the theory of comparative advantage alluded to in the previous chapter. Besides the theoretical benefits of trade liberalization, reference is also sometimes made to the historically positive relationship between trade and economic growth. In this context, the claim is that trade expanded at a much faster pace than domestic production for most industrialized nations during the nineteenth century, with the growth process increasingly transmitted to other parts of the world. One reason was the increase in their demand for primary commodities, with this increased demand outstripping the growth in national income in many instances. The early experience has also demonstrated that the process of transition from low to high per capita income levels tends to be accompanied by shifts in the commodity composition of output, that is, from primary production to manufactures and industrial goods.

Given the peculiar natural resource advantages of developing countries, the implication for them is that export expansion during the early stages of development should take the form of primary commodity exports and that this would be followed by the production and export of industrial goods in later stages. Historically, such export-led development has taken place through various linkages between the export "staple" and related secondary and tertiary activities in the industrial and service sectors, respectively. This has resulted in a generalization that the process of economic growth is initiated through the utilization of natural resources, on the assumption that there are no alternative uses attached to the production of staples or other resource-intensive commodities for export. In this context, staple production is viewed essentially as a process of domestic capital formation in the industries that are linked to the staple.

This linkage process is created through the formation of various backward, forward, and final demand linkages between staple production and other activities. The backward linkages occur when staple production leads to the utilization of other commodities as inputs in the staple-producing activity. Forward linkages occur when there are other production activities requiring staple products as inputs. The final demand linkages refer to the induced household, business, and government expenditures that are generated by staple production. The general assumption is that, over time, the spread effects created by staple production and exports would permeate the entire structure of the economy, thereby providing the momentum required for self-sustained growth (for a fuller discussion, see Hirschman 1977; and David and Scandizzo 1980).

The literature provides several examples of attempts to define, classify, and analyze the nature of these linkages. The general consensus is that the strengths and weaknesses associated with export-led development based on staple production are by no means uniform. However, the ability of the staple to make a meaningful contribution to the transformation process depends on at least two factors. First, the production and export of the staple must increase and remain at a relatively high level. Second, the possibility must exist for the staple products being exported to induce further increases in domestic expenditure through second, third, and fourth round effects. The full working out of the process would therefore result in changes in the structure of demand, production, and factor markets. Further, export expansion based on staple production can set the stage for import substitution industrialization in later stages.


## Labor Allocation
## and Sectoral Employment Patterns

The sectoral changes identified earlier tend to be associated with shifts in the labor force from agriculture and other primary activities to secondary (manufacturing) and tertiary (services) activities or, historically, from those sectors or activities where average labor productivity is low to others where it is higher. The changing patterns of labor force allocation and employment are associated with changes in the composition of demand that, in turn, is due to increasing incomes and intersectoral variations in the rate of labor productivity growth.

In general, the quantity of labor absorbed in a particular sector is closely related to its productivity ratio, that is, its average product per worker relative to the national average. The historical pattern has been for intersectoral productivity differentials to be greater during the early phases of development and to narrow as per capita income increases. Average labor productivity in agriculture is usually lower and generally well below the national average over the entire per capita income range. Nonagricultural sectors normally begin the transformation process with labor productivity well above the national average (Johnston and Kilby 1975).

The growing sector differentials in output per worker may result from an unequal increase in inputs of capital, technology, and other factors among sectors, particularly since intersectoral productivity differentials reflect total factor productivity, that is, the contribution of all inputs and not just labor. Further, sector differences in labor quality may widen with increased age-sex differentials, or growing sector differences in education and training. Other possibilities are that specific product and factor markets may be imperfect, or that opportunities for factor substitution may differ among sectors.

The skill and education differentials mentioned above are related to the fact that economic growth is normally associated with an increasing technological complexity of the overall production process, increasing division of labor, and economies of scale. As Kuznets (1966) points out, the increasing share of services, the introduction of labor-saving technologies in agriculture, and the general rise in education levels and aspirations tend to be associated with increasing skill differentiation. The result is a growth in white-collar, technical, and professional cadres as a proportion of the total labor force.

As in the case of sector output changes, several studies show that the share of employment in primary activities tends to fall as an economy develops, while that in the industrial sector rises (Clark 1957; Maddison 1970; Kuznets 1966; Chenery and Syrquin 1975; and Stern and Lewis 1980). However, the pattern of employment in industry does not necessarily follow the pattern of structural change in output. This is because technological change and investment tend to be concentrated in modern branches of manufacturing, such as chemicals, basic metals, metal products, and machinery.

The results of the study by Stern and Lewis (1980) on the influence on employment patterns produced by changing levels and composition of output show that the direct labor coefficients or labor-output ratios tend to decline for all industries as an economy develops. This decline tends to reduce the employment impact of an expansion in output and is associated with technological progress and the increasing substitution between capital and labor. However, judgments about these and other uniform patterns must be tempered by the fact that country differences in size, resource endowments, development patterns, and external economic policies may be important factors explaining differences in sectoral labor absorption profiles.

Further, there are several reasons that the contemporary experience of developing countries does not necessarily conform to patterns observed for the more developed countries during the early phases of their transformation. The available evidence suggests that the two experiences may not be strictly comparable. During the past two decades, agriculture has accounted for 73 percent of the labor force in low income countries and 46 percent in middle income countries, compared to a mere 7 percent in the developed countries. While labor's share has been declining in each case, the agricultural labor force of the developing countries still remains considerably higher than that of the developed countries during the early phases of their development. In 1900, about 59 percent of the labor force in the now developed countries was employed in agriculture (World Bank 1979).

Further, the labor force growth in today's developing countries has been much more rapid, compared to the historical experience of the developed countries. The current annual growth in the labor force in developing countries is more than 2 percent, compared to a labor force growth of less than 1 percent per annum recorded for the European industrial nations throughout the nineteenth century. It took more than 90 years for the labor force to double in industrial countries, compared to the 30 years it now takes in the developing countries. On average, the industrialized nations were able to absorb about 50 percent of their incremental labor force into industry during the period of their transformation. By contrast, today's developing countries are able to absorb less than 20 percent of their incremental labor force into the industrial sector each year.

These differences are traceable to differential rates of population growth (for an analysis, see World Bank 1980, 1984). The developing countries of today are experiencing population growth rates that are three times as high as that of developed countries. During the 1950–80 period, developing countries experienced an average rate of population growth of about 2.5 percent per annum, compared to 0.8 percent for the developed countries throughout the nineteenth century. Such differences were also replicated in the industrial structure of the labor force. Around 1900, the industrial sector of developed countries accounted for about 22 percent of the labor force. This compares to about 11 percent for contemporary low income countries (World Bank 1980).

In some accounts, the various quantitative and qualitative changes in the labor force are explained in terms of a demographic transition that is inherent in the long-term pattern of structural change. Demographic transition theory posits that there are usually three successive stages of demographic evolution. The first is an agrarian or pre-industrial stage in which birth and death rates tend to balance each other out, with the population remaining relatively stable. However, fertility rates tend to be high during this stage because people adhere to customs and beliefs that promote large family size. This large family size, in turn, tends to counterbalance the mortality levels that are high because of poor diets, inadequate health and sanitation, and, in general, poor basic human needs fulfillment.

The second stage is a transitional one that is marked by a movement from high to relatively low fertility levels. At the outset of the growth process, mortality rates are the first to decline, with fertility rates remaining at traditional levels. This is explained by the fact that nutritional levels and other aspects of basic needs fulfillment tend to improve as per capita incomes increase. Fertility levels begin to fall at a later date and as contraceptive methods become more widely accepted by society. It is also argued that such fertility declines are associated with the growth of impersonal systems of specialization and the emergence of new economic roles outside the home for women. This stage also witnesses increased urbanization. This urbanization, and its correlate (industrialization), is deemed to promote small family size. The underlying assumption is that children are less of an economic asset in an urban setting compared to a rural one.

The third stage is considered to be a stationary one in which both fertility and mortality rates are low and tend to converge. Some of the reasons explaining the low fertility rates include (1) the rise in the education of women, and the corresponding changes in their roles and values; (2) the increasing female participation in industrial labor force, with a secondary importance attached to the child-bearing role; (3) the sustained reduction in infant mortality; (4) the decline in traditional religious beliefs that previously supported high fertility norms; (5) alterations in the role of the extended family system; (6) urbanization and its impact on traditional forms of behavior; (7) the introduction of superior contraceptive methods; (8) the development of old age and other social security systems outside the extended family; and (9) increases in overall socioeconomic mobility (Leibenstein 1974).

There are several reasons that population growth in contemporary developing countries poses a greater economic burden today than it did in the now developed countries during their period of economic transformation. These, in turn, tend to cast doubts on the strict applicability of demographic transition theory. In the first place, birth rates in developing countries are much more rapid than the corresponding rates for Europe, Japan, and North America during the nineteenth century. Population growth in the latter countries hardly exceeded 1 percent a year. The implication is that there will have to be a substantial reduction in developing country birth and population growth rates for any meaningful application of transition theory. Second, the substantial decline in mortality rates, combined with persistently high birth rates, has resulted in a relatively young population profile in developing countries. As further discussed in Chapter 6, this poses a unique kind of labor absorption problem. Third, the large-scale emigration that occurred in nineteenth-century Europe is not possible in today's developing countries. Nearly 45 percent of the increase in the population of the United Kingdom during 1846–1932 emigrated. This compares with a low 0.5 percent of the increase in Asia during the 1970–80 period. Fourth, income in developing countries remains relatively low, human and physical capital is less well built up, and social and political institutions are less well established, compared to the now developed countries during their fastest period of population growth. Fifth, as indicated earlier in this chapter, most developing countries are still largely dependent on agriculture and can no longer draw on large tracts of unused land. Population growth in rural areas of countries like the United Kingdom had come to a halt by the 1880s. Rural population growth in most contemporary Asian and African countries still exceeds 2 percent a year, even when account is taken of the substantial rural to urban migration. This implies a doubling of the population size in rural areas every 40 years (World Bank 1984).

The conventional wisdom teaches us that rapid population growth can slow the pace of development for the following reasons. First, it exacerbates the choice between higher consumption now and the investment needed to achieve higher consumption levels in the future. Rapid population growth usually requires more "demographic investment," that is, additional investment to maintain current levels of per capita income. With rapid population growth, an additional amount of investment is needed to care for the needs of the increasing numbers of dependents in the population, that is, children and old people who are not in the work force. It means that the economy has to support a larger number of people without any change in the means of support provided by its aggregate income or output. Metaphorically speaking, it has to run in order to remain in the same place. A larger amount of investment ("productive") is therefore needed if some modicum of per capita income growth is to be attained. One dimension of this problem concerns the incremental investment needed to raise the "quality" of the population, that is, investment in the "human capital" or the education of skilled manpower needed for economic development.

Another factor, emphasized in Chapter 4, is concerned with the fact that, in many countries, rapid population growth tends to threaten the precarious balance between scarce natural resources and people. Traditional agricultural systems become overloaded, and the risk of environmental damage becomes even greater. These factors, in turn, tend to impose further constraints on the income-earning potential of the poor. The problem is further compounded by the fact that rapid population growth tends to slow the transfer of labor out of low-productivity agriculture into the more progressive agricultural and modern industrial sectors.

While rapid population growth undoubtedly has negative effects on the growth and development potential, there is still no consensus among demographers and economists about the factors responsible for rapid population growth and the direction of causality between such population growth and overall economic development. This is explained both by differences in ideology and the lack of conclusive empirical evidence (see Stavig 1979). First, the process of demographic/economic interaction tends to be a complex one involving the cumulative interplay of a large number of physiological, cultural, institutional, and other socioeconomic variables, with every link in the chain related to others (for a discussion, see Yotopolous 1977). A second viewpoint is that population growth is not so much a cause of underdevelopment, but rather a symptom of the failure of the development process itself. In other words, the endemic and generalized condition of poverty itself heightens the potential to procreate. The implication is that a slowing of population growth is likely to take place as steps are taken to alter the overall parameters of development and underdevelopment. A third is the more iconoclastic viewpoint of Simon (1982), which states that it is perhaps impossible to decide what the optimum population level is, that is, what is too few or too many. One variation on this theme is that population is far from reaching its ultimate level and that rapid population growth may therefore have a beneficial effect on per capita income and output.

## Monetary and Financial Transformation

Finally, and turning to another aspect of the transformation process, it is expected that the structural changes taking place in the real sectors of the economy would be supported by complementary changes in the monetary and financial sectors. The latter changes are predicated on the presupposition that development involves an increase in wage employment, a spread of market transactions, urbanization, commercialization, and other attributes of the modernization process. The overriding philosophy is that this process would be facilitated by the creation of a suitable institutional structure for the mobilization of capital and savings required for real economic growth.

Contextually, one basic structural change in the financial sector is considered to be monetization or the enlargement of the sphere of the money economy. Monetization involves an increase in the proportion of total transactions in the economy that is carried out through the money medium, and therefore the successive growth in various forms of money, ranging from primary money as a medium of exchange through demand deposits in banks to various forms of asset creation, including time and savings deposits. There is a large nonmonetized sector in the majority of developing countries, and the available evidence suggests that the share of the nonmonetized sector in GDP may be as much as 50 percent in some cases.

Such nonmonetized activities tend to predominate in crop production, which is usually based on two subsectors—one large scale and the other traditional. The large-scale sector is usually monetized, while traditional producers market only a part of their output, with portions retained for self-consumption and/or bartered. Besides crop production, examples of activities that are nonmonetized include housebuilding, construction of fences, storage, land reclamation, and certain forms of payment in kind, for example, commodity loans, wages in kind, and sharecropping. While there are statistical problems involved in measuring the extent of nonmonetization, it is generally agreed that nonmonetized activities include elements of both subsistence and commercialized transactions, that is, organized as well as unorganized market transactions. In general, they reflect the dualism and market fragmentation that typify developing economies.

The degree of monetization is usually measured in terms of a monetization ratio that connotes the proportion of the aggregate value of goods and services that is paid for by money (Goldsmith 1969; Chandavar-kar 1977). The path of monetization and corresponding increases in the monetization ratio reflect changes in a given country's financial structure that take place with economic development. Studies of this phenomenon generally show that (1) it is an evolutionary process; (2) it is discontinuous and varies between regions and across countries over time; and (3) increased monetization is closely associated with economic growth, with high monetization ratios closely correlated with high per capita income levels. From this has emerged the generalization that the possibilities for development are closely bound up with the transformation of the nonmonetized sector.

This is also explained in terms of the need to mobilize savings and rechannel these funds to borrowers for the purpose of financing real investment. The underlying argument is that in a developing economy, an increasing distinction tends to emerge between surplus and deficit spending units. Some writers see an inevitability about this dichotomous process traceable to three forms of division of labor in economic activity: (1) production, involving factor services and inputs; (2) accumulation and savings; and (3) intermediation, that is, the specialization between savings and ownership of primary securities (Gurley and Shaw 1964).

These three forms of division of labor are also considered to be interdependent. As an economy develops, there is a differentiation in productive activities and a corresponding specialization in productive functions. Changes in the structure and function take place at different points in space and time so that some economic units would have greater access to financial resources than others. Surplus units would save those funds that remain after consumption requirements are met. Intermediation comes into play as a mechanism for transforming savings into new investment, thereby providing impetus to the cumulative cycle of economic activity.

The process of interaction can be looked at in terms of certain successive stages of financial development. During the early stages of development, savers are the primary users of their own funds, and capital formation takes place without the creation of any new financial assets. There is usually a one-to-one correspondence between the distribution of savings on the one hand, and decisions to invest on the other. However, as an economy develops, this one-to-one correspondence between savings and investment breaks down, and a dichotomous relationship emerges. In this new situation, savers' own demand for funds tends to exceed their supply. A mechanism therefore has to be created for channeling savers' surplus funds to investors whose demand for funds exceeds their own savings. This dichotomous process is usually bridged by the creation of various financial liabilities, for example, bonds, various forms of equity, debt-asset techniques, and so on. These represent indirect claims via financial institutions that channel the surplus funds of savers to those individuals who desire them for real capital investment (Khatkhate 1972).

The general idea, therefore, is that the conditions of net lending and borrowing in the economy tend to be influenced by economic growth and the corresponding changes in the structure of production as well as in the distribution of income and wealth. Thus, as the economy develops, forces are set in motion that make financial intermediation increasingly complex. This is reflected in the growth of a large number of financial intermediaries (banks, insurance companies, building societies, and so on) that bridge the gap between lenders and borrowers in terms of their respective preferences for liquidity, risk, or rates of return.

There is a substantial literature dealing with the linkage between financial intermediation and the overall development process. While there is general agreement that financial intermediation has the potential for increasing savings and, through investment, the pace of economic growth, opinions differ on the direction of causation, or whether specific types of financial intermediation are necessary for economic development. What is generally agreed, however, is that the ability of the financial system to influence the overall process of growth and development hinges on its potential impact on the growth of savings, its ability to provide savings in a financial form, and its capacity for ensuring the most efficient transformation of such funds into real capital investment.

Finally, the process of financial development can also be influenced by the nature of government policies. Some commentators, for example, Shaw (1973) and McKinnon (1973), see the process as being frustrated by the pervasiveness of "financial repression" or the lack of "financial deepening" in the developing countries. They cite as evidence the fragmentation of financial and output markets; the nonspecialization of financial functions by financial intermediaries; the oligopolistic or high-cost structure of the banking system; and a heavy reliance on types of government fiscal, tax, and expenditure policies that tend to place severe restrictions on the efficiency of the private financial sector. What is therefore advocated are policies of financial liberalization as a means of expanding domestic liquidity and foreign reserves through the use of more appropriate pricing, interest rate, and exchange rate policies.

# III

# HETERODOX AND OTHER WORLD VIEWS

# 6

## *Beyond Economic Growth: Joblessness, Poverty, and Inequality*

Since the early 1970s, the international community has become increasingly aware of the failure of the historical growth process to promote authentic and broad-based development for the masses of the population in the developing world. These broad-based changes connote much more than increases in material economic welfare (as measured by per capita income or output performance). They are concerned more with the "content" and "quality" of GNP in relation to its level and rate of acceleration. To some extent, this represents a shift in the development paradigm toward a direct concern for poverty alleviation, employment creation, basic human needs fulfillment, and the reduction of various forms of inequality. It implies a reorientation of development goals and priorities in the direction of human development and the creation of conditions necessary for the fullest realization of the human personality (Haq 1976; Streeten 1981; Timbergen 1976; Seers 1972, 1973).

At the most fundamental level, the need for a shift in emphasis is suggested by a perceived disjuncture between the theory and praxis of economic development. The recent and current development experience shows that in the majority of cases national income growth has been accompanied by an increased immiserization of the masses of the population. In this context, the macroeconomic growth rates achieved by many developing nations since the 1950s are actually higher than the comparable rates for the industrial nations during the latter's take-off period. In the case of a few countries (notably Brazil, Mexico, South Korea, and Taiwan) impressive aggregate growth rates have been accompanied by other noticeable achievements, especially in the growth of manufacturing industry and exports of manufactured goods. The data for the 1960–83 period (Table 6.1) also show that average growth rate trends in the developing world continue to be relatively high, compared to experience of industrial nations.

However, these trends mask the fact that, for the majority of developing nations, the growth process seems to have bypassed the masses of the population and might even have worsened their lot. This is particularly true of the low income countries in Asia and Africa, where nearly 50 percent of the world's population lives. Needless to say, the failure to translate growth achievements into sustained improvements in real living standards and in the overall quality of life continues to have particularly damaging consequences for the poorest segments of society. Many still live under conditions of abject poverty and conditions of life degraded by disease, illiteracy, malnutrition, famine, and squalor. The victims therefore lack the minimum prerequisites of basic human decency.

In many countries, economic growth has been accompanied by a worsening of, or no noticeable improvements in, the pattern of income distribution. Further, problems of unemployment and underemployment might have been exacerbated due to the failure of urban industrial growth to absorb successive increments in the labor force. The latter consequence is traceable, in part, to the neglect of, and, in some cases, the exploitation of, the agricultural sector. This, in turn, has contributed to a noticeable crisis in agricultural productivity, as well as to the overall problems of poverty, especially in the rural areas.

## The Unemployment Problem

In conventional economic analysis, employment creation is treated principally as a consequence of the general process of national income and output expansion. For example, Keynesian theory asserts that the main determinant of employment lies in employers' anticipation of demand for the goods and services that they produce. This "effective demand" provides the motivational force behind the decisions to produce goods and services and to invest in plant and equipment. The realization of both production and investment decisions, in turn, is assumed to promote employment at relatively high wage levels. Accordingly, a relationship is supposed to develop between the demand for goods and the demand for labor, with the relatively high wages paid to workers enhancing their purchasing power over goods and services, thereby augmenting effective demand, and, therefore employment.

However, as Keynes pointed out, this general equilibrium result can be attained only if commodity and labor markets function in the manner

**TABLE 6.1:** Population, GDP per capita in 1980, and growth rates, 1960–83

| Country group | 1980 GDP (billions of dollars) | 1980 population (millions) | 1980 GDP per capita (dollars) | GDP growth rates (average annual percentage change) | | | | | |
|---|---|---|---|---|---|---|---|---|---|
| | | | | 1960–73 | 1973–79 | 1980 | 1981 | 1982 | 1983[a] |
| Developing countries[b] | 2,118 | 3,280 | 650 | 6.3 | 5.2 | 2.5 | 2.4 | 1.9 | 1.0 |
| Low-income | 549 | 2,175 | 250 | 5.6 | 4.8 | 5.9 | 4.8 | 5.2 | 4.7 |
| Asia | 497 | 1,971 | 250 | 5.9 | 5.2 | 6.3 | 5.2 | 5.6 | 5.1 |
| China | 284 | 980 | 290 | 8.5 | 5.7 | 6.1 | 4.8 | 7.3 | 5.1 |
| India | 162 | 675 | 240 | 3.6 | 4.3 | 6.9 | 5.7 | 2.9 | 5.4 |
| Africa | 52 | 204 | 250 | 3.5 | 2.1 | 1.3 | 1.2 | 0.5 | -0.1 |
| Middle-income oil importers | 915 | 611 | 1,500 | 6.3 | 5.6 | 4.3 | 0.9 | 0.7 | 0.3 |
| East Asia and Pacific | 204 | 183 | 1,110 | 8.2 | 8.6 | 3.6 | 6.7 | 4.2 | 6.4 |
| Middle East and North Africa | 28 | 35 | 800 | 5.2 | 3.0 | 4.2 | -2.4 | 5.5 | 2.0 |
| Sub-Saharan Africa[c] | 37 | 60 | 610 | 5.6 | 3.7 | 5.5 | 3.9 | 1.1 | 0.3 |
| Southern Europe | 201 | 91 | 2,210 | 6.7 | 5.0 | 1.5 | 2.3 | 0.7 | -0.9 |
| Latin America and Caribbean | 445 | 241 | 1,840 | 5.6 | 5.0 | 5.8 | -2.3 | -0.4 | -2.2 |
| Middle-income oil exporters[d] | 654 | 494 | 1,320 | 6.9 | 4.9 | -2.4 | 2.4 | 0.9 | -1.7 |
| High-income oil exporters | 228 | 16 | 14,250 | 10.7 | 7.7 | 7.4 | 0.0 | NA | NA |
| Industrial market economies | 7,463 | 715 | 10,440 | 4.9 | 2.8 | 1.3 | 1.3 | -0.5 | 2.3 |

N.A.: Not available.

[a] Estimated

[b] Data for 1982 and 1983 are based on a sample of 90 developing countries.

[c] Does not include South Africa.

[d] The estimated 1983 data exclude Angola, the Islamic Republic of Iran, and Iraq.

*Source:* World Bank (1984).

described by classical and neoclassical economists, that is, if aggregate demand were maintained. Where disequilibrium exists in the economic system, that is, with prices diverging from their equilibrium values, only those consumer demands that are backed by purchasing power will be met. Firms in a disequilibrium state will not be able to realize their desired sales and would therefore face a shortage of finance required to employ the productive resources needed to meet consumer requirements. Under such circumstances, the excess demand that normally governs price adjustments will be inappropriate.

Where aggregate demand is not maintained, the economy is therefore likely to face a persistent disequilibrium in labor markets, and consequently high rates of involuntary unemployment. Keynes therefore challenged the orthodox viewpoint that a free market economic system has a built-in mechanism that promotes stable equilibrium growth and full employment. Such an economy, if left on its own, could not sustain a high enough level of investment to bring about full employment. Therefore, some measure of government stimulation becomes necessary. However, Keynes did emphasize, along orthodox lines, that such public investment should be limited to the market environment, with individual economic agents left free to pursue their own economic interests.

The nature of the economic disequilibrium is somewhat starker and takes on different forms in the developing countries of today. The typical experience suggests that rapid growth in national output and high levels of consumer demand have not been translated into correspondingly high levels of employment and wages. Not only do high levels of open and involuntary unemployment persist, but the unemployment phenomenon has invariably taken on a different dimension. This is traceable to a variety of structural and institutional rigidities that characterize developing economies.

The general experience suggests that there has been a trade-off between economic growth and employment, and not necessarily a positive correlation between these two economic aggregates. At the conceptual level, it can be shown that if growth in national output is accompanied by a shift in the sectoral composition of GNP, or by a change in production techniques, for example, through the use of more capital-intensive or labor-saving technologies, then a trade-off between national output growth and employment creation becomes a real possibility. For any given economy or production sector, several alternative output growth-employment mixes are possible. This depends on available production techniques and factor substitution possibilities. In the majority of developing countries, the national and sector output mixes have shown a pro-capital bias and a concomitant undervaluation of labor and the returns to employment.

There are at least three possible explanations for this phenomenon. The first is related to the general belief, mentioned in Chapter 4, in fixed factor proportions and the related generalization that capital-intensive techniques tend to be more efficient than labor-intensive ones (for a discussion, see White 1978). A second possibility is that the basic technologies used in modern production processes tend to be capital-intensive and leave the developing countries very little technological choice. This is complicated by the nature of the mechanisms governing the international transfer of technology and by the fact that such technologies have a pro-capital bias. A third possibility is that the majority of developing countries have not addressed, in any meaningful sense, the issue of technological appropriateness and have been content to rely on imports.

We will return to the issue of technological dependence in the next chapter. The general argument, however, is that the technology used in many developing countries is inappropriate to their domestic social and economic structures, as reflected in relative factor availabilities. With relatively plentiful supplies of labor, the importation and use of capital-intensive technologies tend to bar a potentially large number of workers from effectively participating in the production process. Inappropriate patterns of technological use, and the corresponding reduction in opportunities for productive employment, are typically associated with a distorted pattern of development, or what is sometimes termed a "structural deformity." This is exemplified by the coexistence of a few growth enclaves in a sea of poverty and underdevelopment.

As mentioned earlier, the unemployment problem facing the majority of developing countries is related to certain structural disequilibria that cannot be removed through the normal process of economic growth. One such structural phenomenon manifests itself in open unemployment, which results from a disequilibrium between the growing working-age population and the availability of suitable employment opportunities. As discussed in the previous chapter, this aspect of unemployment is explained, in part, by the slow sectoral transformation of the labor force due to rapid population and labor force growth. This is related to the unusually slow expansion in industrial employment and the corresponding failure of the industrialization process to provide remunerative employment opportunities. The modern, urban, and usually capital-intensive sector has proved incapable of absorbing large numbers of people, resulting in an absolute increase in the number of potential workers remaining unemployed or underemployed in the rural and urban informal sectors of the economy.

The combined effect of rapid labor force growth and poor sectoral absorption of the labor force has been a concentration of unemployment among literate youth (especially those with a primary and secondary education) and women. In the case of youth unemployment, several case studies have recorded unemployment rates in excess of 20 percent in major urban areas in the developing countries, with the unemployed usually concentrated in the 15–24 age group. One factor in the youth unemployment problem is the lack of any significant correlation between the education received and employment prospects. Many young persons therefore form part of a "reserve army" of "educated unemployed" due to the cumulative interplay of the following factors: (1) poor educational quality; (2) inappropriateness of the education received and the inability of the economy to create employment opportunities that match the skills of the educated; and (3) the creation of false aspiration levels by the education system itself.

In the case of women, the evidence suggests that the growth process has resulted in limited improvements in their economic status. In the majority of cases, labor force participation rates tend to be lower for women compared to men. This is explained by the structural factors previously mentioned, as well as by some specific sociocultural factors limiting their access to employment. In many developing countries, female participation in the labor market depends on the availability of assistance for child care and household responsibilities through the extended family system. As a result, there is a tendency for female labor force participation to be higher in predominantly agricultural societies with strong extended family systems, compared to more urbanized societies with a larger proportion of full-time wage labor. A situation common to most developing countries is one in which the growth process, by emphasizing urban industrialization, has tended to inhibit the growth of nonagricultural labor market opportunities that are compatible with home production. In many cases, female labor market participation is also adversely affected by institutional factors such as labor market segmentation and discrimination.

The unemployment problem can be interpreted from the perspective of sectoral dualism and, in particular, from the insights provided by both the dual labor surplus models (Lewis 1954; Fei and Ranis 1964; Ranis 1973) and others concerned with factors underlying rural-urban migration (Harris and Todaro 1970; Yhap 1975). The implications of the Lewis model for savings and capital accumulation were mentioned in Chapter 4. A few other basic features are now highlighted as a means of emphasizing the implications for the unemployment problem. As previously indicated, in the Lewis version of the labor surplus model, the economy is subdivided into a modern capitalist sector and a traditional or pre-capitalist subsistence sector. The model assumes that the traditional sector is characterized by surplus labor with a low or zero marginal productivity and that the labor supply is infinitely elastic. This implies that, with production techniques and other productive resources remaining unchanged, it is possible to

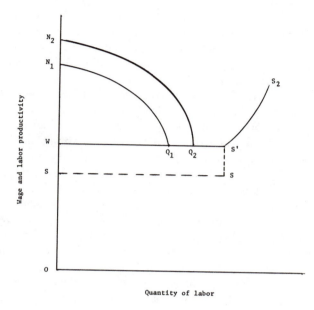

**Figure 6.1**: Wage determination and surplus labor in the Lewis model

withdraw surplus labor from the traditional sector without any loss of output. This surplus labor then becomes available for employment in the modern sector at the low wages that reflect productivity at the margin, that is, low cost per man-hour.

The situation is illustrated in Figure 6.1 in which *OS* measures subsistence income, *OW* is the minimum pay received by hired labor, $N_1Q_1$ is the initial marginal productivity of labor, and $N_2Q_2$ the marginal productivity after the savings of capitalists have resulted in a larger investment. Thus, $N_1Q_1W$ represents the initial amount of capitalist income, and $N_2Q_2W$ their enlarged income after their savings are transformed into increased investment, and as the labor productivity curve moves from $N_1Q_1$ to $N_2Q_2$. The supply curve *SS* is infinitely elastic up to the point where everyone who is able and willing to work finds employment. After that point, the labor supply curve turns sharply upward, and it is at this point that the labor surplus phenomenon comes to an end. This is the "turning point" at which surplus labor is no longer available to the modern sector at a constant wage rate, as shown by the behavior of the curve $WS_1S_2$.

The dual labor surplus model is based on the assumption that unemployment and dualism represent temporary aberrations that will disappear with rural to urban migration, that is, the employment by modern sector capitalists of workers from the traditional subsistence sector. The model turns on the following premises. Assuming that labor is homogeneous in quality and that perfect information exists, rationality dictates that workers in the agricultural sector where the marginal productivity of labor is below its social opportunity cost (defined in terms of the prevailing urban wage rate) will move to a situation where they become equal. The equilibrium adjustment is brought about by rural-urban migration, or what has been termed the force of the "invisible foot" (Nugent and Yotopolous 1979). In the denouement of this process, the marginal productivity of those workers remaining in the agricultural sector would be raised and that of urban sector workers lowered. With new capital investment, more and more labor can be absorbed in the urban sector, leading ultimately to the elimination of the labor surplus and dualism.

However, the experience of the majority of developing countries suggests that equilibrium has not been achieved by the increased shift of the population. The persistently high rates of migration from rural to urban areas have been accompanied by increasing urban unemployment and rural underemployment. Second, despite the high rates of urban unemployment, wage differentials between urban and rural areas have been maintained, or have even increased. The migration factor, far from bringing about equilibrium between the two sectors, has added fuel to the process of cumulative disequilibrium. The situation has been compounded by the "urban bias" underlying the development strategies pursued by most developing countries (see Lipton 1976).

Another type of explanation focuses on the nature of the migration process itself. As explained by Nugent and Yotopolous (1979), migration is a highly selective process and, contrary to traditional thinking, does not necessarily represent a movement of homogeneous and faceless persons from country to town. Compared to indigenous urban workers who are unemployed, the average earnings profile of migrants tends to be higher, and they do not remain unemployed for long periods of time. Migrants tend to be young, ambitious, and better-than-average educated. They do not remain for long in the urban unemployment line and quickly move to the head of the line, thereby appropriating the better paying jobs. This causes employers to upgrade the skill requirements of middle and higher paying jobs so that more marginal workers are displaced or otherwise forced to join the "reserve army" of the urban unemployed.

To the extent that this is true, migration has at least two noticeable effects on the prospects for employment and growth. On the one hand, the employment of migrants in the urban sector leads to a marginalization of previously employed workers and heightens the polarization in this sector. On the other hand, the departure of migrants from the rural areas tends to rob the agricultural sector of potentially valuable human capital, thereby accentuating the decline of the rural sector and increasing the polarization between the agricultural and industrial sectors.

Even with substantial rural to urban migration, the rapid population and labor force growth in the rural sector has resulted in a rural labor surplus in relation to land and other productive resources. This has given rise to various forms of disguised unemployment or underemployment. While economists do not agree about the exact nature of this phenomenon or how it should be defined, it is generally related to a disequilibrium between factor availability (land, capital, technology, and so on) and rural population size. Given factor availabilities, labor time is not optimally spent, resulting in low productivity, low incomes, and sporadic employment.

One commonly cited factor is the land fragmentation and the skewed land distribution patterns that are typical in many rural areas. It is also sometimes thought that the constraints posed by small and fragmented holdings could be removed by drawing labor away from the land, and/or by consolidating holdings. However, the historical experience suggests that consolidation is not necessarily a prerequisite for increasing productivity and that drawing labor away from the land does not necessarily reduce unemployment and underemployment. There are other factors that tend to militate against the transfer of labor from the rural sector. Many people dislike wage labor and show a preference for self-employment. Some may belong to a social division of labor within the extended family, tribe, or village. As in the case of self-employment, others may be desirous of preserving their freedom and independence, and/or avoid the impersonal relationships of urban factory work. The incidence of these and related factors suggests that the only answer lies in the design and execution of programs of balanced national and regional development, including agrarian and land reform, and rural industrialization.

## The Seamless Web of Poverty

One assumption underlying conventional thinking is that economic growth tends to be positively correlated with employment creation, income generation, and reductions in poverty. In other words, with higher GDP growth rates, more people will be employed so that the number of unemployed people living in poverty will also be substantially reduced. The implicit assumption is that income is more or less equally distributed among all classes in society. However, as indicated in Chapter 1, the majority of people living in the developing world still experience various forms of absolute and relative deprivation. One reason is that the goals of economic growth do not necessarily imply an equal sharing of poverty by all groups in society.

The measurement of poverty and its incidence has always posed several intractable theoretical and empirical problems. These are not addressed here. The most general approach, however, is to measure poverty in terms of some minimum income level. The assumption is that income can be spent on the satisfaction of different kinds of needs and therefore provides a reasonable indicator of overall socioeconomic welfare. On this basis, one internationally accepted yardstick is one that defines the incidence of absolute poverty in terms of the minimum income necessary to purchase a nutritionally adequate diet. The income standard, or "poverty line," is therefore set in relation to food intake and minimum consumption baskets considered necessary for a normal and healthy life.

On the above basis, a conservative estimate is that there are now more than one billion people living in absolute poverty in the developing world. The majority of the poor are located in the poorer, low income, or "least developed" countries in sub-Saharan Africa and Asia. These two regions of the world account for about two-thirds of the world's population. The data in Table 6.2 show income and poverty profiles for a select group of countries. The data indicate a close correlation between per capita income attainment and poverty levels.

The absolute poverty measure is one that tries to measure the number of people with inadequate means, that is, insufficient income. Alternatively, the problem could be looked at in terms of consequences, that is, the implications for the provision of basic human needs of health, education, nutrition, housing, and so on. In this context, of the 800 million or more people considered absolutely poor in the developing countries during the early 1980s, about 600 million, or 75 pecent, were illiterate. Further, only about 40 percent of the children in these countries complete more than three years of primary education. In 1980, nearly 550 million people or more were living in countries where life expectancy was less than 50 years, and about 400 million in countries where the child death rate (1–4 years) was more than 200 per 1,000 live births. This is a rate about 20 times that encountered in the developed world (World Bank 1980).

Some of these consequences of poverty are highlighted in Table 6.3, which shows select country performances in terms of longevity, literacy, and overall physical quality of life. The general picture that presents itself

**TABLE 6.2:** Income and poverty profiles–select countries

| Country | GNP per capita U.S.$ 1975[a] | Percent of population in poverty | Share of income received by lowest 40 percent |
|---------|------------------------------|----------------------------------|-----------------------------------------------|
| Bangladesh | 200 | 64 | 20 |
| Ethiopia | 213 | 68 | 17 |
| Burma | 237 | 65 | 16 |
| Indonesia | 280 | 59 | 16 |
| Uganda | 280 | 55 | 15 |
| Zaire | 281 | 53 | 15 |
| Sudan | 281 | 54 | 15 |
| Tanzania | 297 | 51 | 7 |
| Pakistan | 299 | 43 | 17 |
| India | 300 | 46 | 17 |
| Kenya | 413 | 55 | 9 |
| Nigeria | 433 | 35 | 13 |
| Philippines | 469 | 33 | 12 |
| Sri Lanka | 471 | 14 | 20 |
| Senegal | 550 | 35 | 10 |
| Egypt | 561 | 20 | 14 |
| Thailand | 584 | 32 | 12 |
| Ghana | 628 | 25 | 11 |
| Morocco | 643 | 26 | 11 |
| Ivory Coast | 695 | 25 | 10 |
| South Korea | 797 | 8 | 17 |
| Chile | 798 | 11 | 13 |
| Zambia | 798 | 10 | 13 |
| Colombia | 851 | 19 | 10 |
| Turkey | 914 | 14 | 9 |
| Tunisia | 992 | 10 | 11 |
| Malaysia | 1,006 | 12 | 11 |
| Taiwan | 1,075 | 5 | 22 |
| Guatemala | 1,128 | 10 | 11 |
| Brazil | 1,136 | 15 | 9 |
| Peru | 1,183 | 18 | 7 |
| Iran | 1,259 | 13 | 12 |
| Mexico | 1,429 | 14 | 8 |
| Yugoslavia | 1,701 | 5 | 19 |

[a]The GNP figures are based on adjusted estimates to take account of some nonmentary components (Kravis, Heston, and Summers 1982).

*Source:* Ahluwalia, Carter, and Chenery (1979).

**TABLE 6.3**: Quality of life and related indicators of broad-based development

| Country<br>(1) | Physical<br>quality<br>of life<br>index[a]<br>early 1980s<br>(2) | Life<br>expectancy<br>at birth (yrs)<br>1982<br>(3) | Infant<br>mortality<br>rate (aged<br>under 1 yr)<br>1982<br>(4) | Adult literacy<br>rate (percent)<br>1982<br>(5) |
|---|---|---|---|---|
| Somalia | 19 | 39 | 184 | 60 |
| Ethiopia | 20 | 47 | 122 | 15 |
| Nigeria | 25 | 50 | 109 | 34 |
| Senegal | 25 | 44 | 155 | 10 |
| Liberia | 26 | 54 | 91 | 25 |
| Zambia | 28 | 51 | 105 | 44 |
| Tanzania | 31 | 52 | 98 | 79 |
| Zaire | 32 | 50 | 106 | 55 |
| Ghana | 35 | 55 | 86 | NA |
| Bangladesh | 35 | 48 | 133 | 26 |
| Haiti | 36 | 54 | 110 | 23 |
| Pakistan | 38 | 50 | 121 | 24 |
| Kenya | 41 | 57 | 77 | 47 |
| India | 43 | 55 | 94 | 36 |
| Egypt | 43 | 57 | 104 | 44 |
| Zimbabwe | 46 | 56 | 83 | 69 |
| Indonesia | 48 | 53 | 102 | 62 |
| Peru | 62 | 58 | 83 | 80 |
| Malaysia | 66 | 67 | 29 | 60 |
| Brazil | 68 | 64 | 73 | 76 |
| Thailand | 68 | 63 | 51 | 86 |
| China | 69 | 67 | 67 | 69 |
| Philippines | 71 | 64 | 51 | 75 |
| Chile | 77 | 70 | 27 | NA |
| Sri Lanka | 82 | 69 | 32 | 85 |
| South Korea | 82 | 67 | 32 | 93 |
| Singapore | 83 | 72 | 11 | 83 |
| Jamaica | 84 | 73 | 10 | 90 |
| Cuba | 84 | 75 | 17 | 95 |
| Yugoslavia | 84 | 71 | 34 | 85 |
| Argentina | 85 | 70 | 44 | 93 |
| Hong Kong | 86 | 75 | 10 | NA |

NA: Not available

[a]The Physical Quality of Life Index is an unweighted average of life expectancy at birth, infant mortality, and adult literacy. It ranges between 0 (the lowest score) and 100 (the highest score). The index in the table has been calculated from figures different from those shown in columns 3–5.

*Source:* Column 2–Morris (1979); Columns 3 to 5–World Bank (1984).

is that poverty is a "seamless web" and involves the decumulative effects of low incomes and other socioeconomic indicators alluded to earlier. A schematic picture of this seamless web is presented in Figure 6.2, which shows the cumulative interdependence among the various indicators of socioeconomic well-being. Some of the implications for development theory are pointed out in the next two chapters of this study.

It should be mentioned, however, that the poor do not comprise a homogeneous group, but represent people who are open to different forms of vulnerability. Some poor people have incomes above the minimum, while others exist at the margin of survival. The majority live in rural areas and depend on agriculture as the principal means of subsistence. In general, they have limited access to resources, with the majority landless and near landless. They are usually unemployed or underemployed, and, in the latter case, they have no alternative but to work for long hours and at very low levels of productivity and incomes. The lion's share of the meager incomes earned goes toward food consumption. In the majority of cases, the poor have no alterative but to subsist on limited diets of cereals, tubers, and starchy roots.

The malnutrition that results impairs their ability to work and lowers their resistance to disease, and, consequently, large numbers tend to suffer from a variety of tropical diseases. There is no doubt, therefore, that poverty is a major cause of malnutrition in the developing world. In general, the evidence suggests that both the inability to purchase sufficient quantities of food in the marketplace, as well as the high incidence of protein-caloric deficiencies, can be traced to the seamless web. The malnourished predominate in areas that are characterized by the cumulative interplay of low incomes, high levels of unemployment and underemployment, inappropriate land tenure systems, and heavy population pressure.

However, the stark picture presented above should be tempered by the fact that the absolute incomes of the poor have been rising, or the consequences of poverty substantially reduced, in two types of developing countries: socialist-oriented countries such as Cuba, the Peoples Republic of China, North Vietnam, Sri Lanka, and Tanzania, and high-growth capitalist-oriented countries such as South Korea, Taiwan, Hong Kong, and Singapore. While these countries have different political and economic structures, their combined experience points to some of the more important sets of factors explaining the possibilities for poverty alleviation.

First, social services in the form of education, health care, and sanitation and pure water supplies have been made available to all segments of the population as a part of deliberate government policy. This could be contrasted with the general pattern observed in the majority of

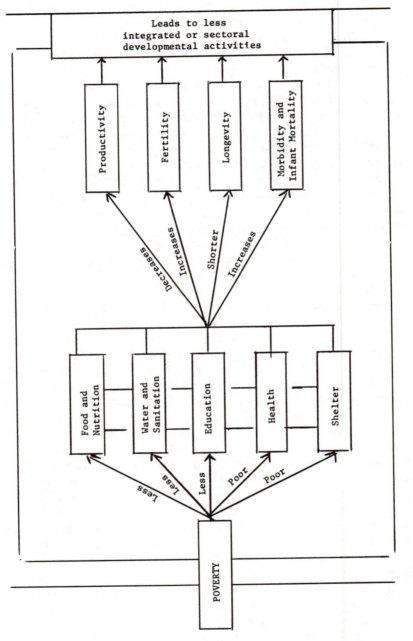

**Figure 6.2:** The seamless web of poverty
*Source:* Compiled by the author.

developing countries, especially those that came under colonial rule. Good illustrations can be found in the fields of education and medical care.

In the immediate postcolonial period, many countries in the developing world were faced with severe shortages of skilled and professional manpower to fill the upper echelons of the civil service and to meet the demands of major firms in the private sector. The policymakers therefore accepted the prevailing economic philosophy that espoused a causal linkage between high levels of schooling (secondary and university education) and economic growth. As a result, emphasis was placed on formal education with an elitist orientation. Education was therefore considered not so much as a factor in economic development per se, but more of a mechanism for individual social mobility. Further, the system effectively blocked the expansion of basic education. One explanation is that the ruling elites became more interested in maintaining their own privileges, with the latter reinforced by the existing political and social structures.

The education facilities that were provided therefore tended to widen disparities because of the unequal opportunities for educational advancement. Over time, it was recognized that the system of formal education was, by and large, irrelevant to the development needs of the countries concerned. This, together with the impact produced by changing development ideologies, resulted in a shift toward basic education and its universalization. In this context, there has been an increased realization that education is both a consumption and an investment good, with both aspects crucial to the development process. This is based on the need to combine several educational activities (formal, nonformal, and informal) in a comprehensive manner so that the recipients will be equipped with skills for communication, production, and for improvements in the overall quality of life.

In the case of health care, the tradition has been to establish and nurture highly urbanized and relatively expensive delivery systems, staffed by a few medical specialists. This meant that large segments of the population, especially in the rural areas, do not have access to basic medical services. While this remains true for the majority of developing countries, those mentioned earlier have increasingly decentralized their health care systems, with an emphasis on widespread and inexpensive medical treatment.

While the emphasis so far has been on absolute deprivation and its consequences, it should be mentioned that there are fundamental differences as well as linkages between it and relative deprivation. As mentioned earlier, economic prosperity does not necessarily imply that poverty will be shared equally by all groups in society.

Second, the respective degrees of emphasis placed on either absolute or relative deprivation must ultimately depend on country-specific situations, for example, a particular country's sociopolitical environment, its level of development, and its development priorities. On this basis, if countries were to be arranged along a hierarchical continuum from richest to poorest, a reasonable assumption is that the elimination of absolute poverty would pose the most urgent problem in the poorest, with the emphasis shifting toward relative deprivation as one moves to countries with higher income levels.

At the national level, the link between absolute and relative deprivation becomes obvious when it is considered that the prior distribution of political power and wealth can have a profound impact on the prospects for reducing absolute poverty. This aspect is addressed in the next section of this chapter. At the international level, the revolution of rising expectations (based on the observation of progress in the developed countries) has brought developing countries to the realization that the possibilities for reducing or eliminating poverty must go beyond the mere satisfaction of minimum standards of living. The implication is that international contrasts in economic deprivation and well-being should be based on relative criteria (for a fuller discussion, see Sen 1980).

## Growth, Income Distribution, and Equity

Most of the discussion so far has focused on some of the factors explaining extremes of poverty. Another side of the same coin is concerned with extremes of wealth, or how income and assets are distributed in society. A direct and positive relationship between economic growth and equity (measured in terms of the pattern of income and asset distribution) is usually assumed in conventional economic thinking. This implies that any policy designed to enhance economic growth would automatically lead to a reduction in income inequality and poverty. For example, if a country chooses a low growth path, both output and equity will be at low levels, and vice versa. The explanation is that both income and employment levels will be low in low growth situations, resulting in an increase in poverty. The reverse is assumed to be true under a high growth scenario.

However, it can also be shown on both theoretical and practical grounds that a negative growth-equity relationship is a real possibility, that is, that there may be a trade-off between growth and equity. This is likely to occur, for example, if economic growth is accompanied by changes in the sectoral composition of output that lead to increasing income

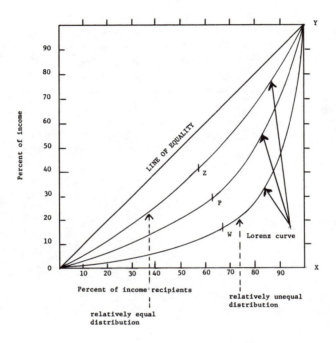

**Figure 6.3**:   The Lorenz curve and the Gini coefficient

concentration and labor displacement due to increasing capital intensity in the production process. This result also becomes particularly evident when it is considered that income is not distributed equally across all classes in society and that the wages of a large number of people are institutionally determined. Factor payments may be distorted by the presence of dualism and monopoly elements in the production structure. Further, the fragmentation of capital and labor markets has further helped to concentrate the benefits of economic growth in a relatively few hands.

As in the case of poverty, there is a great deal of controversy over the appropriateness of alternative measures of income inequality (see, for example, Atkinson 1975; Sen 1973; and Szal and Robinson 1977). A discussion of this issue would take us too far afield. However, the most commonly used measure is the Gini coefficient of income concentration. As shown in Figure 6.3, it is derived from the Lorenz curve and measures the relationship between the percent of income earners in each income group (percentiles) and the percent of total income received. The diagram

**TABLE 6.4:** Income distribution profiles—select countries

| | Percent share of income received by household income groups | | |
|---|---|---|---|
| | Lowest 20 percent | Highest 20 percent | Highest 10 percent |
| Bangladesh | 6.9 | 42.2 | 27.4 |
| Nepal | 4.6 | 59.2 | 46.5 |
| Malawi | 10.4 | 50.6 | 40.1 |
| India | 7.0 | 49.4 | 33.6 |
| Kenya | 2.6 | 60.4 | 45.8 |
| Thailand | 5.6 | 49.8 | 34.1 |
| Philippines | 5.2 | 54.0 | 38.5 |
| Malaysia | 3.5 | 56.1 | 39.8 |
| Korea, Rep. of | 5.7 | 45.3 | 27.5 |
| Brazil | 2.0 | 66.6 | 50.6 |
| Mexico | 2.9 | 57.7 | 40.6 |
| Argentina | 4.4 | 50.3 | 35.2 |
| Israel | 6.0 | 39.9 | 22.6 |
| Hong Kong | 5.4 | 47.0 | 31.3 |
| Trinidad and Tobago | 9.1 | 50.0 | 31.8 |
| Ireland | 7.2 | 39.4 | 25.1 |
| Spain | 6.0 | 42.2 | 26.7 |
| Italy | 6.2 | 43.9 | 28.1 |
| United Kingdom | 7.0 | 39.7 | 23.4 |
| Japan | 8.7 | 36.8 | 21.2 |
| United States | 4.6 | 50.3 | 33.3 |
| Sweden | 7.2 | 37.2 | 21.2 |

*Source:* World Bank (1984).

presents three alternative illustrations of the coefficient, which are measured by the ratios of the areas *OWY, OPY,* and *OZY,* respectively, to that of *OXY.* The coefficient can vary between zero (perfect income equality) and one (perfect income inequality). In practice, countries with highly unequal income distributions typically have Gini coefficients ranging between, say, 0.50 and 0.90, while the range is between, say, 0.20 and 0.40 for countries where the distribution pattern is more equitable.

There are relatively few reliable comparative statistics on the nature of these coefficients and their behavior over time. However, as the data in Table 6.4 show, the income distribution still remains highly unequal in the majority of developing nations, and it is only marginally better in some developed market economies. As shown in the table, the income distribution profile has remained relatively unequal even in the fastest growing developing nations. For developing countries as a group, the earnings of the larger majority of income recipients are stuck at the lower end of the income range, and there is very little convergence to the national average. There is therefore a positive correlation between income inequality and the incidence of poverty.

In the above context, many empirical studies have examined the relationship between economic growth and income distribution at various per capita income levels or stages of development. Some are based on an extrapolation of the historical experience of industrial nations, while others compare countries at different income levels, based on cross-sectional and time series data. One of the most well-known is the study by Kuznets (1955). On the basis of long-term patterns of change in the industrial nations, he hypothesized that countries pass through three stages: a pre-industrial stage of relative income equality, an industrialization phase of relative income inequality, and a modern or developed phase of reduced income inequality. This "inverted S-curve" relationship is explained as follows: First, during the early phases of development, the income distribution is relatively equal because most of the population derives its income from its own labor. Average income is low, and the absolute minimum income for subsistence provides the basis for equalization among lower income groups.

Second, increased income concentration can be expected during the industrialization phase due to the differential effects of capital accumulation, education, and the increasing division of labor.

Increased income concentration can also be expected at this stage because the differential savings hypothesis comes into play. There is a higher level of savings and investment by the capitalist class and a corresponding widening of the income gap between capitalists and workers.

Third, income concentration is expected to lessen during the modern or developed phase for the following reasons: (1) a decrease in population growth, (2) reduced savings among higher income groups due to waste, (3) the concentration of new enterprises due to the failure of existing ones to adjust sufficiently to changing economic conditions and times, and (4) state intervention in the system of distribution.

The Kuznets S-curve relationship has been supported by the results of several studies, including Weisskoff (1970), Paukert (1973), Adelman and Morris (1973), and Griffin and Khan (1978). However, there is still a divergence of opinion about the nature of inequality that accompanies economic growth. For example, the studies by Adelman and Morris and by Griffin and Khan view the relationship as conflicting, with increases in both absolute and relative inequalities over time. By contrast, the studies by Chenery et al. (1974) conclude that while relative inequalities might have increased, this was not necessarily the case for absolute inequality. The general explanation is that the absolute levels of income of the poorest groups in society tend to rise more slowly than the average.

While there is no consensus on whether the income distribution profile might have worsened in developing countries, the evidence suggests that the majority are somewhere in the second Kuznets' phase with relatively unequal distribution profiles. Some of the factors explaining this situation may now be recounted. The first such explanatory variable is the unequal distribution of productive assets such as capital and land. Second, and in the light of the perspectives on income distribution outlined in Chapter 2, the pattern of ownership and entitlement rights might have been worsened by the pursuit of pro-capital, savings-centered, and dualistic strategies of development.

As previously explained, this approach is usually rationalized on the grounds that savings and investment rates tend to differ among the various classes in society, with capitalists having a higher propensity to save than workers. The implication is that total savings and investment would be reduced if the share of income going to that income class with a lower savings rate were to be raised. Accordingly, since the presumption is that owners of capital save more than do workers, development strategies favoring the capital factor and capital-intensive methods of production would generate higher returns to capital, higher savings, and therefore higher aggregate growth rates. As emphasized elsewhere (David 1985), this philosophy has been operationalized through inward-looking strategies of import substitution industrialization that (1) protect the modern urbanized sectors and groups in the economy at the expense of the urban and rural poor and (2) create monopoly rents for the wealthy through various trade restrictions and exchange controls.

In general, countries in which the growth pattern is relatively unbalanced tend to be poor achievers in terms of overall socioeconomic progress and income distribution (David and Scandizzo 1980). As emphasized earlier, the unbalanced development path followed by many developing countries reflects, in part, the dualistic and fragmented nature of their economic and social structures. This is, in turn, a reflection of the pattern of property rights and the unequal sharing of economic power.

Third, besides the pro-capital bias of development strategies and the concomitant undervaluation of the labor factor, unequal distribution is also explained by the effects of population growth and increased rural-urban migration, with the oversupply of the less-skilled workforce depressing the average wage rate and the overall compensation accruing to the labor factor vis-à-vis capital. The situation is further complicated by the increasing demand for skilled labor by the industrial sector. This has resulted in income inequality because the supply of skilled labor continues to expand rather slowly in the majority of developing nations.

The developing countries that have been able to achieve some measure of broad-based and equitable growth are the ones that placed emphasis on human resource development early in the development process. The empirical evidence reveals that relative income shares tend to be most closely correlated with the quality of human resources. Research studies done at the World Bank have shown that income shares of the poorest 80 percent of the population tend to be positively related to education levels and its availability and that the share of income going to the poorest 40 percent of the population is most significantly correlated with primary school enrollment. A similar relationship holds between secondary school enrollment and the share of income going to the middle 40 percent of income recipients.

Finally, it may be useful to interpret the concern for "growth with equity" from the perspective of the "meliorist" or "social-democratic" models of development policy, as suggested by Meade (1964) and World Bank researchers (Chenery et al. 1974). The general framework underlying this model is one in which growth and distribution are combined in a single index of economic welfare based on changes in the income shares of various groups, with the latter defined in terms of their asset holdings, income levels, and economic roles. The rate of increase in society's welfare, as an index of broad-based or equitable development, is then defined as the weighted sum of the growth of income shares of all groups, as follows:

$$G = w_1g_1 + w_2g_2 + w_3g_3 + w_4g_4 + w_5g_5 \qquad (6.1)$$

where $G$ is the index of total development welfare, $w_1$ through $w_5$ are the weights given to income growth at different levels of income, and $g_1$ through $g_5$ the respective growth rates of income of the various income groups in society. The subscripts (1–5) represent rankings from the richest ($w_1$) to the poorest ($w_5$) income groups. The problem is therefore one of maximizing $G$, with the $w$s defined as the initial shares of each income group in national income.

If the emphasis of policy is on maximizing the income growth of the poorest members of society, the weight for the poorest group ($w_5$) would be set equal to one, with the weights for the other groups ($w_1$–$w_4$) set equal to zero. Several other alternatives are possible. For example, the income growth of the lower and middle income groups (say, $w_3$, $w_4$, $w_5$) may be given positive and equal weights, with the weights for the relatively rich (say, $w_1$, $w_2$) remaining at zero; or, alternatively, each income group may be given an equal weighting based on criteria such as household size and other demographic characteristics.

What is evident is that the choice of distributional weights cannot be decided on an *a priori* basis, and value judgments would have to be made in each society about the relative degrees of distributional emphases considered desirable or feasible. Assuming that such a choice can be made, there is also a problem surrounding the time horizon over which the relevant distributional adjustments are allowed to take place, and over whether they will be based on gradualist, activist, or revolutionary policy thrusts.

# 7

## Center-Periphery, International Resource Flows, and the Transnational Process

A general conclusion emerging from the previous chapter is that the cumulative benefits of economic growth have not "trickled down," or have not otherwise been sufficiently "diffused" to the masses of the population in the developing world. This reflects a general lack of socioeconomic progress. The general absence of socioeconomic transformation has been associated with various forms of dualism, a neglect of the agricultural and rural sectors, a failure of the industrialization process, and increasing external dependence by the developing countries.

As articulated by Nugent and Yotopolous:

> Instead of the optimistic mechanisms of the melting pot or the communicating vessels that lead to uniformity and homogenization . . . economic development, at least in its early stages, acts like a suction principle in inducing biformity. It nourishes the towering heights of polarity at one extreme; at the same time it creates marginalization at the other extreme. Just as cream rises to the top, development trickles up for a while to benefit those who are well-endowed, and as sediment becomes mired at the bottom, the victims of development are crowded into the periphery (Nugent and Yotopolous 1979, p. 543).

The focus of this chapter is on some broad factors and processes underlying the structure and functioning of the international economy and their development consequences. The point of departure is the emergence of center-periphery relations. This is followed by a delineation of broad trends and patterns in trading relationships between the developed and the developing world. Finally, some perceptions about the role of transnational corporations in the development process are discussed.

## The Evolution of Center-Pheriphery Relations

There are three broad historical periods during which the majority of developing nations were successively incorporated into the international economic order. The first was the mercantilist period (roughly between 1500 and 1800) when European colonial powers penetrated tropical and subtropical lands with the expressed purpose of finding cheap sources of raw materials and export markets. This was associated with foreign investment in agricultural and other primary activities and led to the creation of a modern enclave sector comprising mines, plantations, and other enterprises related to the process of primary commodity extraction. These, in turn, became linked to metropolitan centers through primary commodity exports and a network of financial, political, and other institutional arrangements.

As Beckford (1972) and others have documented, the process of historical incorporation led to the creation of a "plantation" or "hinterland" economy in parts of Asia, Africa, Latin America, and the Caribbean. The "hinterland" economy, it is argued, was not only tied to the economy of the metropole through a system of "metropole/satellite" relations, but all domestic institutions as well as all major phases of the history of the developing world evolved in response to the requirements of the metropole.

From its very inception, this hinterland economy was a dependent one, passively responding to external stimuli, trade, and investment. It formed the locus of a triangular system of trade and production, dependent on the metropole for capital and markets, and on Africa for slave labor. As is well-known, the process of enslavement saw the transportation of about 50 million Africans to the Americas, the transshipment of indentured East Indian laborers to various parts of the world (Malaysia, Sri Lanka, East Africa, Mauritius, Fiji, and the Caribbean), and the importation of Chinese labor to work in South African gold mines and to build railroads on the West Coast of the United States.

Second, the age of mercantilism was followed by an era of free trade that saw the international expansion of trade and investment and a further consolidation of the metropolitan-satellie linkage process. This later period in the evolution of the hinterland economy saw its vertical integration into the international system of resource allocation and mobilization. This was achieved through increased foreign ownership and investment, a process that further reinforced the subordinate role of the hinterland and encouraged a substantial outflow of the surplus that it generated. This was part of a process in which the dominant colonial powers increased their specialization in the production of manufactured goods and the hinterland its production of raw materials and staples.

A third broad historical period has been the post-World War II era, which has been shaped by several interrelated developments. One such has been the popular use of import substitution industrialization strategies by the developing countries. There was an earlier use of such strategies in Latin America between the 1930s and 1950s. The basic presupposition was that, by following the patterns of early European and North American development, developing countries would experience growth at first and later national development. The period after World War II has also witnessed a phenomenal growth in the manufacturing capacity of the United States, Japan, and other Western developed nations. This has also been accompanied by the tremendous growth and spread of transnational corporations.

Thus, the historical integration of developing nations into the world economic system was accompanied by their increasing specialization in primary commodity production and export, and, on a concomitant basis, a process whereby the wealthier nations exploited their own comparative advantage in industrial production. This type of international division of labor has been rationalized on at least three grounds. One claim is that it was less costly and easier than internal trade in the developing world so that international specialization proved to be more beneficial to the parties concerned than the pursuit of internal forms of specialization along regional lines. The reasoning is that various internal bottlenecks common to the developing countries of the day tended to militate against promoting intracountry trade vis-à-vis international trade.

Another claim is that the historical growth of primary commodity production was largely induced by the growth in demand for such products by the industrialized nations and was partly a result of their industrialization process. As mentioned in Chapter 5, this process was accompanied by increasing real incomes, population growth, and related changes in consumption and production patterns. In such a situation, the internal allocation of resources and expansion of factor supplies in the developing world tended to raise output for exports. Their increased participation in international markets therefore required a shift in resources of land and labor away from subsistence production and toward the production of cash crops for export.

It was in this context that trade was expected to become an "engine of growth," with the industrial nations "exporting" their growth to primary producing countries. A third related claim was based on an extrapolation of the historical experience of the industrialized nations, that is, that there would be successive shifts in the commodity composition of production and exports—from primary products through labor-intensive manufactures to more sophisticated and capital-intensive industrial goods. A pertinent issue is therefore whether it is still realistic to expect the developing countries to use trade as a major development catalyst. This issue is taken up again in the next section of this chapter. However, its resolution must hinge on one's perception about how the international economy functions.

In historical terms, reference may be made to the general "structuralist" thesis that underdevelopment is primarily the result of the process whereby developing countries were integrated into the world economy. During the late 1920s, Sombart advanced the idea that "We must ... distinguish a capitalist center—the central capitalist nations—from a mass of peripheral countries viewed from the center; the former are active and directing, the latter, passive and serving. England constituted the capitalist center in the first half of the nineteenth century; later, in the longer period of High Capitalism, Western Europe [joined England]. ... Finally, in the last generation, the eastern part of the United States has moved up [to the center]" (quoted in Love 1980, p. 63).

A similar reference to the asymmetrical nature of center-periphery relations was also made by Manoilesco (1931), who contended that the international division of labor and the classical theory of comparative advantage worked to the disadvantage of peripheral economies. The reasoning is that productivity and exports of these economies tend to be inferior to those of their central counterparts because the former are primarily agricultural and the latter industrial. He therefore recommended that the excess labor be transferred out of the agricultural sector of these "backward" countries to the industrial sector where productivity was considered to be higher. The argument is in the spirit of the Soviet industrialization debate raised in Chapter 5.

In Western economic circles, the "center-periphery" thesis owes its popularity to the works of Prebisch (1950) and Singer (1950), and to some extent that of Lewis (1954, 1955, 1978). As mentioned earlier, the general thesis is that the process of historical integration has resulted in the division of the world into two basic sectors: an advanced and relatively developed *center* at one pole and a less developed and predominantly agrarian *periphery* at the other. The growth and development of center nations has been largely endogenous and based on an internal dynamism characterized by rapid capital accumulation, technological progress, and high employment and productivity levels. By contrast, the same process in the periphery has been retarded by low capital accumulation, little or no technical progress, low productivity, and high levels of unemployment and underemployment.

The relations between the center and the periphery are viewed in terms of an unequal exchange. This is because the periphery functions mainly as a purveyor of primary products to the center that provides it with industrial products in exchange. As discussed below, the conditions of unequal exchange are explained in terms of an argument that posits a secular tendency of the terms of trade to turn against countries exporting primary products and importing manufactures. Further, Prebisch has argued that income growth in the center has not been accompanied by a corresponding diffusion of technological progress to the periphery, that is, the central nations have not been "exporting" their growth to the periphery. In this context, the argument is that the uneven spread of technological progress was the major factor responsible for the division of the world into an industrial center and a primary producing periphery.

As Prebisch states:

> Reality is undermining the outdated schema of the international division of labor, which achieved great importance in the nineteenth century . . . . [While] the reasoning on the economic advantage of the international division of labor is theoretically sound . . . it is based on an assumption which has been conclusively proved false by the facts. According to this assumption, the benefits of technical progress tend to be distributed alike over the whole community . . . if by "community" only the great industrial countries are meant, it is indeed true that the benefits of technical progress are gradually distributed among all social groups and classes. If, however, the concept of community is extended to include the periphery of the world economy, a serious error is implicit in the generalization. The enormous benefits derived from increased productivity have not reached the periphery in a measure comparable to that obtained by the peoples in the great industrial countries. Hence, the outstanding differences between the standards of living of the masses of the former and the latter and the manifest discrepancies between their respective abilities to accumulate capital . . . . Thus, there exists an obvious disequilibrium, a fact which destroys the basic premise underlying the schema of the international division of labor (Prebisch 1950, p. 1).

## Trade Relations Stylized:
## Optimism or Pessimism?

The evidence suggests that during the past two decades, there has been a tremendous growth in world trade. This has been growing at about 8 percent per annum in real terms compared to about 0.9 percent per annum between 1913 and 1939, and less than 4 percent between 1873 and 1913 (Lewis 1980). This pattern has been accompanied by notable shifts in the structure of exports of the developing countries, with their share of manufactures in total exports increasing from around 8 percent in the 1950s to over 20 percent during the 1970s (for a discussion see Riedel 1984).

However, a relatively few small countries in Asia (South Korea, Taiwan, Hong Kong, and Singapore) were primarily responsible for more than 60 percent of this expansion. The remainder is accounted for by two groups of developing countries: (1) the "newly industrializing countries" (NICs), such as Argentina, Brazil, Greece, India, Israel, Mexico, Portugal, Spain, and Yugoslavia, and (2) the "new exporting countries" (NECs), including Cyprus, Colombia, Indonesia, Jordan, Malaysia, Morocco, Peru, Philippines, Sri Lanka, Thailand, and Tunisia. Some writers see this as a reason for rejecting the "export pessimism" thesis and for adopting a more optimistic view of the export prospects for developing countries (e.g., Havrylyshyn and Alikhani 1982).

However, one reason for continued export pessimism is suggested by the patterns of vertical trading that define the relationships between the developing and the developed world. These are exemplified by (1) relatively high export commodity concentration ratios, with one or two primary commodities responsible for the lion's share of export revenues; (2) relatively high partner concentration ratios, with the larger share of exports going to two or three nations in the industrial world; and (3) a highly positive vertical trade index, indicating a high concentration of primary commodities and unsophisticated manufactured goods in exports, a high concentration of processed goods in imports, and, in general, technological backwardness in output and trade.

The best examples of countries displaying a lack of diversification in their production and trade structures can be found in Africa, which is more dependent on primary commodity exports than any other world region. Thirty major resource commodities now account for about 70 percent of the region's nonfuel exports, compared to about 35 percent for all developing countries and about 10 percent for the entire world (World Bank 1981). In both Africa and the developing world as a whole, the high commodity concentration ratios and export coefficients have been accompanied by wide fluctuations in export earnings and in the terms of trade.

Before discussing some of the underlying factors at work, we take up again the original Prebisch-Singer thesis about the secular decline in the net barter terms of trade between primary products and manufactured goods, and therefore between the developed and the developing nations. A similar inference can be drawn from Lewis' dual labor surplus model. The model suggests that as long as conditions of labor surplus ("unlimited supplies of labor") in the traditional subsistence sector depress real wages throughout the economy, any gains from productivity increases in the export sector are likely to accrue to the importing countries. Further, where surplus labor exists at the ruling wage rate, prices tend to give the wrong signals to resource allocation in general and to the international division of labor in particular.

In the Prebisch-Singer version, the primary concern was with the historical decline over the long-term period prior to World War II, but it was also predicted that there would be a progressive and inexorable deterioration in the terms of trade as long as asymmetrical trading relationships persisted between developed and developing nations. It was also argued that a persistence of the historical downward trend would adversely affect the distribution of gains from trade received by primary producing countries, resulting in a stagnation in their income levels.

There has been a considerable debate on the terms of trade issue and, in particular, the empirical or *statistical* problem whether the net barter terms of trade (NBTT) of the developing countries has shown a secular decline (e.g., see Ellsworth 1956, Baer 1969, Lipsey 1963; and Bairoch 1975). While the details of the debate would take us too far afield, a few general comments may prove useful. A basic problem concerns the measurement of the NBTT, how it compares with other terms of trade measures, and its usefulness as an indicator of center-periphery relations.

In this context, the most widely used measure of the NBTT is the ratio of prices of primary commodities to that of manufactured goods. A second measure is the ratio of exports from the developing countries to exports from the developed ones. The latter measure better illustrates the structure of trading relationships between the two groups of countries. In practice, however, the unit value index of exports divided by the unit value index of imports of the developing countries is usually taken as a proxy for the second measure.

The statistical evidence on historical trends in the NBTT shows a relatively strong decline for the period between 1871 and 1938. However, the evidence for the period after 1950 is far less conclusive. No firm conclusions can therefore be drawn about long-term trends in the NBTT. Over some periods, and for some commodities, it has either deteriorated or remained constant, while it has improved in other cases (for a discussion, see Spraos 1979, 1980).

However, as the data in Table 7.1 show, the situation is a generally adverse one and might have worsened considerably in more recent times. The disruption in world trade caused by increased oil and food prices after 1973, as well as the successive world recessions after that period, must be considered important explanatory factors. These and other factors help to explain why there is a regular cyclical fluctuation in the terms of trade index. Studies show that this tends to be correlated with a high incidence of export earnings instability facing the developing nations.

Both the partner and commodity concentration of trade tend to be positively correlated with export earnings instability. The latter is in turn related to commodity price fluctuations caused by both demand and supply factors. For the majority of commodities exported by the developing nations, the influence operates primarily from the demand side, with the price fluctuations traceable to changes in economic activity (booms and

**TABLE 7.1**   Changes in export prices and in the terms of trade, 1965-84 (average annual percentage change)

| Country group | 1965–73 | 1973–80 | 1981 | 1982 | 1983[a] | 1984[b] |
|---|---|---|---|---|---|---|
| *Change in export prices* | | | | | | |
| Developing countries | 6.0 | 14.7 | -2.5 | -6.1 | -3.7 | -1.0 |
|   Manufactures | 5.1 | 10.9 | -5.0 | -1.9 | -4.2 | -2.8 |
|   Food | 5.8 | 8.0 | -12.1 | -17.4 | 10.2 | 7.3 |
|   Nonfood | 4.0 | 10.3 | -13.5 | -8.1 | 4.8 | -3.4 |
|   Metals and minerals | 1.8 | 5.8 | -10.5 | -9.5 | 0.5 | -4.9 |
|   Fuels | 7.9 | 27.2 | 12.5 | -3.2 | -12.4 | -2.4 |
| High-income oil exporters | 7.4 | 24.8 | 8.3 | -2.7 | -11.3 | -1.6 |
| Industrial countries | | | | | | |
|   Total | 4.7 | 10.1 | -4.6 | -4.0 | -3.2 | -1.5 |
|   Manufactures | 4.7 | 10.9 | -6.0 | -2.1 | -4.3 | -2.3 |
| *Change in terms of trade* | | | | | | |
| Developing countries | 0.5 | 2.0 | 0.5 | -1.1 | -0.6 | 1.0 |
|   Low-income countries | 0.4 | -1.5 | -0.2 | -1.5 | 0.9 | 4.1 |
|    Asia | 0.8 | -1.6 | 1.3 | -2.2 | 0.4 | 3.5 |
|    Africa | -0.7 | -1.0 | -7.2 | 1.1 | 4.2 | 7.8 |
|   Middle-income oil importers | -0.2 | -2.3 | -5.0 | -2.2 | 3.7 | 0.4 |
|   Middle-income oil exporters | -0.4 | 9.0 | 11.7 | 1.7 | -8.5 | 0.9 |
| High-income oil exporters | 2.9 | 12.3 | 14.6 | 2.3 | -8.6 | -1.0 |
| Industrial countries | -0.5 | -3.5 | -2.1 | 2.0 | 2.1 | -0.2 |

[a]Estimated.
[b]Projected.
*Source:* World Bank (1985).

recessions) in the industrial nations that are the primary purchasers of primary commodities. The fluctuations are also sometimes caused by supply forces, for example, output fluctuations brought about by the influence of changes in weather, climate, or temperature. The serious price fluctuations facing some of the major commodities exported by developing countries are illustrated in Table 7.2. Moreover, many of these commodities, for example, sugar, normally experience long periods of depressed prices.

As alluded to earlier, fluctuations in the terms of trade and in primary commodity prices bear a close relationship to the unfavorable effects of the international business or trade cycle. A general proposition, advanced by Prebisch during the 1940s, was that national trade cycles (of Argentina) were primarily a reflection of those of industrialized trading partners, and especially that of the United States, which was considered the "cyclical center" of the international economy (see Love 1980). The argument can be extended to the contemporary world environment as follows. First, the evidence suggests that when the cycle turns into a recessionary phase, it is the primary producing countries that tend to be most affected. The lack of market power by these countries means that they have to absorb severe losses due to price reductions that take place during periods of recession. By contrast, the oligopolistic control of markets by developed country firms enables large exporters of manufactured goods to maintain prices in line with their cost structure, thereby guaranteeing normal profits. This represents part of a vicious structural situation in which increases in relative prices during the upswing of the business cycle tend to favor producers of manufactures more than proportionately, without equally compensating losses during periods of contraction.

The argument is that the demand, supply, and price trends obtaining in world markets are such that primary commodity exporters tend to lose proportionately more than their industrial counterparts when market conditions are unfavorable. Further, even where prices of primary commodities increase, this tends to be proportionately less than the cost-induced and technology-based prices of industrial products. The impact of technology is further explored in the next section of this chapter.

It is sometimes claimed that the NBTT is a very poor measure of a country's economic well-being, or of the gains that can be derived from trade. Using again as a measure the ratio of export prices (of primary commodities) to import prices (of manufactures), export prices may fall because productivity has increased in the producing countries, or, alternatively, import prices may rise if the quality of imported goods has improved. The former situation reflects a transfer of productivity gains from the exporting to the importing countries. The latter case, it can be argued, is merely a reflection of a statistical problem of adjusting the price index. Further, the lower price of exports may be accompanied by an increase in export volume, resulting in a rise in the income terms of trade (the ratio of export values of primary commodities to import prices of manufactures).

On the other hand, whether or not the prices of primary products fall relative to those of industrial goods, a theoretical possibility exists for developing countries to attempt to increase their export earnings through

**TABLE 7.2:** Purchasing power index of primary commodities exported by developing countries in terms of imported manufactures, 1948–84[a] (Constant dollars; 1977–79 = 100) (Annual averages)

| (Weights % Share)[b] | Petroleum | 33 Commodities (excluding energy) (100.0) | Total (71.8) | Agriculture | | | Food | | | | | Metals & minerals (23.3) |
|---|---|---|---|---|---|---|---|---|---|---|---|---|
| | | | | Total (58.3) | Beverages (26.5) | Cereals (7.5) | Fats & oils (8.6) | Other (15.6) | Nonfood (13.6) | Timber (4.8) | | |
| 1948 | 50 | 117 | 124 | 118 | 62 | 174 | 174 | 155 | 149 | 58 | | 107 |
| 1949 | 43 | 117 | 121 | 117 | 72 | 180 | 135 | 155 | 137 | 64 | | 114 |
| 1950 | 44 | 156 | 169 | 152 | 106 | 196 | 163 | 203 | 243 | 77 | | 134 |
| 1951 | 37 | 159 | 169 | 143 | 98 | 179 | 163 | 192 | 280 | 95 | | 141 |
| 1952 | 36 | 137 | 135 | 122 | 91 | 174 | 133 | 145 | 189 | 69 | | 159 |
| 1953 | 40 | 131 | 130 | 124 | 97 | 182 | 141 | 133 | 153 | 66 | | 150 |
| 1954 | 43 | 142 | 144 | 142 | 141 | 172 | 133 | 135 | 154 | 93 | | 147 |
| 1955 | 42 | 139 | 134 | 122 | 109 | 149 | 121 | 132 | 185 | 73 | | 167 |
| 1956 | 41 | 138 | 132 | 124 | 112 | 147 | 121 | 136 | 164 | 68 | | 172 |
| 1957 | 39 | 132 | 131 | 126 | 98 | 134 | 116 | 176 | 153 | 63 | | 147 |
| 1958 | 35 | 112 | 109 | 104 | 85 | 129 | 104 | 123 | 134 | 57 | | 130 |
| 1959 | 33 | 115 | 112 | 101 | 79 | 129 | 118 | 115 | 160 | 71 | | 132 |
| 1960 | 30 | 113 | 110 | 97 | 74 | 120 | 110 | 117 | 164 | 76 | | 132 |
| 1961 | 30 | 107 | 102 | 93 | 70 | 128 | 113 | 103 | 139 | 78 | | 129 |
| 1962 | 28 | 108 | 103 | 94 | 68 | 143 | 107 | 107 | 141 | 87 | | 127 |
| 1963 | 28 | 127 | 130 | 130 | 67 | 143 | 113 | 241 | 130 | 84 | | 124 |
| 1964 | 26 | 124 | 119 | 117 | 75 | 138 | 114 | 179 | 129 | 70 | | 149 |

| Year | | | | | | | | | | | |
|---|---|---|---|---|---|---|---|---|---|---|---|
| 1965 | 25 | 114 | 99 | 92 | 71 | 135 | 126 | 90 | 126 | 81 | 170 |
| 1966 | 24 | 111 | 93 | 87 | 66 | 144 | 116 | 81 | 120 | 80 | 173 |
| 1967 | 24 | 103 | 91 | 86 | 63 | 150 | 108 | 83 | 113 | 84 | 143 |
| 1968 | 25 | 111 | 97 | 91 | 67 | 156 | 111 | 89 | 125 | 92 | 156 |
| 1969 | 25 | 120 | 106 | 100 | 68 | 153 | 109 | 122 | 132 | 88 | 169 |
| 1970 | 23 | 114 | 101 | 99 | 72 | 126 | 116 | 122 | 112 | 85 | 160 |
| 1971 | 27 | 100 | 93 | 91 | 58 | 112 | 108 | 126 | 104 | 80 | 127 |
| 1972 | 28 | 102 | 99 | 99 | 58 | 109 | 96 | 167 | 98 | 72 | 115 |
| 1973 | 33 | 128 | 126 | 124 | 62 | 187 | 165 | 179 | 130 | 105 | 140 |
| 1974 | 110 | 160 | 166 | 178 | 57 | 216 | 152 | 381 | 116 | 101 | 152 |
| 1975 | 94 | 111 | 113 | 118 | 48 | 148 | 89 | 240 | 89 | 67 | 115 |
| 1976 | 100 | 109 | 109 | 109 | 89 | 119 | 93 | 147 | 110 | 88 | 110 |
| 1977 | 101 | 113 | 117 | 120 | 139 | 101 | 107 | 105 | 103 | 92 | 105 |
| 1978 | 86 | 92 | 93 | 92 | 88 | 103 | 96 | 92 | 95 | 79 | 91 |
| 1979 | 112 | 98 | 94 | 92 | 82 | 97 | 99 | 103 | 102 | 125 | 105 |
| 1980 | 169 | 115 | 115 | 117 | 67 | 107 | 84 | 223 | 108 | 139 | 108 |
| 1981 | 199 | 98 | 95 | 95 | 58 | 119 | 84 | 151 | 98 | 109 | 102 |
| 1982 | 196 | 83 | 76 | 74 | 61 | 88 | 69 | 91 | 88 | 111 | 95 |
| 1983 | 177 | 88 | 84 | 80 | 64 | 98 | 85 | 96 | 102 | 107 | 98 |
| 1984 | 168 | 84 | 80 | 76 | 71 | 92 | 96 | 66 | 97 | 118 | 91 |

[a]Computed from unrounded data and deflated by manufacturing unit value (MUV) c.i.f. index.

[b]Weighted by 1977–79 developing countries' export values.

*Note:* The commodities included in each group are beverages—coffee, cocoa, tea; cereals—maize, rice, wheat, grain sorghum; fats and oils—palm oil, coconut oil, groundnut oil, soybeans, copra, groundnut meal, soybean meal; other foods—sugar, beef, bananas, oranges; nonfoods—cotton, jute, rubber, tobacco; timber—logs; metals and minerals—copper, tin, nickel, bauxite, aluminum, iron ore, manganese ore, lead, zinc, phosphate rock.

*Source:* World Bank, Economic Analysis and Projections Department, Commodity Studies and Projection Division.

the mechanism of higher prices brought about by restrictions on production and export volume. The theoretical outcome depends, of course, on the elasticity of demand for their exports and would only prove beneficial if they face a relatively elastic demand. Orthodox economists criticize the restrictionist option on the grounds that such actions tend to reduce world welfare (in the sense of Pareto optimality). Some also argue that a nondistorting direct transfer of money from consumers to producers would, on grounds of economic welfare, be preferable to lower output and higher prices for primary commodities.

In general, the theoretical possibility does not provide a realistic choice. This becomes evident when account is taken of the multiplicity of factors that distort the structure of trade between primary producing and industrial nations. This structure is affected in one way or another by government action in both the developed and developing nations, the activities of transnational corporations, oligopsonistic (few buyers) market structures, and, in general, by impefections in international commodity markets. Contextually, the call by developing countries for more and better international commodity agreements could be interpreted as an attempt to mobilize greater countervailing power.

The foremost example of these market distortions is provided by the large number of trade controls—mostly tariff and nontariff barriers—that are imposed by the developed nations on commodity imports from the developing world. As is well known, a common feature of nominal tariff rates is that they tend to escalate in proportion to the degree of processing, from raw materials through semifinished products to finished goods. This tends to raise effective tariff rates (measured in relation to value-added in the exporting countries) considerably above the corresponding nominal tariff rates. An illustration of the escalation of developed country tariff rates by degree of processing is provided in Table 7.3. In general, the escalation of tariff rates as products become more highly processed tends to encourage the imporation of unprocessed primary products or semi-finished manufactured goods into the developed contries. This tends to reduce imports of many finished products in which developing countries may have a comparative advantage, with a potentially negative impact on their income growth.

The caveat should be added that the protection in industrial countries against manufactures and other processed goods has been largely against the threat of imports from other industrial countries for products such as steel, cars, and electronics. Protection against manufactured goods from the developing countries is directed mainly against imports of apparel and footwear, as presently covered under the Multi-Fibre Agreement. In the case of agricultural commodities, protection by industrial countries has also been mainly directed against imports from other industrial countries.

**TABLE 7.3:** Developed country tariff rates on selected commodities

|  | Product group | European Economic Community | Japan | United States |
|---|---|---|---|---|
| Coffee | Green roasted | 5.0 | 0.0 | 0.0 |
|  | Coffee extracts | 18.0 | 17.5 | 0.0 |
| Cocoa | Cocoa beans | 3.0 | 0.0 | 0.0 |
|  | Powder and butter | 12.2 | 4.9 | 0.3 |
|  | Chocolate | 27.0 | 27.4 | 6.5 |
| Cotton | Raw cotton | 0.0 | 0.0 | 1.9 |
|  | Cotton yarn | 6.0 | 3.6 | 6.8 |
|  | Cotton fabrics | 10.0 | 5.9 | 7.4 |
|  | Cotton clothing[a] | 13.7 | 13.2 | 8.8 |
| Sisal | Fibers | 0.0 | 0.0 | 0.1 |
|  | Cordage | 11.7 | 7.7 | 2.3 |
| Iron | Iron ore | 0.0 | 0.0 | 0.0 |
|  | Pig iron | 2.2 | 4.3 | 1.5 |
|  | Steel ingots | 5.7 | 5.0 | 2.5 |
|  | Mill products | 4.9 | 5.2 | 4.4 |
|  | Special steels | 5.3 | 4.9 | 3.2 |
| Copper | Copper ore | 0.0 | 0.0 | 0.0 |
|  | Unwrought copper | 0.0 | 4.8 | 1.0 |
|  | Wrought copper | 6.0 | 6.8 | 2.6 |
| Manganese | Manganese ore | 0.0 | 0.0 | 0.0 |
|  | Ferromanganese | 2.0 | 4.8 | 1.7 |
| Aluminum | Bauxite | 0.0 | 0.0 | 0.0 |
|  | Alumina | 5.7 | 4.9 | 0.0 |
|  | Unwrought aluminum | 5.8 | 8.5 | 0.0 |
|  | Wrought aluminum | 9.7 | 11.7 | 2.9 |
| Wood | Rough wood | 0.0 | 0.0 | 0.0 |
|  | Plywood | 2.8 | 4.6 | 6.3 |
|  | Wood manufactures | 5.1 | 4.1 | 5.3 |
| Paper | Wood pulp | 0.0 | 0.0 | 0.0 |
|  | Paper preparations | 0.0 | 2.1 | 0.0 |
|  | Paper products | 9.4 | 4.6 | 3.5 |
| Rubber | Natural rubber | 0.0 | 0.0 | 0.0 |
|  | Rubber products | 5.3 | 4.8 | 5.3 |
| Leather | Hides and skins | 0.0 | 0.0 | 0.0 |
|  | Leather | 3.9 | 6.2 | 3.7 |
|  | Leather goods | 11.7 | 11.0 | 14.4 |
| Tobacco | Unmanufactured | 0.0 | 55.0 | 18.0 |
|  | Manufactured | 54.5 | 16.8 | 12.1 |

[a]SITC 841.1—Textile clothing, not knit.
*Source:* Data provided by GATT.

The industrial countries do provide a large number of tariff preferences to most agricultural commodities imported from the developing world, though this is by no means a uniform or universal practice. However, there are some important exceptions. One is the case of cane sugar, which has to compete with sugarbeet grown in the temperate zone, and other substitutes such as high fructose corn syrup (see McNally, David, and Flood 1984). Fruits and vegetables coming from developing countries close to European and North American markets are another example.

Third, some other commodities grown in developing countries, for example, oilseeds, fibers, rubber, and tobacco tend to face competition in industrial countries either with similar products, close substitutes, or synthetic substitutes (for a fuller discussion, see Duncan and Lutz 1983; Lutz and Bale 1980).

There is a general consensus that nontariff barriers constitute a more serious impediment than tariff barriers to the free flow of international trade. These nontariff barriers take a variety of forms, including (1) open-ended subsidies for specific industries in the developed countries, for example, steel, chemicals, motor vehicles, and shipbuilding; (2) quantitative restrictions in the form of voluntary export restraints and orderly marketing arrangements negotiated between exporting and importing countries. These arrangements generally violate the principles of open trade underlying the General Agreement on Tariffs and Trade (GATT); (3) variable levies on agricultural imports and price supports for agricultural crops, for example, in the European Economic Community and the United States; and (4) various types of qualitative restrictions on imports from the developing countries (see Baldwin 1970; Nowzad 1978; Yeats 1979).

Estimates of the percentage of imports affected by nontariff barriers are provided in Table 7.4. These protective measures have negative consequences for both developed and developing countries. In the former case, the protective measures tend to insulate inefficient and at times declining industries in the developed countries from international competition, with negative consequences for the growth of world trade. Nontariff barriers also produce a systematic bias against exports from developing nations. The historical evidence suggests that producers in these countries are in general less able to surmount a given set of nontariff barriers compared to their counterparts in the more developed countries. The majority still lack the requisite commercial experience and, in some cases, cannot adequately deal with the complicated issues posed by these barriers. They frequently lack appropriate information about these barriers and, as a consequence, have to incur unanticipated selling costs. In addition, exports from the developing countries are often subject to

**TABLE 7.4:** Percentage of industrial countries' imports covered by nontariff barriers

| Importer | Imports from | |
|---|---|---|
| | Developed countries | Developing countries |
| United States | 13.0 | 5.5 |
| Japan | 19.2 | 5.4 |
| Switzerland | 22.6 | 48.8 |
| Sweden | 1.0 | 7.0 |
| Norway | 8.2 | 10.9 |
| Austria | 15.0 | 8.1 |
| EC[a] | 15.1 | 11.8 |
| Denmark | 9.4 | 19.2 |
| Ireland | 15.0 | 9.5 |
| France | 20.1 | 7.1 |
| United Kingdom | 14.9 | 14.3 |
| Italy | 12.5 | 7.0 |
| Germany, Fed. Rep. | 12.6 | 8.5 |
| Netherlands | 16.1 | 19.8 |
| Belgium and Luxembourg | 19.2 | 29.7 |

[a]Weighted average; excludes Greece.

*Note:* This table is based on detailed information on nontariff barriers available in UNCTAD. The figures measure the value of imports affected by nontariff measures in relation to total imports. Import figures are from 1980, whereas the information on nontariff barriers applies to 1983. If a country's import restrictions are rigorous, it imports little and few of its imports are affected by restrictions. Thus, these figures provide little basis for comparison among countries in the total amount of restrictions.

*Source:* World Bank (1984).

inordinately stringent health and quality standards that tend to introduce direct cost biases against them.

The high incidence of protectionism in industrial market economies can be interpreted from the wider perspective of political and social considerations governing international trading relationships. Economists have for some time recognized the fact that trade policy has become less concerned with the technical issues of comparative advantage and more with the political realities underlying the domestic and foreign policy interests of major industrial countries (Cooper 1972; Balassa 1980; Johnson 1967). The argument for the national management of trade has a long history and is traceable to the classical mercantilist doctrine of the seventeenth and eighteenth centuries. As is well known, the statesmen of the day advocated domestic industrialization policies as a means of strengthening the state and reducing dependence on foreign imports. For example, the creation of tariff walls to develop national industry was proposed in both Alexander Hamilton's *Report on Manufactures* (1791) and Friedrich List's *National System of Political Economy* (1841). List is usually credited as being the father of the "infant industry" argument for protection, that is, that the high initial costs of production in a new industry could be reduced over time through economies of scale and external economies (see Corden 1965).

In more modern times, policies based on the national management of trade have come to be associated with various forms of neomercantilism. Neomercantilism, like its predecessor (mercantilism) is exemplified by the following strategies: (1) the quest by the developed nations for balance-of-payments surpluses through protectionist and related measures designed to expand their world market shares and to insulate their domestic industries from competitive imports; (2) on a related basis, the increasing concern for domestic unemployment and the use of adjustment assistance and other measures to protect domestic industry from what is perceived to be unfair competition from imports produced with "cheap labor" in the developing countries; and (3) the pursuit of economic and other policies by the two superpowers as a means of preserving the international balance of power (Bergsten and Krause 1975).

## The Transnational Process:
## General Considerations

As indicated earlier, the evolution of the international economic order has been accompanied by an increasing transnationalization of economic activity. This continues to have important implications for the movement of goods and factors across national boundaries, and therefore for the development process itself. The most important element underlying the transnational process has been the growth and spread of large nationwide and multinational firms. While competition is not altogether absent from the activities of these firms, the majority of these transnational corporations (TNCs) tend to be monopolistic or oligopolistic enterprises whose general characteristics and behavior are identified below.

First, there is a concentration of ownership of foreign investment in the metropolitan countries so that corporate decision making tends to be centralized in the world's leading financial capitals. Second, there is a concentration of economic activity in specific industries (extractive and manufacturing) and in particular countries. A third feature is the centralization of foreign holdings in the largest corporations. This implies that discretionary control over vast resources is centralized in relatively few hands (Bergsten et al. 1978).

An important aspect of the debate on TNCs concerns their influence on international resource flow patterns, as well as the basis of involvement of developing countries in the global political economy. In this context, several features of the transnational process (e.g., the concentration of economic activity, economies of scale, and product differentiation) raise questions about orthodox explanations of the factors governing international economic relations in general and the impact of the transnational process on developing countries in particular.

To put the matter in its proper perspective, it is necessary to return to the orthodox view that stresses the need to increase capital movements among nations as a means of maximizing global economic welfare, as well as that of individual countries. This line of thinking, traceable to views expressed by Ohlin (1933), Iverson (1936), and others, is based on the general assumption of international factor mobility and explains international investment relationships in terms of each country's capital endowments and the differential rates of return on this factor. The basic hypothesis is that the abundance of capital relative to other factors of production in capital-surplus countries makes its price and rate of return lower there compared to capital-deficit countries. Under the circumstances, capital-surplus countries are likely to earn higher levels of income by exporting their capital to capital-deficit countries, rather than by investing at home. Such a capital outflow, it is argued, would result in a more optimal mix of factors of production and their more efficient use, both nationally and internationally.

The above analytical framework is at the heart of orthodox (neoclassical) explanations of the international spread of economic activity and the reasons that private firms invest abroad. As in the case with commodity flows and comparative advantage, the assumption is that perfect competition prevails and that the firm has perfect knowledge of the prices, costs, and revenues attached to future investment. Assuming that its behavior is governed by the profit maximization rule, the rational investing firm attempts to maximize the difference between the discounted stream of earnings (benefits) and the discounted stream of costs of alternative investment projects. The neoclassical or accepted rule is that investment would be profitable to the firm as long as the rate of return (the marginal productivity of capital) is higher than the rate of interest (the price of capital). Therefore, the rule governing the decision to invest abroad becomes one whereby the rate of return abroad is higher than the corresponding rate for the domestic economy. Under such circumstances, interest rate differentials become the primary determinants of capital movements among countries. This, in turn, results in an optimal allocation of capital throughout the world.

It is evident that this perspective treats international investment purely in terms of international capital flows, that is, portfolio investment, with other forms of investment regarded as a special case. This limited view of international investment was later broadened to include capital flows as well as other resource flows among countries. Further, it has come to be recognized that intercountry differences in rates of return on capital provide only a partial explanation of the motives behind international investment. Underlying the rate-of-return analysis is the neoclassical assumption of a riskless world. However, the degree of risk and uncertainty associated with alternative investment opportunities is now considered important in the determination of international capital movements.

One important variation on this theme concerns the possibility that imperfect competition rather than competitive market equilibrium better explains the conditions governing the international transfer of resources. As mentioned earlier, the transnational process is defined by various forms of noncompetitive behavior. Some economists view this situation in terms of a need for a paradigm shift away from the macrotheory of international capital movements to a consideration of the behavior of the transnational firm and related international resource flows as part of industrial organization theory and the international influence of monopolistic and oligopolistic market structures (Hymer 1976; Kindleberger 1969, 1970; Caves 1982).

A firm's decision to invest abroad is usually governed by a multiplicity of factors and typically takes place in a complex international environment characterized by various degrees of risk and by laws and regulations imposed by governments and financial institutions. Given this situation, a general hypothesis advanced by the economists mentioned above (Hymer, Kindleberger, and Caves) is that a firm's foreign earnings should be high enough to compensate it for the risks inherent in foreign investment. In other words, there must be some special advantages accruing to the firm that compensate it for the disadvantages and additional costs associated with operating in a foreign environment. In this context, Hymer claims that the decision to invest abroad is motivated by the same factors explaining barriers to entry in U.S. industry. These include economies of scale, absolute cost advantage, and product differentiation (Bain 1956). These barriers to entry, combined with various forms of buyer and seller concentration in industry, are considered to be the major determinants of market structure, conduct, and performance. The reasoning is that monopolistic and oligopolistic firms are able to maintain prices well above competitive levels for considerable period of time by establishing new barriers to competition and by institutionalizing these and other forms of market imperfection.

From the perspective of imperfect competition, there are at least four types of international investment strategies that TNCs pursue as a means of satisfying their global objectives. First, they make *horizontal investments* in foreign production of the same goods produced in the home market. This is an example of oligopoly with product differentiation. Such horizontal operations involve the global or transnational integration of economic activities on the basis of intracorporate specialization.

Second, there are *vertical investments* where raw materials and other inputs for the domestic production process are produced abroad. Dunning (1971) distinguishes between two types of such vertical investment operations: backward vertical (cost-oriented) and forward vertical (market-oriented). Investments of the former type involve the securing and exploitation of raw material supplies for various uses. Such investments usually take two forms. In one case, the firm may be able to purchase cheaper or more reliable supplies of raw materials or processed goods. The second variety takes place mostly in extractive industries, with the firm's primary objective being one of supplying finished products in world markets. The forward vertical operations are an extension of the purchasing function mentioned above. In this case, the firm's primary objective is to enhance and protect its markets, as well as to facilitate its domestic production activities.

Third, there are *defensive investments* whereby firms take steps to protect their oligopoly position or market power, or otherwise raise various barriers to entry to potential competitors by using measures designed to control input sources.

Fourth, there may be *cross investments* among firms specializing in different commodities and resources. This is usually done in the pursuit of greater structural diversification and as a means of gaining greater control of the international environment. For a fuller discussion, see Kindleberger (1969).

The various types of investments described above have come to have important consequences for global production, finance, and trade. One general element of the transnational process is the linkage of production structures across countries and the incorporation of resources from several countries into an integrated global production structure. Since an increasing proportion of total world product is being produced across countries, there is probably a reduced need for transnational investors to take account of national policies. This is because production and related decisions tend to be based on overall global strategies and much less on circumstances facing individual affiliates, subsidiaries, or national governments.

Examples of backward and forward linkages of international production structures are legion. In the case of U.S.-based TNCs, there is substantial backward integration between domestic and foreign activities in petroleum, steel, copper, aluminum, and other resource-based industries. Forward integration exists in a number of sales, services, and assembly operations in foreign countries (Bergsten et al. 1978).

Investments in production activities are usually associated with short- and long-term flows of equity capital. This has helped to stimulate the growth of international finance through deposits in foreign banks, investments in the Eurodollar market, and, in general, through the growth of various forms of money and quasi-money. The growth and spread of TNCs is therefore linked to the evolution of international money and capital markets, which have provided these firms with continued access to the savings of many nations. The linkage of production and finance is part of a larger cumulative process in which the demand for liquid resources by the TNCs is linked to the continuous mobility of capital across national boundaries (Wachtel 1977).

This process has encouraged the development of various forms of transnational banking and the integration of short- and long-term capital markets. The related process of financial intermediation has been associated with various forms of international money (e.g., Eurodollars and petrodollars) that are usually deposited in major international banks and then recirculated throughout the world in the form of loans. It has been argued that while these forms of money have helped to augment international liquidity, their constant movement across national boundaries tends to destabilize international financial markets and militates against the ability of sovereign governments to pursue autonomous monetary and financial policies. The overall result has been the "denationalization" of capital and its increasing "internationalization" (Hymer 1972; Wachtel 1977).

Finally, mention must be made of the fact that an increasing proportion of world trade now takes the form of intrafirm transactions among the affiliates and subsidiaries of transnational corporations. While few reliable statistics are available on the nature of these trade flows, the available evidence suggests the following kinds of patterns. As far back as 1970, intrafirm trade among U.S.-controlled TNCs accounted for about 10 percent of all world trade in manufactures, and about 30 percent of U.S. manufacturing trade is handled through internal transactions of such firms. Such intrafirm trade also accounts for more than 40 percent of the total exports of the world's largest TNCs (Goldsbrough 1981).

As further discussed in the next section of this chapter, such intracorporate transactions have important implications for a given country's trade to respond to changes in economic activity and relative competitiveness. This is particularly true of developing countries with less flexible industrial and trade structures. The point of emphasis is that where trade flows are generated by TNCs with affiliates and subsidiaries in several countries, they may not respond as rapidly to relative prices as the trade of independent producers operating under more competitive conditions and in more open markets.

One explanation is that the accounting prices used in the intracorporate transactions of TNCs are usually "transfer prices" rather than market prices determined by the forces of supply and demand. While these transfer prices are recorded in international trade statistics, their determination is a matter that is purely internal to the TNC and is based on a process of intracorporate bargaining and the necessity to allocate costs among various affiliates and subsidiaries.

It is generally believed that the transfer pricing mechanism helps to determine the distribution of global as well as intracorporate profits. The typical TNC therefore has an incentive to manipulate these prices so as to minimize its global tax burden. Under the circumstances, it can minimize its overall tax bill, or maximize its global after-tax earnings, by inflating profits of affiliates in those jurisdictions where the tax burden is lowest, and vice versa. It has been shown that a corporation with plants in an importing and exporting country, in the attempt to minimize its overall tax and tariff burden, will choose the lowest or highest possible transfer price, depending on whether the relative differential in corporate tax rates is less or more than the import tariff on the product. Transfer prices on intracorporate imports may be overstated and those on intracorporate exports understated as a means of transferring profits from those countries that impose restrictions on profit repatriation (United Nations 1974, 1978).

While there is very little empirical evidence on the actual extent of overinvoicing or underinvoicing, one area in which transfer pricing tends to distort the international allocation of resources is in transportation. In the majority of cases, transportation facilities are provided by the corporate network so that there is no means of determining true market transportation costs. Another is in the area of technological transfer where intracorporate resource flows take the form of packages of collective and indivisible inputs.

In the latter case, the possibility exists that a quantitatively significant element of the cost of technology transfer is disguised through the manipulation of transfer prices and passed on to purchasers in other countries. The evidence suggests that this can form a significant element of international income flows in some industries. For example, a study by

Vaitsos (1974) of intracorporate imports into Colombia estimated that the weighted average of overpricing ranged between 25–50 percent for chemical, electrical, and rubber products to 100 percent for pharmaceuticals. In the latter case, the absolute amount of overpricing for the foreign firms studied amounted to six times their royalties and 24 times their declared profits.

Finally, many scholars are of the view that the impact of the transnational process in the determination of international trade flows tends to be most keenly felt in the area of technology transfer. The view is that the concentration of technological knowledge in the hands of a few transnational firms provides one of the best explanations of their monopoly power. Such monopoly power is usually acquired through the process by which these firms gain monopoly rights over proprietary technology, for example, through patent laws. It is further thought that such power tends to become entrenched in the monopoly rents that are appropriated through the creation of new products and processes based on such a technology. On an overall basis, therefore, the ownership of technology, and the control of product and process innovations associated with it, essentially enable these corporations to maximize their share of the market in which they operate (Parry 1977).

According to Vernon (1970, 1972, 1974), these sources of market control can be explained in terms of the behavior of two types of international oligopolies—innovation-based and mature. The former type is characterized by relatively high expenditures on the services of engineers, scientists, and other cadres involved in research and development. This leads to some special advantages that are derived from the introduction of new products as well as from differentiating existing ones. This type of transnational oligopoly normally plays a dominant role in the manufacture and trade in those commodities associated with high levels of innovation and development effort. Over time, many innovation-based oligopolies develop into mature ones. The market advantage of mature oligopolies is derived not so much from product innovation but more from barriers to entry stemming from economies of scale in production, transportation, and marketing.

In the above context, technological know-how and change are now considered as explicit trade-determining variables. Most technological know-how tends to be generated in highly industrialized countries and then consciously transferred, or indirectly diffused, to other countries. Where technology is considered a trade-determining variable, it is a reflection of international market imperfection, and therefore calls into question the assumption underlying orthodox trade models that factors and outputs are internationally mobile (see Helleiner 1978).

One related explanation is provided by the *product life cycle* model (Vernon 1966; Wells 1972). The model postulates that countries achieve temporary positions of comparative advantage as a result of technological leadership, product differentiation, and the early exploitation of economies of scale. Their ability to maintain this comparative advantage depends on the extent to which new products and product variations can be continuously created through research and development. Large firms in the industrialized nations are in a much better position to create and maintain such temporary monopoly position, because of the following factors that are associated with the research and development process.

First, large firms with significant and high-income markets are usually able to minimize the risks associated with expensive and time-consuming research and development. As a consequence, they are able to create new products and technology on a continuous basis. This provides them with an opportunity to exploit economies of scale in production. Second, they are frequently members of the oligopolistic markets in their home countries and are able to protect their technological findings through patent laws. Third, the diffusion of technological innovation, even without the benefits of legal protection, requires considerable financial resources and time.

The product life-cycle occurs because a new product will be first produced in the country of its creation, and exports will start as other markets accept the product. As the market grows, local production will begin either on a licensing basis or in production facilities owned by the original producer. The product might ultimately be exported back to the country of origin. Thus, over time, a shift takes place as competing products appear and the initial monopoly position disappears. However, the monopoly advantage of the original producer might be prolonged by means of a secondary product cycle based on process innovations that are superimposed on the first (product innovation) cycle. Eventually, however, cost advantages will begin to favor centers of production in low-wage countries.

As indicated earlier, the product cycle model emphasizes the importance of technology in international trade flows and the prominent role played by large transnational firms in this process. This technology factor is usually ignored in orthodox trade theory, which implicitly assumes that technological knowledge is perfectly mobile and therefore equally accessible to all countries, irrespective of their levels of development. This implies that production functions are similar in all countries and that international cost differentials are a result of differences in factor endowments. However, there is reason to believe that the technological base, and therefore production functions, tend to differ significantly among countries. This opens up the possibility for differential rates of progress among countries at different levels of development. It also has implications for differential price movements between primary products and industrial goods, and therefore for the terms of trade between developed and developing nations.

## Transnational Corporations and Foreign Investment in Developing Countries

As is well known, the debate on the relationships between TNCs and the developing countries, and therefore their potential role in economic development, has been a long and at times highly charged one. The underlying issues are complicated by the fact that both the nature of the investments and the environment in which they take place have undergone significant changes during the past three decades or more. In this context, the role of TNCs in the development process is discussed in terms of the factors influencing what is known as private direct foreign investment (PDFI), and the fact that such investments have costs and benefits to both home and host countries. Further, as the perspectives presented in Table 7.5 indicate, opinion is equally divided on the positive and negative consequences of the transnational process for economic development.

The past few decades have witnessed significant changes in the form and rate of flow of private direct foreign investment to the developing countries. As indicated in an earlier section of this chapter, such investments date back to colonial times, with foreign resources concentrated in mines, plantations, and other extractive activities. This pattern continued right up to the late 1950s and early 1960s. The latter period witnessed a very slow growth in direct foreign investment to developing countries due to the changing political climate in these countries. One explanatory variable was the rising tide of opposition to foreign economic control that accompanied the attainment of political self-determination.

The pace picked up again during the late 1960s to the late 1970s. Net inflows of direct foreign investment to the developing countries increased from an average of about $2 billion per year during the early 1960s to an average of around $13 billion per year during 1979–81 due to (1) the rapid economic growth experienced by several developing countries during this period, and especially by the middle income countries to which most of the investment flowed, and (2) changing attitudes on the part of both TNCs and home and host country governments. This created an environment in which the costs of foreign investment flows were reduced and corresponding benefits increased for both home and host countries (Billerbeck and Yasugi 1979).

**TABLE 7.5:** Perspectives of private direct foreign investment and transnational corporations

| Approaches | Assumptions, characteristics |
| --- | --- |
| Business school | Based on free enterprise ethic. Concerned with increasing private profitability of foreign investment through minimizing tax burdens and providing incentives. |
| Neoclassical | Shares above assumptions. Emphasizes the need for free international resource flows as a means of maximizing world welfare and that of individual countries. |
| Post-Keynesian | Stresses divergence of interests of foreign investors and host countries due to imperfect competition, and other behavioral and environmental constraints in the world economy. |
| Structuralist-institutionalist | Questions the validity of assumptions underlying free market system. Like post-Keynesianism, emphasizes the unequal exchange relations underlying international resource flows. Advocates national and international reforms. |
| Dependency | Like structuralist perspective, views foreign investment as perpetuating economic and other forms of dependency. Foreign investment cannot lead to authentic development. |
| Marxian | Based on a total rejection of foreign investment. Analysis in terms of imperialism and capitalist expansion on a world scale. Advocates nationalization and other revolutionary changes. |

*Source:* Compiled by the author.

However, the period since the early 1970s has witnessed a marked decline in the relative importance of direct foreign investment in the overall capital flows to developing countries. While direct investment has continued to increase in absolute terms, bank credit has become much more dominant in private capital flows. In 1973, direct foreign investment was responsible for financing about 20 percent of the combined current account deficits and net accumulation of reserves of nonoil developing countries, compared to an average of about 10 percent in 1983. (Goldsbrough 1985). Further, as the data in Table 7.6 show, the shift in the composition of financing has resulted in a significant change in the structure of external liabilities of these countries. The share of direct

**TABLE 7.6:** Foreign direct investment and external debt in developing countries, 1973–83

| | Stock of foreign direct investment[a] (In billions of dollars) | | Total outstanding external debt[b] | Share of foreign direct investment in total gross external liabilities[c] (In percent) |
|---|---|---|---|---|
| | 1973 | 1983 (Estimate) | 1983 | 1983 |
| Seven major borrowers | 20.0 | 59.6 | 350.1 | 14.5 |
|    Argentina | 2.5 | 5.8 | 44.4 | 11.6 |
|    Brazil | 7.5 | 24.6 | 88.0 | 21.8 |
|    Indonesia | 1.7 | 6.8 | 30.4 | 18.3 |
|    Korea | 0.7 | 1.8 | 38.9 | 4.4 |
|    Mexico | 3.1 | 13.6 | 89.4 | 13.2 |
|    Philippines | 0.9 | 2.7 | 23.9 | 10.9 |
|    Venezuela | 3.6 | 4.3 | 35.1 | 10.9 |
| Nonoil developing countries | 47.0 | 140.9 | 685.5 | 17.0 |

[a]The 1983 end of year stock figures equal the estimated book value of the stock of direct investment from industrial countries at the end of 1978 plus total direct investment flows during 1979–83.

[b]End of year. Includes short-term debt, but not reserve-related liabilities.

[c]Total gross external liabilities are defined as stock of foreign direct investment plus total outstanding external debt.

*Source:* Goldsbrough (1985).

foreign investment in the gross external liabilities (the stock of direct foreign investment plus total external debt) of nonoil developing countries declined from around 27 percent in 1973 to 17 percent in 1983, while the share of debt to private institutions rose from 10 to 25 percent.

It should also be noted that the lion's share of direct foreign investment is concentrated in a relatively few countries with large natural resource endowments and domestic markets or other significant advantages as a base for export-oriented production. For example, five countries (South Africa, Mexico, Brazil, Malaysia, and Singapore) accounted for about 50 percent of the stock of direct foreign investment to nonoil developing countries during the early 1980s. Other countries that either have large domestic markets (e.g., India and China) or that have successfully pursued export-oriented development strategies (e.g., South Korea) are much less reliant on such investment.

The above country experiences could be contrasted with that of many African and Caribbean countries that, despite significant incentives to foreign investors, have not been able to attract them in any large numbers. The reason is probably their small domestic markets. However, it should also be mentioned that this factor has not proved a deterrent to the foreign investment process in small Asian countries, such as Hong Kong and Singapore where the bulk of the foreign investment has been in export-oriented production activities. Besides the relatively low wages obtaining in these countries, they also tend to maintain more open and liberal policies toward foreign investors.

The changing structure of direct foreign investment has also been accompanied by changes in the relationships with developing countries. Traditionally, most forms of such foreign investment were based on ownership and control of foreign affiliates and subsidiaries through equity and management participation. However, two noticeable shifts have taken place in these forms of association. First, there have been shifts from equity participation and control to financing in the form of loans and/or suppliers credits. Second, there has been a shift from direct control and ownership by the parent company to various forms of management participation, management contracts, technical assistance agreements, and so on.

Under the new arrangements, TNCs try to achieve some measure of effective participation in management, but this is usually separated from the objective of ownership or equity participation. Further, while these corporations are still interested in earning adequate returns on their investments, they are also willing to participate in new agreements due to the growing size of investment projects and other factors in the international investment climate. As a means of distributing the financial burden and spreading investment risks, these firms have shown an increasing willingness to enter into joint ventures and co-financing arrangements with other partners (Moran 1973).

Given the above considerations, the remaining and crucial issue concerns the potential impact of direct foreign investment on the development process. In general, its resolution depends on how one views the role of foreign firms. Within the context of the perspectives outlined in Table 7.5, the issue can be addressed by juxtaposing the goals of TNCs against those of host countries in the developing world as a means of highlighting areas of conflict.

It was stated earlier that TNCs make horizontal, vertical, defensive, and cross investments across national boundaries. The objectives behind the transfer of the requisite resources go beyond those of the profit maximization behavior that is usually attributed to the neoclassical firm. They are also related to the perceived need of these corporations to (1) safeguard their supplies of raw materials in agricultural, mining, and other extractive activities; (2) exploit, where possible, conditions favorable to export-oriented production, for example, cheap labor costs and raw materials; and (3) undertake those activities that are supportive of those of the parent company or affiliates elsewhere, for example, banking, insurance, transportation, and related services.

These activities tend to have far-reaching effects on the development process since they tend to have differential impacts on a relatively large number of developmental parameters. These include (1) macroeconomic parameters such as income, foreign exchange, tax revenues, and the balance of payments; (2) the employment potential of both the modern and traditional sectors of the economy; (3) the regional, personal, and functional distribution of income; (4) the pace and pattern of industrialization, for example, the types of industries and appropriateness of technology; and (5) the political superstructure and sociocultural values. These are also areas that pose the greatest source of conflict between foreign investors and developing countries. We elaborate on some pertinent issues below and again in Chapter 8.

Historically, the main bone of contention between TNCs and developing countries has centered around the claim that foreign investment is not normally subject to nationally defined objectives nor necessarily supportive of the overall development efforts of host countries. In this context, the claim is that the typical foreign producing sector tends to function as an enclave, and therefore has failed to develop substantial consumption, production, and fiscal linkages in the host country economy. To the extent that the requisite linkage effects operated mainly between satellite companies in the periphery and parent institutions in the metropole, the requisite demand for mass-consumption, intermediate, and capital goods in the host country were not satisfactorily met.

While there has been some change in attitudes over the years, it can be commented that the typical foreign investor does not normaly perceive its role in terms of the total development of the host country, but rather from a more limited perspective of generating tax revenue that could then be used to finance plans for national development. While this is a rational response, the total tax take available to host countries depends on how the firm makes its pricing and cost allocations among affiliates in several countries. As emphasized earlier, to the extent that the accounting or transfer prices used diverge from notional market prices, host countries may lose substantial revenues.

Besides the tax yield, the total tax revenues available to the host country also depend on the corporate tax rate. Over the years, there has been no uniform definition of taxable income among developing countries so that both the tax base and the tax yield varied substantially among countries. Under the circumstances, firms have been able to allocate their global income in such a manner as to reduce their total tax bill. In more recent times, however, the force of the tax minimization objective might have been weakened by international action to equalize tax rates across countries. However, these and other international initiatives designed to regulate the activities of TNCs have not borne much fruit (for a further discussion, see Billerbeck and Yasugi 1979).

The tax revenue problem is related to others concerning the outflow of capital from the developing countries and the potentially negative consequences for the balance of payments. In the typical case, the initial inflow of capital that is associated with a foreign investment normally benefits the host country's balance-of-payments position. However, as the investment begins to generate income in later stages, there is an increasing outflow of factor incomes. Tensions have arisen between foreign firms and developing countries because, in some cases, net income outflows have tended to surpass new inflows in these later stages, contributing, in part, to balance-of-payments deficits and foreign exchange shortages. This is particularly true for investments in certain extractive industries.

The negative consequences of net investment income outflows (repatriated profits, dividends, interest on loans associated with past investments, and so on) should be considered in the much wider context of the factors that cause balance-of-payments deficits in the developing countries. These include (1) the outflow of other factor incomes, for example, the payment of various commissions, fees, and other remuneration to expatriate personnel of foreign firms; (2) the negative effects on the balance of trade that might arise because of the higher than normal prices paid for a wide variety of consumption, intermediate, and capital goods associated with a foreign investment; and (3) the sluggish and sometimes erratic behavior of export earnings.

Net investment income is also affected by the fact that developing countries compete for foreign investment and therefore have to offer a wide range of investment incentives. These incentives include (1) tax concessions, for example, generous tax write-off provisions, and concessions on sales, exports, and licensing fees; (2) tariff concessions, for example, protective tariffs, tariff reductions on imported inputs; and (3) financial incentives, including investment grants, local loans at subsidized interest rates, subsidies on exports and wages and the participation of local private and public organizations in financing new ventures.

There is always some question whether these incentives do in fact help to create a sound investment climate. Given the financial constraints facing many developing countries, the opportunity costs of the tax revenues foregone may be quite high. Further, there may be an indirect cost in the sense that a part of the foregone tax revenue may be eventually taxed by the foreign firm's home country. To the extent that this occurs, it can be considered a transfer of tax revenue from developing to developed countries. In general, these incentives have not proved useful in determining the distribution of private foreign investment among developing countries. One reason is that the majority of these countries tend to maintain similar and competing incentive structures. Other factors may have a more important impact on the foreign investment decision, for example, the host country's overall sector and development policies, its location, the political ideology of its government, and the degree of political stability that it enjoys.

In conclusion, most developing countries are in a relatively weak bargaining position vis-à-vis TNCs and are caught on the horns of a dilemma. On the one hand, rationality dictates that they should take every opportunity to maximize national returns from foreign investment and the overall transnational process. On the other hand, they are caught in the bind of having to maintain a climate favorable to foreign investment. While this dilemma persists, there has been an intensification of the competition among the developing countries to attract foreign investment. In this process, the countries that seem to fare the best are the "newly industrializing" or semi-industrialized ones with large internal markets, a favorable physical and social infrastructure, and supportive managerial and administrative systems. The larger majority of developing nations are still handicapped by their relatively weak bargaining power vis-à-vis TNCs. This is explained by factors such as their limited market size and resource endowments, poor infrastructural facilities, the lack of managerial skills and human capital formation, and relatively weak administrative systems.

# 8

# Unequal Exchange, Dependency, and Uneven Development

A general conclusion emerging from Chapters 6 and 7 is that trade, income levels, and overall resource utilization in developing countries tend to be lower than they would be under conditions of Pareto optimality, and if goods and factors were completely mobile across countries. This suboptimality defines the conditions of uneven development, that is, the inherent tendency for inequality to increase, both nationally and internationally. This chapter looks at this phenomenon in a more systematic manner and makes use of the insights provided by the structuralist, dependency, and Marxian perspectives of development. While no full-fledged or unified theory of center-periphery relations or uneven development is presented, the objective is to highlight some essential ingredients and building blocks. An attempt is also made to identify some of the major similarities and differences between the structuralist and dependency perspectives on the one hand and the more radical heterodox or Marxian perspective on the other.

## Structuralist Arguments and Hypotheses

The phenomenon of uneven development is reflected in the slow growth or stagnation, unemployment, worsening income distribution, and disequilibria in terms of particular properties of domestic and foreign demand, production relations, and other structural rigidities facing developing countries. Explanations of these conditions are provided in several interrelated varieties of structuralist thought, including (1) Lewis' dual labor surplus model; (2) the center-periphery thesis of Prebisch and Singer; (3) the balanced growth theories of Nurske (1953) and Rosenstein-Rodan (1943); and (4) the disequilibrium theories of Myrdal (1957), Hirschman (1958), Myint (1971), and Balogh (1974). These economists seem to agree that the equilibrating mechanisms of the price system have failed to produce steady growth, external equilibrium in trade and payments, and desirable levels of employment and income distribution in the developing countries.

First, it is necessary to restate a set of basic structuralist hypotheses and domain assumptions. These can be subdivided into three basic groups. A first set is concerned with structural parameters and factor supplies in developing countries. A second group is concerned with price relations and, in particular, with the income and price elasticities of developing country exports and imports. A third set places more emphasis on the cumulative effects of polarization and the unequalizing influences produced by the differential impacts of spread and backwash effects, or the operation of centrifugal and centripetal forces.

The first set of hypotheses highlights the fact that the economies of developing countries (the South or periphery) display a duality in the structure of production and in the supply of factors of production, as compared to the more homogeneous structure typically encountered in the more developed countries (the North or center). Taking as a point of departure the assumptions underlying Lewis' dual labor surplus model, the duality in the production structure of the South is reflected by technological dualism (with a capital-using modern sector and a noncapital-using subsistence sector), capital dualism (based on the differential rates of savings between capitalist and workers), and an elastic labor supply. In Lewis' model, it is assumed that labor has an infinitely elastic supply and that the real wage is pegged at some subsistence level. In other models, for example, Chichilnisky (1981), this assumption is relaxed, and the economy of the South is characerized by abundant labor, that is, the supply of labor is responsive to the behavior of real wages.

The second set of assumptions is concerned with the price relations governing the South's imports and exports. Here the basic explanation turns on the different income elasticities of demand for primary and industrial goods. As explained in Chapter 5, this is an extrapolation of Engels' Law that the proportion of income spent on food and other primary commodities tends to fall as income rises. The generalized version of Engels' Law (also supported by balanced growth theorists) states that consumer demand for food and other primary commodity groups is mainly a function of income and is only slightly affected by the behavior of relative prices.

On the above basis, Prebisch and Singer hypothesized that the income elasticity of demand for the South's exports tends to be lower than that for the North's exports and that technical progress in manufacturing results in a rise in incomes in the North, while that in the production of food and raw materials in the South resulted in a fall in prices. This unequal exchange is explained in terms of a general proposition that technological progress tends to be diffused more uniformly, and at a faster pace, in industrial activities compared to primary production, with costs of production diminishing more rapidly in the former case. Under such circumstances, one should expect the ratio of relative prices to become more favorable to primary producers, resulting in a more favorable impact on their terms of trade. However, the argument is that the presence of monopoly elements in the production and pricing structures of central economies enables them to retain the benefits of technological progress in the form of higher relative prices and rising factor incomes.

Contextually, while the North is able to use its monopoly privileges to maximize factor incomes, the gains in productivity in the South take the form of price reductions. Further, due to the differential effects of technological change, the allocation of gains arising from productivity increases tends to favor industrial products at the expense of primary commodities. In the former case, the result has been relatively higher prices and therefore relatively higher payments to factors of production. By contrast, the process has resulted in relatively lower prices for primary commodities and a concomitant reduction in factor rewards.

It is interesting to note that formal models of "immiserizing growth" are also based on assumptions about different elasticities of demand for primary commodities vis-à-vis industrial products (see Bhagwati 1968, 1972; and Mundell 1968). The general assumption is that exports of the developing countries face inelastic demands in international markets, while the demands for developed country exports tend to be more elastic. On this basis, it is argued that if developing countries attempt to grow faster than their more developed counterparts, the prices of their exports will fall significantly, with negative consequences for their terms of trade and growth efforts.

The implication is that where developing countries rely on trade as an engine of growth, the faster growth of the developed countries may very well be a precondition for the success of such an approach. This is because the faster growth of the developed relative to the developing countries may be a necessary prerequisite for preventing the terms of trade from worsening, or even for guaranteeing its potential improvement. The models of "immiserizing growth" are based on assumptions about a given international structure of demand. Unlike structuralist approaches, they fail to consider the fact that the internal structures of each of these groups of countries tend to have certain effects on the structure of international markets (Chichilnisky 1981).

The final set of structuralist hypotheses rests on the claim that central and peripheral economies tend to experience differential and unequal outcomes from their participation in the international economic system due to the impetus and peculiar character of cumulative circular causation (Myrdal 1957). The general proposition is that the dynamics of the societal system, at both national and international levels, is determined by the fact that, among all the conditions that are internal to the system (endogenous ones), there tends to be a "cumulative causation" or state of "circular interlocking interdependence." This means that if there is a change in any one condition, others will change in response. The secondary changes will in turn cause new changes all around, with responses reaching back to the original conditions of change. The process then cumulates in future rounds. The cumulative effects arise because the feedbacks from the initial changes tend to produce two types of repercussions. First, they tend to operate in the same direction of cumulative growth or decline, as the case may be. Second, this cumulative growth or decline tends to be out of proportion to the initial impulse of change (Myrdal 1974).

The principle of cumulative causation can be further explained in terms of the contradictory influences of "spread" and "backwash" effects, or the operation of centrifugal and centripetal forces at both national and international levels. The general point of emphasis is that in the relationships between the North and South, as well as between advanced and backward regions in the South, the backwash or unfavorable effects tend to predominate, with the spread of favorable effects remaining relatively weak. Moreover, the backwash effects tend to be relatively strong, and the spread effects relatively weak, at lower levels of development compared to higher levels.

As Myrdal states:

> . . . I refer to all relevant adverse changes, caused outside the locality, as the "backwash effects" via migration, capital movements, and trade as well as the effects of the whole gamut of other social relations exemplified above (non-economic factors) . . . the higher the level of development a country has already attained the stronger the spread effects will usually be. For a higher level of development is accompanied by improved transportation and communications, higher levels of education, and more dynamic communication of ideas and values—all of which tend to strengthen the forces for centrifugal spread of economic expansion or remove obstacles for its operation (Myrdal 1957, pp. 30, 34).

From another angle, Hirschman defines the effects of spread and backwash in terms of the nature of the "trickle down" and "poliarization" that are typically associated with unbalanced growth between regions or countries. These effects are explained by contrasting a region experiencing growth (the North) with a lagging region (the South).

Hirschman states:

> The favorable effects consist of the trickling down of Northern progress; by far the most important of these effects is the increase of Northern purchases and investment in the South, an increase which is sure to take place if the economies of the two regions are at all complementary. In addition, the North may absorb some of the disguised unemployment of the South and thereby raise the marginal productivity of labor and per capita consumption levels in the South ... on the other hand, several unfavorable polarization effects are also likely to be at work. Comparatively inefficient, yet income-creating Southern activities in manufacturing and exports may become depressed as a result of Northern competition. To the extent that the North industrializes along lines in which there is no Southern production, the South is likely to make a bad bargain since it will now have to buy Northern manufactures, produced behind tariff walls, instead of goods previously imported from abroad at lower prices (Hirschman 1958, pp. 187–88).

The structuralist world view and its domain assumptions have provided the building blocks for a growing number of formal models dealing with the relationship between unequal exchange and uneven development (e.g., Findlay 1973; Bacha 1978; Krugman 1981; and Chichilnisky 1981). While the details of these models are not explored here, they generally show how the process of uneven development cumulates when there is a lack of homogeneity in the production structures and demand conditions facing the economies of the North vis-à-vis those of the South. Under conditions of abundant labor supplies and generalized dualism in the South, as well as different capital/labor ratios and rates of technological diffusion between the North and the South, it is demonstrated that trade between the two world regions typically leads to a worsening of the terms of trade, unemployment, and income distribution in the South and an overall cumulation of the process of uneven development.

In other words, factor prices would not be equalized, nor the terms of trade improved, as orthodox predictions based on export-led growth strategies would lead one to believe. The latter result can take place only if it is assumed that production structures are homogeneous across countries and regions. The implications for nations in the periphery have been stated as follows:

It may seem paradoxical that what is in general considered the relative advantage of the South, its abundant labour and labour intensive exports, may be a handicap in export policies, bringing about a worsening of its terms of trade, and reinforcing North-South factor price inequality. It follows that relative advantages based on inequalities are not necessarily self-destructing: in some cases they may actually be self-perpetuating. The opposite of the conventional wisdom on this matter seems closer to the truth, in the sense that a strong domestic market structure (with the associated high productivity and wages) is a better basis for a long-term success in export policies than the cheap and abundant labour provided by widespread poverty (Chichilnisky 1981, p. 184).

## Perspectives of Dependency and Dependent Development

The dependency perspective is based on the general structuralist thesis concerning international inequality. This, it is argued, has been associated with a process of national stratification and the widespread marginalization of subject peoples. As highlighted below, the process is thought to have taken many forms and was aided and abetted by several types of socioeconomic influences.

In general, it is reflected by two basic types of polarization: at the international level between the more developed and industrialized center economies at one pole and the relatively underdeveloped and peripheral economies at the other; and nationally, between advanced and modern groups, sectors, and regions on the one hand and relatively backward, marginal, and generally less advanced groups, sectors, and regions on the other. Accordingly, dependency theorists argue that the process has resulted in a restriction of the benefits of development to certain groups and economic activities associated with foreign interests, but with a serious marginalization of other groups and activities. They point to the negative consequences for the masses of the population, as reflected in their limited access to various forms of opportunity. It is also sometimes argued that this marginality has been reinforced by a social system that tends to perpetuate various patterns of differentiation along class, ethnic, color, and caste lines.

In the attempt to explain the significance and ramifications of dependency, we draw primarily from the writings of members of the Latin American dependency research program (notably Furtado 1967, 1970,

1973; Sunkel 1969, 1972, 1973; Dos Santos 1970; Pinto and Knakal 1972; Cardoso and Faletto 1979; Caporaso and Zare 1982; and Palma 1978). While there is not always agreement about the precise theoretical significance or empirical validity of the dependency concept, a few generalizations can nevertheless be advanced.

In a general sense, dependency connotes an unequal or asymmetrical relationship between entities in various spheres: objects, individuals, groups of persons, individual economic sectors, national economies, and so on. In the typical case, this relationship between any two such entities can be conceptualized in terms of an asymmetry defined by differentials in economic status, power, and prestige. This, in turn, gives rise to a complex process of interaction and unequalizing influences in several other spheres. In terms of the center-periphery dichotomy, the state of dependency generally connotes a situation in which the possibilities for sustained development in the periphery are primarily determined by advanced center nations and institutions, without the periphery being able to exert an equal amount of countervailing influence on its own development situation, either autonomously, or by changing the nature of the relationship between itself and the center (Evans 1979). In this context, the basic condition for a nation's dependency and underdevelopment is presumed to lie in its openness to various forms of vulnerability linked to its poor standing in the stratified international hierarchy.

In the early evolution of the dependency concept, the primary focus was on external economic relationships. As mentioned earlier, the root cause of dependency and underdevelopment was considered to be factors underlying the historical integration of the periphery into the world economic system. This, it is argued, has resulted in dependent relations in trade, division of labor, investment, and related economic arrangements. These dependency relations are exemplified, in turn, by the following structural features of underdevelopment, among others: (1) the fact that the majority of dependent economies are still at a pre-capitalist stage of development, generally lack industrial development, are unable to generate indigenous technological capabilities, or otherwise use domestic resources optimally; (2) the fact that the majority of dependent economies experience increased economic stagnation due to the operation of exogenous economic influences; and (3) the fact that their development choice possibilities tend to be restricted.

The links between external vulnerability and restricted choice are brought out in the following quotation:

> Given that a country depends on the external sphere for completion of its economic cycle, we can ask whether it depends on actors in one country

or several and further, how unevenly its reliances are distributed among these actors ... the more concentrated (i.e., the less uniformly distributed) the external reliances the more severe the pattern of dependency. Concentration of reliances is tied to two other important concepts of dependency—vulnerability and restricted choice. The greater the concentration of reliance, the greater the vulnerability of an actor for the simple reason—the greater the difficulty the actor would have in adjusting to a break in relations (Caporaso and Zare 1982, p. 49).

The reasoning is, therefore, that the more externally oriented an economy is, the more open it becomes to various forms of vulnerability and the more restricted are its economic choice possibilities. The pattern and concentration of external reliances reflect a situation of "external dependency" in the areas of trade, finance, technology, and even in terms of political and social ideology. These, in turn, are considered to have certain internal developmental consequences. The latter can be thought of as "internal dependency" and is generally reflected by internal fragmentation, a lack of integration among economic and social sectors, and underdevelopment.

Some of the major external reliances and their internal consequences are illustrated in Table 8.1. Aspects of trade dependency have been discussed in the previous chapter. We also touched upon the technology issue as part of the discussion of the activities of transnational corporations. In elaboration, a large part of the international market for technology has been commercialized, with proprietary rights acquired for the requisite technology. This process has invoved both legal and nonlegal restrictions that protect the owners of technology and limit the free international flow of technological know-how. A point emphasized in our previous discussion of the subject is that the international market for technology has become highly imperfect, with the monopoly power of technology suppliers entrenched in patents and trademark protections associated with different products and industrial processes and related oligopolistic pricing arrangements. This has placed developing countries in a situation of more or less permanent technological import dependency. It has also deprived them of the multiplier effects that typically result from the pursuit of domestic research and development (R & D) programs.

This technological dependency is also linked to the failure of the developing countries themselves to develop appropriate forms of technology. This is related to the factor proportions problem discussed in Chapter 4. Evidence of technological inappropriateness can be found in the overcapitalizatin of the modern sector vis-à-vis the subsistence sector. With most modern (imported, capital-intensive) technology concentrated in modern industrial enclaves or otherwise among more progressive farmers, the subsistence sector is generally starved, further exacerbating the growth

**TABLE 8.1:** External reliances and internal consequences

| A. *External Reliances* | *Characteristics* |
|---|---|
| 1. Trade | High proportion of trade in GNP. |
| 2. Commodity trade concentration | High percentage share in total exports and GNP of two to three most important commodity exports. |
| 3. Trade partner concentration | Relatively high proportion of trade with one country or region. |
| 4. Vertical trade disposition | High proportion of unprocessed to processed exports, with high ratio of processed goods in total imports. |
| 5. Export earnings instability | Wide year-to-year fluctuations in export prices and earnings. |
| 6. Technological | All technologically sophisticated products and processes have to be imported. |
| 7. Food imports | Historical changes in net food and grain trade, with increasing proportion of basic food items imported. |
| 8. Financial | High proportion of capital imports in domestic capital formation, and high external public debt. |
| B. *Internal Consequences* | *Characteristics* |
| 9. External control | High percentage of external control of production. |
| 10. Sectoral disarticulation | Uneven development across sectors and regions. |
| 11. Monocultural attachment | High proportion of labor force in traditional sectors. |
| 12. Export crop concentration | Neglect of food subsector and rural production. |
| 13. Low incomes | Low and stagnating GNP per capita. |

*Source:* David (1985).

margins between the two sectors. Further, subsistence sector stagnation is normally associated with a situation in which the requirements of consumer demand emanating from this sector tend to be translated into demands for modern sector products. This, in turn, tends to heighten the need to import modern sector technology.

This process reflects a structural maladjustment, that is, the inappropriateness of the technology to the domestic social and economic structure as reflected in relative factor availabilities. In a situation of labor surplus, the importation of capital-intensive technologies tends to bar the larger majority from effective participation in the production process. As emphasized in Chapter 6, the lack of opportunity for productive employment is typically associated with a distorted pattern of development, reflected by the coexistence of islands of growth enclaves in a sea of poverty and underdevelopment.

While dependency takes many forms, perhaps its most prevalent contemporary manifestation is the increasing financial dependency of the developing world on both private and official international lending agencies. This aspect has been discussed in detail elsewhere (David 1985). Like its correlates on the real side of the economy, financial dependency has resulted from the cumulative interplay of both internal and external factors. At the internal level, it is a reflection of the institutional maladjustments and inefficiencies that have become endemic to the domestic process of financial intermediation. This has resulted in sustained outflows of domestic capital to metropolitan centers. This forms part of a much broader scenario in which externally controlled commercial and industrial investments have become linked to large-scale movements of financial capital. In addition, the deepening of external financial reliances has been accompanied by skyrocketing balance-of-payments deficits and external debt, with increasing accommodation sought from the International Monetary Fund (IMF) and private multinational banks.

Besides those mentioned earlier, the following other systematic effects of dependency are usually discussed in the literature. In some instances, some commentators point to the adverse effects on the domestic industrialization process that has accompanied the flow of financial capital to the periphery. This flow, it is argued, was to some extent stimulated by the relatively abundant supplies of cheap labor and the ability of foreign investors to forge a new international division of labor among manufacturing activities in several countries. Other factors included the availability of financial and business incentives and the willingness of local private and public institutions to participate in the financing of business ventures. In the latter context, mention is sometimes made of the role played by local class and political alignments in setting a favorable investment climate and tone (Cardoso and Faletto 1979).

This kind of interest linkage is usually viewed in the context of the coalescence of a worldwide technocratic and political bureaucracy and, more generally, in terms of the existence of a network of interests and interactions that link certain social groups and classes across countries. An important element in the vector of such interest linkages is thought to be exhibited by the nature of the political system and the power of the state in managing the economy of peripheral countries. In this context, it is argued that most states in developing countries are "dependent capitalist states" that lack a development-oriented "national bourgeoisie" (Cardoso and Faletto 1979). This is explained by the fact that the most powerful political actors tend to be most closely tied to foreign capital and related international interests. Under the circumstances, the local ruling elite becomes "structurally inhibited" from undertaking sound domestic reforms since the latter are likely to transform the status quo, alter the prevailing patterns of resource allocation and distribution, and thereby reduce the power, influence, and overall economic security enjoyed by these cadres.

Some scholars view the interest linkage in terms of the influence of foreign investment and the transnational process on value formation in the periphery. According to Villamil et al. (1978), the process has resulted in the upsurge of a new "transnational ideology," which is fostered by transnational firms and other international actors that share common sets of interests, beliefs, values, and norms. This "transnationalization of culture," it is argued, has been translated into beliefs about the legitimacy of certain kinds of economic arrangements, development priorities, life-styles, and consumption patterns. The general argument is that members of the "transnational community" who are located in the periphery have come to realize that their very existence depends on the strength of the linkages that are maintained with the wider transnational system. As a consequence, they vigorously promote such links through their own life-styles and generally champion development priorities that perpetuate the linkage process.

In other instances, the marriage between foreign investment and domestic forms of participation is thought to have resulted in the following readily identifiable forms of dependent development. One type is represented by the former colonial enclaves in the mining and plantation sectors, which are now either controlled domestically through nationalization or other forms of public participation, or externally by the affiliates of transnational corporations. This suggests only marginal changes in the traditional patterns of export dependence. In the majority of cases, the prevalent feature of dependent development continues to be reflected in the monocultural pattern of production and export, with a predominance of subsistence activities utilizing pre-capitalist methods of production.

The persistence of these conditions, that is, monocultural modes of production and export reliance on a few primary commodities, is sometimes interpreted as a failure of the export-led growth model (see Chapter 5). The general argument is that the implementation of this model has not resulted in a sustained and integrated pattern of domestic development, but rather in a disarticulated production structure with relatively few and insignificant backward and forward linkages or multiplier effects.

A second aspect of dependent development pertains to the negative consequences for agricultural and rural development throughout the developing world. Over the years, the lion's share of investment has been channeled into large farms or plantations that have an internal comparative advantage in terms of soil fertility, the use of modern technology, and access to modern production inputs, forms of finance, and management. Further, patterns of infrastructural development, communications systems, bulk storage, processing and distribution facilities, and even the requirements of international commodity agreements have been dictated by the needs of the export enclave sector. One noticeable consequence has been the failure of peripheral economies to develop flexible systems of mixed farming as a means of moderating the sharp dichotomy between the modernized export sector and the traditional rural sector.

The system of monocultural export production has built certain inflexibilities into the agricultural sector, and these have tended to militate against meaningful employment creation. While this form of economic activity has provided employment opportunities for a limited number of hired agricultural laborers, the overall result, in many cases, has been the dismantling of traditional farm economies based on family labor. As emphasized in Chapter 6, most of this displaced labor migrates to urban areas where it remains marginally unemployed or underemployed. Alternatively, some members of this group are reabsorbed into the traditional subsistence sector where they heighten the competition for the limited resources available and create further pressures for the subdivision of relatively small agricultural holdings.

The neglect of the traditional agricultural and rural sector has meant that it has not been able to keep pace with the burgeoning food needs of a rapidly growing population. Evidence of this is the high food import dependency, with many developing countries having to import grain to meet their domestic food consumption needs. In many cases, the ruling political elite seems to have made a conscious political decision to rely on food imports rather than provide the incentives necessary for domestic farmers to increase production. This is part of a larger process in which some leaders in the developing world, as a means of offsetting the worsening food situation, have shown a willingness to neglect the rural sector in favor of imports on concessional terms. One explanatory variable in this case lies in the necessity of ensuring the availability of cheap food to middle-class urban groups on whom they have to rely for political support.

Agricultural and rural neglect represent only one side of the dependency equation. The other side is reflected in a heavy reliance on an urban-oriented, externally propelled, industrialization strategy. This is linked to dependency because it has increasingly represented a development approach in which the building of the industrial base is linked to a heavy reliance on foreign investment. One form of such investment is exemplified by industrial platforms where foreign firms choose particular locations for low-skilled processing and/or assembly operations. In addition, there may be certain outposts where skills, technology, and/or industrial components are readily available, with the possibility for the products that are manufactured to be shifted to industrial platforms for assembly or to larger export markets. In yet other cases, the foreign investments may be associated with the stimulation of demand for new consumer products in expanding domestic markets, especially in heavily populated developing countries.

In many instances, these forms of investment are rationalized on the grounds that they represent an integral part of a country's import substitution industrialization strategy. However, subscribers to the dependency perspective argue that the pursuit of such strategies has resulted in a significant growth in manufacturing activity and the related emergence of a domestic commercial class (especially in Latin American countries) at the expense of increased foreign penetration and the heightening of external influence and control. They cite as evidence of this "failed logic" of import substitution the following consequences: (1) the transfer of the benefits of industrialization abroad in the form of profit repatriation, excessive payments for imported intermediate and capital goods, interest on foreign loans, and the like; (2) some modernization and expansion of capital-intensive economic activities and the disruption of labor-intensive ones; and (3) the widening of the development gap between high-income groups in the urban and modern sectors on the one hand and low income segments of the population in the urban informal and rural sectors on the other.

In the latter context, it is also argued that the industrialization of dependent economies has resulted in wage and labor market segmentation between the relatively high-wage cadres in the manufacturing sector, a less well-paid segment in the mining and agricultural sectors, and a marginalized residual group. A further contention is that the process has been accompanied by the growth in professional forms of employment, with a basic dichotomy emerging between an enlarged state bureaucracy on the one hand and a privileged sector in the private sector on the other. Members of the latter group are seen as constituting a "dependent bourgeoisie" whose interests take precedence over those of the majority of workers as the general process of foreign penetration proceeds.

In conclusion, it can be commented that economists in the United States and Western Europe still find it difficult to accept the dependency concept and its ramifications. One reason is ideological and is related to the overall issue of paradigm tenacity discussed in Chapter 1 of this study. Second, some economists do not consider it a useful concept for analyzing development, on the grounds that it does not sufficiently establish that there is a necessary logical connection between external reliances and domestic forms of underdevelopment (Lall 1975). To the extent that this is true, it may be merely a reflection of the fact that there are few empirical studies that attempt to test various dependency relationships. While there is still no formal theory of dependency, the perspective still provides a useful methodological framework for analyzing concrete conditions of development and underdevelopment (see Palma 1978; and Seers 1981).

Under the structuralist (Prebisch-Singer model) and dependency research programs, both center and periphery nations are presumed to share in varying degrees in the benefits of world income, production, consumption, and trade. However, the general model posits that various forms of market imperfection and unequal exchange have resulted in the center appropriating the lion's share of the benefits. Underdevelopment of the periphery is traced to its reliance and dependency on the wider world economy and the role played by the ruling elite in blocking broad-based and authentic forms of development. Activist policies geared toward national and international reforms are therefore advocated as a means of breaking the development impasse.

This view should be contrasted with the "new orthodox" position, which is based on a resurrection of the neoclassical competitive model (e.g., Balassa 1977, 1982 and Little 1982). The argument is that, even if we accept the presence of various forms of dependency, underdevelopment in the periphery is related to some systematic disequilibria and internal market distortions produced by inappropriate domestic economic policies. The price, monetary, and financial policies of the state are thought to have produced market imperfections that frustrate the development of free commodity and factor markets, thereby leading to a suboptimality in the allocation of resources.

Contextually, policy reforms are advocated as a means of making market signals perform their proper allocative role and to effect smooth adjustments in demand, supply, and prices in all sectors of the economy. As discussed in greater detail elsewhere, the policy measures usually include (1) pricing policies designed to eliminate taxes and subsidies on major commodities; (2) monetary and fiscal policies that allow the market rate of interest to reflect the opportunity cost of capital; (3) wage reduction (repression) to make market wage rates reflect the true opportunity cost of labor; and (4) devaluation of the foreign exchange rate, tariff changes, and reductions in quantitative restrictions. The overall objective is to introduce policy changes that would gradually move the economy toward its potential production possibility frontier by making its exports more competitive in international markets (David 1985).

First, as discussed in Chapter 2, the neoclassical theories on which these prescriptions are based are confined to the realm of exchange relations. Further, as argued earlier in this chapter, the underlying world view does not pay attention to structural rigidities that are embedded in the prevailing system of national and international economic relations. These relations give rise to specific institutional environments and demand and supply conditions. This brings us to the Marxian or radical heterodox perspective in which international markets are considered to be the very mechanisms through which developing countries are exploited. As further outlined in the final section of this chapter, supporters of this perspective argue that the neoclassical paradigm focuses on too narrow a set of demand, supply, and exchange relations, and neglects a consideration of the historical forces that have produced national and international relations of production based on class exploitation.

## Radical Heterodoxy
## and the Development of the Underdevelopment

As indicated elsewhere in the study, the radical heterodox or Marxian paradigm stands in direct opposition to orthodoxy, both in terms of the sociology of knowledge to which it subscribes as well as the interpretation given to the factors and processes underlying development and change. In the latter context, underdevelopment is not viewed in terms of a benign "dependency" of the periphery on the center, but more fundamentally in terms of what is perceived to be a dialectical unity between development and underdevelopment, or what Frank (1967) calls "the development of the underdevelopment." This is in turn traced to the set of historical forces associated with capitalist expansion on a world scale, the international linkage of dominant classes, and the contradictory relationships that have emerged between dominant and exploited classes.

According to Frank:

Underdevelopment is not just a lack of development. Before there was development there was no underdevelopment. This relationship between development and underdevelopment is not just a comparative one, in the sense that some places are more developed or underdeveloped than others: development and underdevelopment are also related both through the common historical process that they have shared during the past several centuries and through the mutual, that is, reciprocal influence they have had, still have, and will continue to have, on each other throughout history (Frank 1975, p. 1).

The general proposition, therefore, is that development and underdevelopment are simultaneous and related products of the historical evolution on a world scale of a single integrated capitalist system. The system is considered to be integrated in the sense that all parts of the world are integrated so that the possibilities for development and change become endogenous to the system itself. It is also argued that while the system is an integrated one, one part exploits the other by expropriating the economic surplus from the many, with a corresponding appropriation by the few. This is the case even though some of the benefits of the economic and cultural development derived from such exploitation are diffused back to the periphery.

The exploitation is thought to have resulted in an antithetical development process at both international and national levels. In the international context, reference is often made to the growing inequality between the developed centers and the relatively underdeveloped peripheries, and at the national level between developed sectors, regions, and groups on the one hand and underdeveloped sectors, regions, and segments of the population on the other. The general claim is that at both national and international levels, improvement in the material conditions of a powerful minority not only coexists with the stagnation and retrogression of the majority, but that this has been taking place at a time when the needs and wants of the latter group continue to grow. This, it is argued, has given rise to a basic contradiction in the periphery between the desire for rapid economic growth on the one hand and the need to establish a good, equitable, and sustainable society on the other (Baran 1957; Goulet 1977).

At the outset, it is necessary to put this world view in the wider context of Marx's materialist conception and interpretation of history as well as his theory of societal evolution. There is a vast literature on this subject, and our account is highly selective. See, for example, Marx (1967 edition), Sweezy (1956), Mandel (1970), Gurley (1976), Dobb (1963), Baran and Sweezy (1966), and Heilbroner (1980), among others. In the Marxian schema, what distinguishes human beings from animals is that they have the ability to consciously engage in purposeful productive activity as a means of survival. The level of their productive ability depends on what he terms the "forces of production," including both physical and human instruments used in the production process. The nonhuman factors include natural resources, raw materials, machines, tools, and so on, while the human factors encompass knowledge, skills, aspirations, and needs.

These productive forces develop through the labor that people use in extracting a living from the natural environment. In this process, people strive to make a living and develop their own capabilities simultaneously.

While human activity is an essential part of the productive forces, the argument is that people tend to be constrained by the material conditions of life. The other element in the ongoing process of productive activity is called the "relations of production." The relations refer to the social arrangements and institutions that are most closely associated with the manner in which goods are produced and exchanged.

Marx emphasized that these social relations are by and large determined by the stages of development of society's material forces of production. Included in social relations are (1) property relations; (2) the mechanisms for organizing, recruiting, and compensating labor; (3) the markets and other mechanisms for exchanging the products of labor; and (4) the institutions of power and hierarchy that define how the ruling social classes distribute the surplus product. The social relations of production essentially reflect society's class structure that is, in turn, embodied in the mode of production or work process. The social classes are therefore defined in terms of the common relationships that members hold to the production and distribution process (capitalists, landlords, laborers, and so on) and are considered to have unequal and antagonistic relationships with each other.

In this context, it is argued that at a certain stage of development, the material productive forces of society come into conflict with the existing relations of production. Thus, as the productive forces grow and people further develop their capabilities, the developing productive forces come into conflict with the social relations of production, that is, the prevailing class structure. This means that the new mechanisms that people develop to earn a living become incompatible with older ways in which they relate to one another in the production process. It is this conflict that leads to social revolution in the Marxian sense.

The materialist interpretation of history is also linked to dialectical materialism, which is used as a method for understanding the processes of historical evolution, as well as to demonstrate the historical inevitability of certain modes and patterns of change. The philosopher Hegel is credited with providing the first classical statement of the dialectics in his attempt to formulate the principles of logic underlying the historical process. The notion of change is central to the Hegelian conception of dialectics, and reality is defined by its changefulness. This involves quantitative alterations in the nature of reality through the conflict of opposites or contradictions. For an elaboration, see Heilbroner (1980).

Hegel construed dialectical development primarily in terms of "thought" and "spirit" and showed very little concern for its practical applications. However, dialectical laws cannot be used as a substitute for empirical facts, or to predict events without a concrete interpretation of the facts in question. This brings us to the Marxian conception of dialectical materialism that, as is often stated, is based on a turning upside down of the Hegelian dialectic. In his application of this philosophy to the study of human history, Marx postulated that the evolution of all human society, past and present (with the possible exception of primitive society), is based on class struggles stemming from contradictions between the forces and social relations of production. This provided one pillar for his revolutionary conception of change, in contrast to Hegel, who saw change in evolutionary terms.

In the Marxian schema, the possibilities for revolutionary change in a conflict-ridden society are interpreted in terms of a moving synthesis or idea of organic change. Conflicts arise from the inner contradictions of the social system, and as these are resolved, the system reaches a new equilibrium level. This, in turn, generates new conflicts, resulting in new disequilibria and systems adjustments. There is therefore a deterministic feature in the historical evolution of the social system. This means that future configurations of the system are contained within, and reflect, the resolution of past and present forms of conflict.

Following from this is a theory of societal evolution (shown in Figure 8.1). Within this framework, the problems of development and underdevelopment are linked to the historical process of capitalist expansion on a world scale. In economic terms, the related theory of economic growth is concerned with explaining the factors underlying the contradictory development of the capitalist mode of production on a world scale. There are at least three interrelated elements of this theory. The first concerns the use of historical time vis-à-vis the logical time of neoclassical theory. As stated by one writer, this notion of time

> . . . conceives of the entire period of capitalist development as a whole and attempts to distinguish within its development the crucial period or epochs into which it necessarily divides. The theory is, therefore, "historical"—not in the sense that it conceives of disequilibrium situation, but in the sense that it grasps not only the quantitative growth of the system but also its qualitative development over time. The historically distinct periods within the development of the capitalist economy are defined *theoretically* by the form which the growth process takes—the tendencies which dominate that process. In particular, the quantitative growth of the economy runs up against impediments which arise out of the historically given structure of the economic relations of the different periods. The stages of economic growth are defined by these impediments and therefore by these structural relations. It is, furthermore, the pressure of the growth process itself which breaks apart these barriers, thereby establishing the expansion of the economy on a new basis (Levine 1975, pp. 49–50).

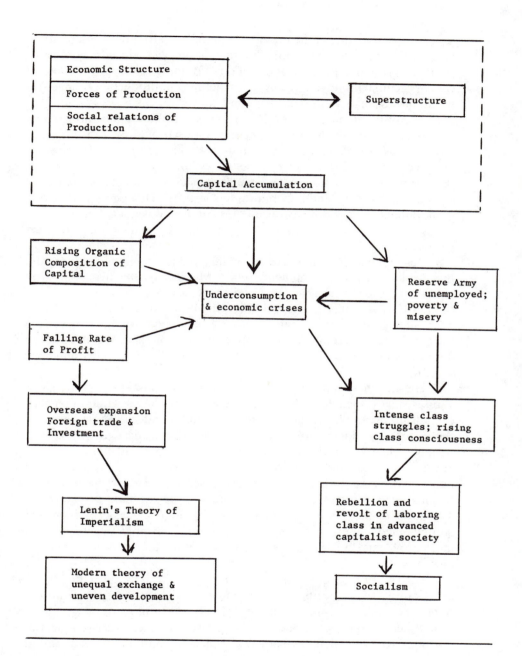

**Figure 8.1**: The Marxian model of societal evolution.

*Source*: Compiled by the author.

A second feature is the primacy of place given to production relations (over exchange relations) and the role of surplus value in generating conflict between capitalists and workers. A third is the pivotal role of capital accumulation and expansion as methods of production change (for useful discussions, see Levine 1975 and Harris 1975).

One of the implications of this theory is that there can be no separate or distinct theory of underdevelopment, or what is termed in this study "The Economics of Developing Nations." Within the Marxian framework, all development theory becomes a theory of transition from stages of pre-capitalist production (communalism, slavery, feudalism) through capitalist production and imperialism to socialism. Though its epistemological foundations are different from those of orthodoxy, it suffers from the same "universalist" orientation as encountered under the orthodox paradigm.

Despite this limitation, there is a large and growing body of literature that explains underdevelopment from a Marxian perspective, that is, in terms of the historical elements and processes underlying international capitalist expansion (e.g., Bagchi 1982, Kay 1975, Foster-Carter 1976, Best 1976, and Resnick 1975, among others). This body of thought can be further explained from the perspective of unequal exchange and uneven development as articulated by Samir Amin (1974, 1976) and Emmanuel (1972).

The starting point is the evolution of the capitalist system through its various stages, including feudalism, mercantilism, industrial and financial capitalism, imperialism, colonialism, and neocolonialism. These phases in the system's evolution are thought to have been associated with corresponding changes in the nature and variety of contradictions between development and underdevelopment. The international spread of monopolies and oligopolies, it is claimed, was accompanied by rising rates of surplus extraction and an increasing tendency toward underconsumption. The latter phenomenon was partly offset by the overseas expansion that accompanied imperialism, wasteful consumption, rapid depreciation of machinery, and increased public expenditure for civil and military purposes.

The rise of monopoly and oligopoly is thought to have resulted in the exploitation of peasants, workers, and small businesspeople in the periphery both by center capitalist firms and a mixture of the local "comprador" bourgeoisie and state capitalist bureaucracies. Members of the latter group are defined by their conspicuous consumption of imported luxury items and their preference for safe "return flow" investments in center countries vis-à-vis domestic forms of expansion. This forms part of a more pervasive "extroverted" or outward-oriented development. As Amin argues, "Outward oriented growth cannot constitute development because of consequential damaging structural changes, and is necessarily unequal, regularly blocked, and too slow to avoid widening gaps among nations."

Since the growth of peripheral economies depends on primary commodity exports, and therefore on changes in demand in metropolitan countries, patterns of trade facing the former tend to be more unequal compared to the latter. The radical heterodox version of this argument can be explained by reference to Emmanuel's *Unequal Exchange* (1972). As in the case of the earlier Prebisch-Singer thesis, he attempts to explain existing economic inequalities among nations in terms of international trading relationships and, in particular, in terms of wage rate differentials between the center and the periphery. In this context, it should be mentioned that while Amin sees rates of capital accumulation in individual countries as determining the unequal wage rates between center and periphery, Emmanuel stresses trade and exchange as the dominant factors of unequal development. Both writers therefore embrace the unequal exchange thesis, but for different reasons.

Emmanuel's approach is based on a reformulation of Marx's formula for the transformation of values into prices, and he uses this to explain why the terms of trade of peripheral economies are consistently unfavorable. While questioning the assumptions of conventional trade theory, he uses a Marxian analytical framework to show that the worsening position of the periphery is attributable to the exploitative nature of trade relations with socialist and capitalist nations alike. The basic explanation is provided in a model that postulates that the motive force behind the structure and functioning of the world capitalist system is a law of price formation that allows for the unequal rewarding of factors of production. The basic thesis is that the capitalist system, in its global operations, compels the workforce in developing nations to exchange the produce of its labor at an unfavorable rate compared to its counterpart in the high-wage developed world. Stated differently, poorer countries are forced to exchange products in which a larger number of labor-hours are embodied, with commodities produced with a smaller number of labor-hours in richer nations. This "unequal exchange" is considered the elementary mechanism underlying the transfer of values from the poor to the rich, and as defining the conditions of underdevelopment in the periphery.

This leads to unequal exchange because of the assumptions Emmanuel makes about the international flow of resources. The first is that capital tends to be internationally mobile and moves around in such a manner as to equalize profit rates. Second, while the capital factor is mobile, labor tends to be immobile. Even though there is a "seepage" of the labor factor across national boundaries, this tends to be insignificant so that wages tend to be unequal both intranationally and internationally. Third, and related to the second assumption, wage rates are determined not by prices, but more by social, historical, and institutional forces. With wage rates in poor countries stagnating at a low level, there is a hidden transfer of resources from poor to rich countries during the trade and exchange process.

At the theoretical level, Emmanuel reverses the traditional Ricardian assumptions about comparative costs and the international division of labor. Ricardo assumed capital immobility and the equalization of wages at subsistence in a full employment economy. Emmanuel's theory is based on the premise that rewards to factors determine exchange values. This forms part of a more general attempt to integrate a new theory of international trade with the classical and Marxian general theory of labor values. As such, the model relies heavily on the assumptions underlying the Marxian labor theory of value. The validity of these assumptions remains a matter of controversy.

Further, as Bacha (1978) and others have demonstrated, one of the conclusions of Emmanuel's model can be derived by using the tools of orthodox neoclassical theory. From this perspective, the issue can be restated as follows. Unequal exchange occurs because real wage rates in the periphery tend to be lower than those obtaining in the center, and labor is internationally immobile. Under the circumstances, trade between the periphery and the center tends to shift the terms of trade against the periphery. As a result, the gains from trade and income levels in the periphery would be lower, compared to some ideal Pareto-optimal situation in which labor is perfectly mobile. In the latter situation, there will be a tendency toward international equality in real wage rates and a corresponding movement in the periphery's terms of trade and income to a more optimal level (see also Chichilnisky 1981).

Be that as it may, the general conclusion emerging from the radical model of unequal exchange is that no matter what the periphery produces, the product of its labor will never fetch the same value in international trade as a product with a comparable amount of labor from the advanced center. Peripheral economies have no internal dynamism of their own, and their economic fate is totally determined by their standing in the international economic hierarchy. This gives rise to unequal and uneven development because of the peculiar nature of the class structure found in the periphery.

As Amin argues, this class structure lacks the classic nature of the industrial-capitalist class found in advanced centers. Capitalists in the periphery tend to be located primarily in the modern sector, that is, in the center of the periphery. The general Marxian argument is that members of this class are products of imperialism and colonialism, which created a mercantile and landlord bourgeoisie out of the traditional upper and middle classes who were the local guardians of international capitalist interests. One result, it is argued, is that the small proletariat in the periphery is relatively well off compared to the large number of marginalized peasants and urban unemployed. Members of this small proletariat are forced to cooperate with landlords and merchants in order to maintain their position of relative affluence. In addition, the blockage of local forms of industrial development has led to the formation of a modern middle class of "petty bourgeoisie" comprising army officials, state bureaucrats, and similar cadres. In terms of the possibilities for sustained economic development, this class is thought to pose the most serious challenge to the landlord class. One reason is the advocacy of various forms of state capitalism. The factors associated with the rise of the latter phenomenon have been described as follows:

> Because of inadequate industrialization and the absence of a foreign bourgeoisie, petty bourgeoisie style strata (civil servants, office workers, sometimes survivors from crafts, small traders, middle class peasants, etc.) acquire great importance. The expansion of the educational system and increasing unemployment give rise to a crisis of the system. The very requirements of accelerated industrialization in order to overcome the crisis lead to the development of a public sector, since the rules of profitability (which determine the flow of foreign capital) and the insufficiency of private local capital hold back the necessary rate of industrialization. The subsequent strengthening of the state bureaucracy can lead to a general application of state capitalism (Amin 1976, p. 349).

Thus, radical and neoclassical thinkers alike would seem to agree that local state capitalism cannot provide an answer to the problems inherent in the quest for sustained economic development. While orthodox thinkers view the problem in terms of lack of market incentives, Marxists argue that local state capitalism represents a system in which the "petty bourgeoisie becomes the transmission belt of imperialist domination" (Amin 1976, p. 380). Whichever world view one supports, it remains true that since the attainment of political independence, the large majority of developing countries have been embracing policies and strategies based on a model of "national developmentalism." Like its counterpart—state capitalism—this is a model in which the ruling elite uses various policy measures to gain and maintain control of the local economy and development process, including increased participation of the state in economic activity, selective nationalization of foreign corporations, and so on.

In general, the implementation of this model has made very little change in the internal process of capital accumulation and development, and only marginal changes, if any, in income distribution, employment creation, and poverty redressal. In some cases, the size of the economic surplus available domestically has been enlarged. However, even in these cases, the lion's share tends to be recirculated among members of the ruling elite class and supporting cadres in the form of rents or open corruption, with the larger majority of the population still left out of the redistributive process. The overall result, in terms of the dynamic effects on development, has been the same as with the implementation of the orthodox model, that is, increased polarization, unequal exchange, and uneven development.

In conclusion, the thesis of uneven and unequal development can be stated in terms of the following propositions. First, there is unequal exchange between center and periphery because commodities exchanged contain unequal labor quantities and qualities, reflecting unequal levels of productivity and differential rates of capital accumulation and technological progress. Second, these inequalities tend to be maintained and perpetuated through the cumulative interplay of the following factors: (1) the maintenance and stagnation of pre-capitalist social formations in the periphery compared to the center, where they have been totally eliminated; (2) the various restrictions imposed on the periphery, which limit and continue to frustrate its ability to penetrate world markets; (3) the control of prices and technology available to the periphery by oligopolistic center firms; (4) the lack of an autonomous class structure in the periphery; and (5) the inadequacy and inappropriateness of local state capitalist or "nationalist developmentalist" models that are proposed for industrialization and development.

# Bibliography

Adelman, Irma, and Cynthia Taft Morris. 1973. *Economic Growth and Social Equity in Developing Countries*. Stanford, Calif.: Stanford.

Ahluwalia, M. S., N. Carter, and H. Chenery. 1978. "Growth and Poverty in Developing Countries." World Bank Staff Working Paper no. 309. Washington, D.C.: The World Bank.

Amin, Samir. 1974. *Accumulation on a World Scale: A Critique of the Theory of Underdevelopment*. New York: Monthly Review.

——— . 1976. *Uneven Development: An Essay on the Social Formations of Peripheral Capitalism*. New York: Monthly Review.

Argyris, Chris. 1957. *Personality and Organization*. New York: Harper & Row.

Atkinson, A. B. 1975. *The Economics of Inequality*. London: Oxford.

Bacha, Edmar. 1978. "An Interpretation of Unequal Exchange from Prebisch-Singer to Emmanuel." *Journal of Development Economics* 5: 319–30.

Baer, Werner. 1969. "The Economics of Prebisch and ECLA." In *Latin America: Problems in Development*, edited by Charles Nesbit, 215–17. New York: The Free Press.

Bagchi, A. K. 1982. *The Political Economy of Underdevelopment*. New York: Cambridge.

Bain, J. S. 1956. *Barriers to New Competition*. Cambridge, Mass.: Harvard.

Bairoch, Paul. 1975. *The Economic Development of the Third World since 1900*. London: Methuen.

Balassa, Bela. 1977. *Policy Reform in Developing Countries*. Oxford. Pergamon.

——— . 1980. "The New Protectionism: Evaluation and Proposals for Reform." In *Challenges to a Liberal International Order*, edited by R. C. Amacher et al., 279–302. Washington, D.C.: American Enterprise Institute.

——— . 1982. "Disequilibrium Analysis in Developing Countries: An Overview." *World Development* 10: 1027–38.

Baldwin, Robert. 1970. *Nontariff Distortions in International Trade*. Washington, D.C.: Brookings Institution.

Balogh, Thomas. 1974. *The Economics of Poverty*. White Plains, N.Y.: M. E. Sharpe.

_____ . 1982. *The Irrelevance of Conventional Economics*. New York: Norton.

Baran, Paul. 1957. *The Political Economy of Growth*. New York: Monthly Review.

Baran, Paul, and E. J. Hobsbawm. 1961. "The Stages of Economic Growth." *Kyklos* 14: 234–42.

Baran, Paul, and Paul Sweezy. 1966. *Monopoly Capitalism*. New York: Monthly Review.

Barnett, Richard, and Ronald Muller. 1974. *Global Reach: The Power of Multinational Corporations*. New York: Simon and Schuster.

Bauer, P. T., and A. A. Walters. 1975. "The State of Economics." *Journal of Law and Economics* 18: 1–23.

Becker, Gary. 1964. *Human Capital*. New York: Columbia.

_____ . 1976. *The Economic Approach to Human Behavior*. Chicago: University of Chicago.

Beckford, George. 1972. *Persistent Poverty: Underdevelopment in Plantation Economies of the Third World*. New York: Oxford.

Bergsten, C. F., and L. B. Krause, eds. 1975. *World Politics and International Economics*. Washington, D.C.: The Brookings Institution.

Bergsten, C. F. et al. 1978. *American Multinationals and American Interests*. Washington, D.C.: The Brookings Institution.

Best, Michael. 1976. "Uneven Development and Dependent Market Economies." *American Economic Review* 66: 136–41.

Bhagwati, Jagdish. 1968. "Distortions and Immiserizing Growth: A Generalization." *Review of Economic Studies* 35: 481–85.

_____ . 1972. "The Theory of Immiserizing Growth: Further Applications." In *International Trade and Money*, edited by M. B. Connolly and A. K. Swoboda, 45–54. London: Allen and Unwin.

Billerbeck, K., and Y. Yasugi. 1979. "Private Direct Foreign Investment in Developing Countries." World Bank Staff Working Paper no. 348. Washington, D.C.: The World Bank.

Blaug, Mark. 1975. "Kuhn versus Lakatos, or Paradigms versus Research Programs in the History of Economics." *History of Political Economy* 7: 399–433.

Boulding, Kenneth. 1968. *The Image*. Ann Arbor, Mich.: Ann Arbor Paperbacks.

————. 1968a. *Beyond Economics: Essays on Society, Religion and Ethics*. Ann Arbor: University of Michigan.

————. 1970. "Is Economics Culture Bound?" *American Economic Review* 60: 496–502.

————. 1973. *Collected Economic Papers*, vol. 3. Boulder, Colo.: Colorado Associated Press.

Brodbeck, May, ed. 1968. *Readings in the Philosophy of the Social Sciences*. New York: Macmillan.

Bronfonbrenner, Martin. 1971. "The 'Structure of Revolutions' in Economic Thought." *History of Political Economy* 3: 136–51.

————. 1976. "Economics in Dialectical Dialect." *Journal of Political Economy* 84: 123–30.

Brown, Lester. 1981. *Bulding a Sustainable Society*. New York: Norton.

Cain, Glen. 1976. "The Challenge of Segmented Labor Market Theories to Orthodox Theory: A Survey." *Journal of Economic Literature* 14: 1215–57.

Caporaso, James, and B. Zare. 1982. "An Interpretation and Evaluation of Dependency Theory." In *From Dependency to Development: Strategies to Overcome Underdevelopment and Inequality*, edited by H. Munoz, 45–55. Boulder, Colo.: Westview.

Cardoso, F., and E. Faletto. 1979. *Dependency and Development in Latin America*. Translated by M. Urquidi. Berkeley, Calif.: University of California.

Caves, Richard. 1982. *Multinational Enterprise and Economic Analysis*. Cambridge: Cambridge.

Chandavarkar, A. 1977. "Monetization of Developing Countries." *IMF Staff Papers* 24: 665–721.

Chenery, Hollis. 1961. "Comparative Advantage and Development Policy." *American Economic Review* 51: 18–51.

———. 1975. "The Structuralist Approach to Development Policy." *American Economic Review* 65: 310–16.

———. 1979. *Structural Change and Development Policy*. New York: Oxford.

Chenery, Hollis, and Michael Bruno. 1962. "Development Alternatives in an Open Economy: The Case of Israel." *Economic Journal* 72: 79–103.

Chenery, Hollis, and Paul Clark. 1964. *Interindustry Economics*. New York: John Wiley.

Chenery, Hollis, et al. 1974. *Redistribution with Growth*. London: Oxford.

Chenery, Hollis, and Lance Taylor. 1968. "Development Patterns among Countries and over Time." *Review of Economics and Statistics* 50: 391–416.

Chenery, Hollis, and Moises Syrquin. 1975. *Patterns of Development, 1950–1970*. New York: Oxford.

Chichilnisky, Graciela. 1981. "Terms of Trade and Domestic Distribution: Export-Led Growth with Abundant Labor." *Journal of Development Economics* 8: 163–92.

Clark, Colin. 1957. *The Conditions of Economic Progress*. London: Macmillan.

Cooper, Richard. 1972. "Trade Policy Is Foreign Policy." *Foreign Policy* 9: 18–36.

———. 1972a. "Economic Interdependence and Foreign Policy in the Seventies." *World Politics* 24: 159–81.

Corden, W. M. 1965. "Recent Developments in the Theory of International Trade." Special Papers in International Economics, International Finance Section, Department of Economics, Princeton University, Princeton, N.J.

Dalton, George. 1968. "Economics, Economic Development, and Economic Anthropology." *Journal of Economic Issues* 2: 173–85.

David, Wilfred L., ed. 1973. *Public Finance, Planning, and Economic Development: Essays in Honor of Ursula Hicks*. New York: St. Martin's.

———. 1977. "Dimensions of the North-South Confrontation." In *Issues and Prospects for the New International Economic Order*, edited by William Tyler. Lexington, Mass.: D. C. Heath.

_____ . 1985. *The IMF Policy Paradigm: The Macroeconomics of Stabilization, Structural Adjustment, and Economic Development*. New York: Praeger.

David, Wilfred L., and Pasquale Scandizzo. 1980. "Agricultural Growth and Structural Transformation." Division Working Paper no. 30. Economics and Policy Division, Agriculture and Rural Development Department, The World Bank, Washington, D.C.

Davidson, Paul. 1972. *Money and the Real World*. London: Macmillan.

_____ . 1980. "Post Keynesian Economics: Solving the Crisis in Economic Theory." *The Public Interest*. Special Issue: 151–73.

Denison, E. F. 1967. *Why Growth Rates Differ? Postwar Experience in Nine Western Countries*. Washington, D.C.: The Brookings Institution.

Diamand, Marcelo. 1978. "Towards a Change in the Economic Paradigm through the Experience of Developing Countries." *Journal of Development Economics* 5: 19–53.

Dixit, A. 1973. "Models of Dual Economies." In *Models of Economic Growth*, edited by J. A. Mirlees and N. H. Stern, 125–52. New York: John Wiley.

Dobb, Maurice. 1963. *Studies in the Development of Capitalism*. New York: International Publishers.

_____ . 1969. *Welfare Economics and the Economics of Socialism: Towards a Commonsense Critique*. Cambridge: Cambridge.

_____ . 1972. *Theories of Value and Distribution since Adam Smith*. Cambridge: Cambridge.

Domar, Evsey. 1946. "Capital Expansion, Rate of Growth and Unemployment." *Econometrica* 14: 137–47.

_____ . 1957. *Essays in the Theory of Economic Growth*. New York: Oxford.

Dos Santos, T. 1970. "The Structure of Dependence." *American Economic Review* 60: 235–46.

Duesenberry, James. 1949. *Income, Saving and the Theory of Consumer Behavior*. Cambridge, Mass.: Harvard.

Duncan, Ron, and Ernst Lutz. 1983. "Penetration of Industrial Country Markets by Agricultural Products of Developing Countries." *World Development* 11: 771–86.

Dunning, John, ed. 1971. *The Multinational Enterprise*. New York: Praeger.

Eichner, A. S., and J. A. Kregel. 1975. "An Essay on Post-Keynesian Theory: A New Paradigm in Economics." *Journal of Economic Lierature* 13: 1293–1314.

Ellsworth, P. T. 1956. "The Terms of Trade between Primary Producing and Industrial Countries." *Inter-American Economic Affairs* 10: 55–57.

Emmanuel, A. 1972. *Unequal Exchange: A Study of Imperialism*. New York: Monthly Review.

Enke, S. 1963. *Economics for Development*. Englewood Cliffs, N.J.: Prentice-Hall.

Evans, Peter. 1979. *Dependent Development: The Alliance of Multinational, State, and Local Capital in Brazil*. Princeton, N.J.: Princeton.

Feder, Gerschon. 1982. "On Exports and Economic Growth." *Journal of Development Economics* 12: 39–73.

Fei, J. C., and G. Ranis. 1964. *Development of the Labor Surplus Economy: Theory and Policy*. Homewood, Ill.: Irwin.

Findlay, Ronald, 1973. *International Trade and Development Theory*. New York: Columbia.

——— . 1975. "Implications of Growth Theory for Trade and Development." *American Economic Review* 65: 323–28.

——— . 1980. "The Fundamental Determinants of the Terms of Trade." In *The World Economic Order: Past and Prospects*, edited by S. Grassman and E. Lindberg, 425–57. London: St. Martin's.

Foster-Carter, Adrian. 1976. "From Rostow to Gunder Frank: Conflicting Paradigms in the Analysis of Underdevelopment." *World Development* 4: 167–80.

Frank, A. G. 1967. *Capitalism and Underdevelopment in Latin America: Historical Studies of Chile and Brazil*. New York: Monthly Review.

——— . 1969. *Underdevelopment or Revolution: Essays on the Development of the Underdevelopment and the Immediate Economy*. New York: Monthly Review.

——— . 1975. *On Capitalist Development*. Bombay: Oxford.

——— . 1978. *Dependent Accumulation and Underdevelopment*. New York: Monthly Review.

Frank, Charles R. Jr., and Richard Webb, eds. 1977. *Income Distribution and Growth in Less-Developed Countries*. Washington, D.C.: The Brookings Institution.

Friedman, Milton. 1957. *A Theory of the Consumption Function*. Princeton, N.J.: Princeton for NBER.

———. 1962. *Capitalism and Freedom*. Chicago: University of Chicago.

Furtado, Celso. 1967. *Development and Underdevelopment: A Structuralist View of the Problems of Developed and Underdeveloped Countries*. Berkeley, Calif.: University of California.

———. 1970. *Economic Development of Latin America: A Survey from Colonial Times to the Cuban Revolution*. Cambridge: Cambridge.

———. 1973. "The Concept of External Dependence in the Study of Underdevelopment." In *The Political Economy of Development and Underdevelopment*, edited by Charles Wilber, 118–23. New York: Random House.

Galtung, Johan. 1971. "A Structural Theory of Imperialism." *Journal of Peace Research* 13: 81–116.

Germani, Gino. 1981. *The Sociology of Modernization*. New Brunswick, N.J.: Transaction Books.

Gerschenkron, A. 1968. *Economic Backwardness in Historical Perspective*. Cambridge, Mass.: Harvard.

Goldsbrough, David. 1981. "International Trade of Multinational Corporations and the Responsiveness to Changes in Aggregate Demand and Relative Prices." *IMF Staff Papers* 28: 973–99.

———. 1985. "Foreign Direct Investment in Developing Countries." *Finance and Development* 22: 31–34.

Goldsmith, Raymond. 1969. *Financial Structure and Development*. New Haven, Conn.: Yale.

Goodwin, R. M. 1967. "A Growth Cycle." In *Socialism, Capitalism, and Growth*, edited by C. H. Feinstein, 54–58. Cambridge: Cambridge.

Gordon, R. A. 1976. "Rigor and Relevance in a Changing Institutional Setting." *American Economic Review* 66: 1–14.

Gordon, Wendell. 1973. *Economics from an Institutional Viewpoint*. Austin: University of Texas.

———— . 1980. *Institutional Economics: The Changing System*. Austin: University of Texas.

Goulet, Denis. 1977. *The Cruel Choice: A New Critique in the Theory of Development*. New York: Atheneum.

Griffin, Keith, and A. R. Khan. 1978. *Poverty and Landlessness in Rural Asia*. Geneva: ILO.

———— . 1978a. "Poverty and the Third World: Ugly Facts and Fancy Models." *World Development* 6: 295–304.

Gruchy, A. G. 1969. "Neo-Institutionalism and the Economics of Dissent." *Journal of Economic Issues* 3: 1–17.

———— . 1972. *Contemporary Economic Thought*. Clifton, N.J.: Augustus M. Kelley.

Gurley, John. 1976. *Challenges to Capitalism: Marx, Lenin, and Mao*. San Francisco, Calif.: San Francisco Book Co.

Gurley, John, and Edward Shaw. 1964. *Money in the Theory of Finance*. Washington, D.C.: The Brookings Institution.

Hagen, Everett. 1962. *The Economics of Development*. Homewood, Ill.: Irwin.

Hanson, James. 1975. "Transfer Pricing in the Multinational Corporation: A Critical Appraisal." *World Development* 3: 857–65.

Harcourt, G. C. 1972. *Some Cambridge Controversies in the Theory of Capital*. Cambridge: Cambridge.

Harris, Donald J. 1975. "The Theory of Economic Growth: A Critique and Reformulation." *American Economic Review* 65: 329–37.

———— . 1978. *Capital Accumulation and Income Distribution*. Stanford, Calif.: Stanford.

Harris, J. R., and M. D. Todaro. 1970. "Migration, Unemployment and Development: A Two Sector Analysis." *American Economic Review* 60: 126–42.

Harrod, Roy. 1933. *International Economics*. Cambridge: Cambridge.

———— . 1939. "An Essay in Dynamic Theory," *Economic Journal* 49: 14–33.

Haq, M. 1976. *The Poverty Curtain*. New York: Columbia.

Havrylyshyn, O., and I. Alikhani. 1982. "Is There Cause for Export Optimism? An Inquiry into the Existence of a Second Generation of Successful Exporters." *Weltwirtschaftliches Archiv* 4: 651–63.

Hayek, F. A. 1948. *Individualism and Economic Order*. Chicago: University of Chicago.

———. 1952. *The Counter-Revolution of Science*. New York: The Free Press.

Heilbroner, Robert L. 1970. "On the Limited Relevance of Economics." *The Public Interest* 21: 80–93.

———. 1980. *Marxism: For and Against*. New York: Norton.

Helleiner, Gerald K. 1978. "World Market Imperfections and the Developing Countries." Occasional Paper no. 11, NIEO Series. Washington, D.C.: Overseas Development Council.

Hempel, Carl. G. 1965. *Aspects of Scientific Explanation*. New York: The Free Press.

Hempel, Carl. G., and Paul Oppenheim. 1948. "Studies in the Logic of Explanation." *Philisophy of Science* 15: 135–75.

Hirschman, Albert O. 1958. *The Strategy of Economic Development*. New Haven, Conn.: Yale.

———. 1968. "The Political Economy of Import Substitution Industrialization in Latin America." *Quarterly Journal of Economics* 87: 1–32.

———. 1973. "The Changing Tolerance for Income Inequality in the Course of Economic Development." *Quarterly Journal of Economics* 87: 544–66.

———. 1977. "A Generalized Linkage Approach to Development with Special Reference to Staples." *Economic Development and Cultural Change* 25 (Supplement): 67–98.

———. 1981. *Essays in Trespassing*. New York: Cambridge.

Hoselitz, Bert F. 1960. *Sociological Factors in Economic Growth*. Glencoe, Ill.: The Free Press.

Huntington, Ellsworth. 1915. *Civilization and Climate*. New Haven, Conn.: Yale.

———. 1962. *Mainsprings of Civilization*. New York: American Library.

Hymer, Stephen. 1970. "Efficiency (Contradictions) of Multinational Corporations." *American Economic Review* 60: 441–48.

_____ . 1972. "The Internationalization of Capital." *Journal of Economic Issues* 6: 91–111.

_____ . 1976. *The International Operation of National Firms: A Study of Direct Foreign Investment*. Cambridge, Mass.: MIT.

I.L.O. 1977. *Employment, Growth, and Basic Needs: A One-World Problem*. New York: Praeger.

Iverson, Carl. 1936. *Aspects of the Theory of International Capital Movements*. London: Oxford.

Johnson, Harry, ed. 1967. *Economic Nationalism in Old and New States*. Chicago: University of Chicago.

Johnston, Bruce F. 1970. "Agriculture and Structural Transformation in Developing Countries: A Survey of Research." *Journal of Economic Literature* 8: 369–404.

Johnston, Bruce F., and Peter Kilby. 1975. *Agriculture and Structural Transformation: Strategies in Late Developing Countries*. New York: Oxford.

Jorgenson, Dale. 1969. "The Role of Agriculture in Economic Development: Classical vs. Neoclassical Models of Growth." In *Subsistence Agriculture and Economic Development*, edited by Clifton Wharton, Jr., 320–48. Chicago: Aldine.

Kaldor, Nicholas. 1955. "Alternative Theories of Distribution." *Review of Economic Studies* 23: 83–100.

_____ . 1957. "A Model of Economic Growth." *Economic Journal* 67: 591–624.

_____ . 1970. "A Case for Regional Policies." *Scottish Journal of Political Economy* 17: 337–48.

_____ . 1972. "The Irrelevance of Equilibrium Economics." *Economic Journal* 82: 1237–55.

_____ . 1975. "What's Wrong with Economic Theory?" *Quarterly Journal of Economics* 89: 347–57.

Kalecki, M. 1939. *Theory of Economic Dynamics*. London: Allen and Unwin.

Kay, Geoffrey. 1975. *Development and Underdevelopment. A Marxist Analysis.* New York: St. Martin's.

Kennedy, Charles, and A. P. Thirlwall. 1979. "Import Penetration, Export Performance and Harrod's Trade Multiplier." *Oxford Economic Papers* 31: 302–23.

Keynes, J. M. 1936. *The General Theory of Employment, Interest, and Money.* London: Macmillan.

Khatkhate, D. 1972. "Analytical Basis of the Working of Monetary Policy in Less Developed Countries." *IMF Staff Papers* 19: 533–58.

Kindleberger, Charles. 1958. *Economic Development.* Homewood, Ill.: Irwin.

––––––. 1969. *American Business Abroad: Six Lectures on Direct Investment.* New Haven, Conn.: Yale.

––––––, ed. 1970. *The International Corporation: A Symposium.* Cambridge, Mass.: MIT.

King, Benjamin. 1981. "What Is a SAM? A Layman's Guide to Social Accounting Matrices." World Bank Staff Working Paper no. 463. Washington, D.C.: The World Bank.

Kravis, Irving B. 1970. "Trade as a Handmaiden of Growth: Similarities between the Nineteenth and Twentieth Centuries." *Economic Journal* 80: 850–72.

Kravis, Irving B., Alan Heston, and Robert Summers. 1982. *World Product and Income: International Comparisons of Real GDP. International Comparison Project. Phase III.* Baltimore, Md.: Johns Hopkins.

Krueger, Anne. 1974. "The Political Economy of Rent-Seeking Society." *American Economic Review* 64: 291–303.

––––––. 1978. *Foreign Trade Regimes and Economic Development: Liberalization Attempts and Consequences.* New York: Columbia for NBER.

Krugman, Paul. 1981. "Trade, Accumulation, and Uneven Development." *Journal of Development Economics* 8: 149–61.

Kuhn, Thomas. 1962. *The Structure of Scientific Revolutions.* Chicago: University of Chicago.

––––––. 1970. *The Structure of Scientific Revolutions.* 2nd edition. Chicago: University of Chicago.

Kuznets, Simon. 1955. "Economic Growth and Income Inequality." *American Economic Review* 45: 1–28.

———. 1966. *Modern Economic Growth: Rate, Structure, and Spread*. New Haven, Conn.: Yale.

———. 1971. *Economic Growth of Nations: Total Output and Production Structure*. Cambridge, Mass.: Belknap.

Lakatos, Imre, and A. Musgrave, eds. 1970. *Criticism and the Growth of Knowledge*. London: Cambridge.

Lall, Deepak. 1976. "Distribution and Development: A Review Article." *World Development* 4: 725–38.

———. 1985. "The Misconceptions of 'Development Economics'" *Finance and Development* 22: 10–13.

Lall, S. 1973. "Transfer Pricing by Multinational Manufacturing Firms." *Oxford Bulletin of Economics and Statistics* 35: 173–95.

———. 1974. "Less Developed Countries and Private Direct Foreign Investment." *World Development* 2: 43–48.

———. 1975. "Is 'Dependence' a Useful Concept in Analyzing Underdevelopment?" *World Development* 3: 799–810.

Leibenstein, Harvey. 1957. *Economic Backwardness and Economic Growth*. New York: John Wiley.

———. 1974. "An Interpretation of the Economic Theory of Fertility: Promising Path or Blind Alley?" *Journal of Economic Literature* 12: 457–79.

Leontief, Wassily. 1971. "Theoretical Assumptions and Non-Observed Facts." *American Economic Review* 61: 1–7.

Leontief, Wassily, et al. 1977. *The Future of the World Economy*. New York: Oxford.

Lerner, Daniel. 1968. "Modernization: Social Aspects." In *International Encyclopaedia of the Social Sciences*, edited by D. Sills, 387–95. New York: Macmillan.

Levine, David. 1975. "Theory and Growth of the Capitalist Economy." *Economic Development and Cultural Change* 24: 47–74.

Lewis, W. A. 1954. "Economic Development with Unlimited Supplies of Labor." *Manchester School of Economic and Social Studies* 23: 139–91.

———. 1955. *Theory of Economic Growth*. London: Allen and Unwin.

———. 1958. "Unlimited Labor: Further Notes." *Manchester School of Economic and Social Studies* 26: 1–32.

———. 1971. *Tropical Development, 1880–1913*. Evanston, Ill.: Northwestern.

———. 1972. "Reflections on Unlimited Labor." In *International Economics and Development: Essays in Honor of Raul Prebisch*, edited by L. DiMarco, 75–96. New York: Academic Press.

———. 1978. *The Evolution of the International Economic Order*. Princeton, N.J.: Princeton.

———. 1980. "The Slowing Down of the Engine of Growth." *American Economic Review* 70: 555–64.

———. 1984. "The State of Development Theory." *American Economic Review* 74: 1–10.

Lipsey, Robert. 1963. *Price and Quantity Trends in the Foreign Trade of the United States*. Princeton. N.J.: Princeton.

Lipton, Michael. 1976. *Why Poor People Stay Poor: Urban Bias in World Development*. Cambridge, Mass.: Harvard.

Little, I. M. 1982. *Economic Development: Theory, Policy, and International Relations*. New York: Basic Books.

Love, Joseph. 1980. "Raul Prebisch and the Origins of the Doctrine of Unequal Exchange." *Latin American Research Review* 15: 45–72.

Lutz, Ernst, and Malcolm Bale. 1980. "Agricultural Protectionism in Industrial Countries and Its Global Effects: A Survey of Issues." World Bank Reprint Series no. 174. Washington, D.C.: The World Bank.

Maddison, Angus. 1970. *Economic Progress and Policy in Developing Countries*. London: Allen and Unwin.

Manoilesco, M. 1931. *The Theory of Protection and International Trade*. London: P. S. King.

Mandel, Ernest. 1970. *An Introduction to Marxist Economic Theory*. New York: Pathfinder.

Marx, Karl. 1859. *A Contribution to the Critique of Political Economy*, edited by M. Dobb, 1970. New York: International Publishers.

––––––. 1967. *Capital*. New York: International Publishers.

Maslow, Abraham. 1957. *Motivation and Personality*. New York: Harper & Row.

McKinnon, Ronald. 1964. "Foreign Exchange Constraints in Economic Development and Efficient Aid Allocation." *Economic Journal* 74: 388–409.

––––––. 1973. *Money and Capital in Economic Development*. Washington, D.C.: The Brookings Institution.

McNally, W., W. David, and D. Flood. 1984. *World Sugar Study*. Economics and Policy Division, Agriculture and Rural Development Department, The World Bank, Washington, D.C.

Meade, James E. 1951. *The Balance of Payments*. London: Oxford.

––––––. 1964. *Efficiency, Equality, and the Ownership of Property*. London: Allen and Unwin.

Meier, Gerald, ed. 1983. *Pricing Policy for Development Management*. Baltimore, Md.: Johns Hopkins.

Meier, Gerald, and Dudley Seers, eds. 1984. *Pioneers in Development*. New York: Oxford.

Miernyk, William. 1965. *The Elements of Input-Output Analysis*. New York: Random House.

Mikesell, Raymond, and J. Zinser. 1973. "The Nature of the Savings Function in Developing Countries: A Survey of the Theoretical and Empirical Literature." *Journal of Economic Literature* 11: 1–26.

Modigliani, Franco, and Albert Ando. 1963. "Life-Cycle Hypothesis of Saving: Aggregate Implications and Tests." *American Economic Review* 53: 55–84.

Moore, Wilbert E. 1963. *Social Change*. Englewood Cliffs, N.J.: Prentice-Hall.

Moran, Theodore. 1973. "Transnational Strategies of Protection and Defense by Multinational Corporations: Spreading the Risks and Raising the Cost of Nationalization in Natural Resources." *International Organization* 27: 273–87.

Morawetz, David. 1977. *Twenty-five Years of Economic Development, 1950 to 1975*. Washington, D.C.: The World Bank.

Morris, M. D. 1979. *Measuring the Condition of the World's Poor: The Physical Quality of Life Index*. New York: Pergamon.

Mundell, Robert. 1968. *International Economics*. New York: Macmillan.

Myint, Hla. 1971. *Economic Theory and Underdeveloped Countries*. New York: Oxford.

Myrdal, Gunnar. 1956. *The International Economy: Problems and Prospects*. New York: Twentieth Century Fund.

———. 1957. *Economic Theory and Underdeveloped Regions*. London: Gerald Duckworth.

———. 1968. *Asian Drama: An Inquiry into the Poverty of Nations*. New York: Twentieth Century Fund.

———. 1970. *An Approach to the Asian Drama: Methodological and Theoretical*. New York: Vintage Books.

———. 1973. *Against the Stream: Critical Essays in Economics*. New York: Vintage Books.

———. 1974. "What Is Development?" *Journal of Economic Issues* 8: 729–36.

Nelson, Richard R. 1956. "A Theory of the Low Level Equilibrium Trap." *American Economic Review* 46: 894–908.

Newlyn, W. T. 1977. *The Financing of Economic Development*. Oxford: Clarendon.

Nowzad, B. 1978. *The Rise of Protectionism*. Washington, D.C.: International Monetary Fund.

Nugent, Jeffrey, and Pan Yotopolous. 1979. "What Has Orthodox Development Economics Learned from Recent Experience?" *World Development* 7: 541–54.

Nurske, Ragnar. 1953. *Problems of Capital Formation in Developing Countries*. New York: Oxford.

Okun, Arthur M. 1975. *Equality and Efficiency: The Big Tradeoff*. Washington, D.C.: The Brookings Institution.

Ohlin, Bertil. 1933. *Interregional and International Trade*. Cambridge, Mass.: Harvard.

Palma, Gabriel. 1978. "Dependency: A Formal Theory of Underdevelopment or a

Methodology for the Analysis of Concrete Situations of Underdevelopment?" *World Development* 6: 881–924.

Parry, T. G. 1977. "Multinational Manufacturing Enterprises and Imperfect Competition." Occasional Paper no. 1, Center for Applied Economic Research, University of New South Wales, Australia.

Parsons, Talcott. 1951. *The Social System*. Glencoe, Ill.: The Free Press.

Paukert, Felix. 1973. "Income Distribution at Different Levels of Development: A Survey of Evidence." *International Labour Review* 108: 97–125.

Pearson, S. R., J. D. Stryker, and C. P. Humphreys. 1981. *Rice in West Africa: Policy and Economics*. Stanford, Calif.: Stanford.

Pinto, A., and J. Knakal. 1972. "The Center-Periphery System 20 Years Later." In *International Economics and Development: Essays in Honor of Raul Prebisch*, edited by L. DiMarco, 97–128. New York: Academic Press.

Piore, Michael. 1983. "Labor Market Segmentation: To What Paradigm Does It Belong?" *American Economic Review* 73: 249–53.

Prebisch, Raul. 1950. *Economic Development of Latin America and Its Principal Problems*. New York: United Nations.

———. 1959. "Commercial Policies in Underdeveloped Countries." *American Economic Review* 49: 251–73.

———. 1964. *Toward a Trade Policy for Development*. New York: United Nations.

———. 1976. "A Critique of Peripheral Capitalism." *CEPAL Review* 1: 9–76.

Pyatt, G., and E. Thorbecke. 1976. *Planning Techniques for a Better Future*. Geneva: I.L.O.

Pyatt, G., and J. I. Round. 1977. "Social Accounting Matrices for Development Planning." *Review of Income and Wealth* 23: 339–63.

Pyatt, G., A. R. Roe, et al. 1977. *Social Accounting for Development Planning: With Special Reference to Sri Lanka*. Cambridge: Cambridge.

Ranis, G. 1973. "Industrial Sector Labor Absorption." *Economic Development and Cultural Change* 21: 387–408.

Resnick, Stephen. 1975. "The State of Development Economics." *American Economic Review* 65: 317–22.

Riedel, James. 1984. "Trade as an Engine of Growth in Developing Countries Revisited." *Economic Journal* 94: 56–73.

Robinson, Joan. 1956. *The Accumulation of Capital*. London: Cambridge.

———. 1971. *Economic Heresies*. New York: Basic Books.

———. 1981. *What Are the Questions? And Other Essays*. Armonk, N.Y.: Sharpe.

Rosenstein-Rodan, P. 1943. "Problems of Industrialization of Eastern and South Eastern Europe." *Economic Journal* 53: 205–16.

Rostow, Walt. 1960. *The Stages of Economic Growth: A Non-Communist Manifesto*. Cambridge: Cambridge.

———. 1971. *Politics and the Stages of Growth*. Cambridge: Cambridge.

Rostow, Walt., et al. 1963. *Economics of Take-Off into Sustained Growth*. London: Macmillan.

Schultz, Theodore. 1975. "The Value of the Ability to Deal with Disequilibria." *Journal of Economic Literature* 13: 827–46.

———. 1980. "Nobel Lecture: The Economics of Being Poor." *Journal of Political Economy* 88: 639–51.

Schumpeter, Joseph. 1949. "Science and Ideology." *American Economic Review* 39: 345–59.

———. 1978. *History of Economic Analysis*. New York: Oxford.

Seers, Dudley. 1972. "What Are We Trying to Measure?" *Journal of Development Studies* 8: 21–36.

———. 1973. "The Meaning of Development." In *The Political Economy of Development and Underdevelopment*, edited by Charles Wilber, 6–14. New York: Random House.

———, ed. 1981. *Dependency Theory: A Critical Reassessment*. London: Francis Pinter.

Sen, A. K., ed. 1971. *Growth Economics*. London: Penguin.

———. 1973. *On Economic Inequality*. Oxford: Clarendon.

———. 1980. "Levels of Poverty: Policy and Change." World Bank Staff Working Paper no. 410. Washington, D.C.: The World Bank.

_____ . 1981. *Poverty and Famines: An Essay on Entitlement and Deprivation.* Oxford: Clarendon.

_____ . 1983. "Development: Which Way Now?" *Economic Journal* 93: 745–62.

Shaw, Edward. 1973. *Financial Deepening and Economic Development.* New York: Oxford.

Simon, Julian. 1982. *The Ultimate Resource.* Princeton, N.J.: Princeton.

Singer, Hans. 1950. "The Distribution of Gains between Investing and Borrowing Countries." *American Economic Review* 40: 473–85.

Solo, Robert. 1975. "What Is Structuralism? Piaget's Genetic Epistemology and the Varieties of Structural Thought." *Journal of Economic Issues* 9: 605–25.

Solow, Robert M. 1956. "A Contribution to the Theory of Economic Growth." *Quarterly Journal of Economics* 70: 65–94.

_____ . 1957. "Technical Change and the Aggregate Production Function." *Review of Economics and Statistics* 39: 312–20.

Sombart, Werner. 1915. *The Quintessence of Capitalism.* Translated and edited by M. Epstein. London: T. F. Unwin.

Southworth, Herman, and Bruce Johnston, eds. 1967. *Agricultural Development and Economic Growth.* Ithaca, N.Y.: Cornell.

Spraos, John. 1979. "The Theory of Deteriorating Terms of Trade Revisited." *Greek Economic Review* 1: 15–42.

_____ . 1980. "The Statistical Debate on the Net Barter Terms of Trade between Primary Commodities and Manufactures." *Economic Journal* 90: 107–28.

Sraffa, Piero. 1960. *Production of Commodities by Means of Commodities: Prelude to a Critique of Economic Theory.* Cambridge: Cambridge.

Stavig, Gordon. 1979. "The Impact of Population on the Economy of Countries." *Economic Development and Cultural Change* 24: 735–50.

Stern, Joseph, and Jeffrey Lewis. 1980. "Employment Patterns and Income Growth." World Bank Staff Working Paper no. 419. Washington, D.C.: The World Bank.

Streeten, Paul. 1972. *The Frontiers of Development Studies.* New York: Halstead.

_____ . 1974. "Social Science Research on Development: Some Problems in the

Use and Transfer of an Intellectual Technology." *Journal of Economic Literature* 12: 1290–1300.

―――― . 1981. *Development Perspectives*. New York: St. Martin's.

―――― . 1982. *First Things First: Meeting Basic Needs*. New York: Oxford.

Sunkel, Osvaldo. 1969. "National Development Policy and External Dependence in Latin America." *Journal of Development Studies* 6: 23–48.

―――― . 1972. "Big Business and 'Dependencia': A Latin American View." *Foreign Affairs* 50: 517–31.

―――― . 1973. "Transnational Capitalism and National Disintegration in Latin America." *Social and Economic Studies* 22: 132–76.

Sweezy, Paul. 1956. *The Theory of Capitalist Development*. New York: Monthly Review.

Szal, Richard, and Sherman Robinson. 1977. "Measuring Income Inequality." In *Income Distribution and Growth in Less Developed Countries*, edited by Charles R. Frank, Jr., and Richard Webb, 491–533. Washington, D.C.: The Brookings Institution.

Taylor, Lance. 1979. *Macro Models for Developing Countries*. New York: McGraw-Hill.

Taylor, Lance, and Edmar Bacha. 1976. "The Unequalizing Spiral: A First Growth Model for Belindia." *Quarterly Journal of Economics* 90: 197–218.

Thirlwall, A. P. 1979. "The Balance-of-Payments Constraint as an Explanation of International Growth Rate Differences." *Banca Nazionale del Lavoro Quarterly Review* 128: 44–53.

―――― . 1980. "Regional Problems Are 'Balance-of-Payments Problems.'" *Regional Studies* 14: 419–25.

Timbergen, Jan. 1976. *RIO: Reshaping the International Order*. New York: E. P. Dutton.

Timmer, C. Peter, Walter Falcon, and Scott Pearson. 1984. *Food Policy Analysis*. Baltimore, Md.: Johns Hopkins.

Toynbee, Arnold J. 1947. *A Study of History*. New York: Oxford.

―――― . 1966. *Change and Habit: The Challenge of Our Time*. New York: Oxford.

United Nations, Statistical Office. 1968. *A System of National Accounts*. Studies in Methods, Series F, No. 2, Rev. 3. New York: United Nations.

United Nations, Department of Economic and Social Affairs. 1974. *Multinational Corporations in World Development*. New York: Praeger.

United Nations, Center for Transnational Corporations. 1977. *Survey of Research on Transnational Corporations*. New York: United Nations.

_____ . 1978. *Transnational Corporations in World Development: A Re-Examination*. New York: United Nations.

Vaitsos, Constantine. 1974. *Inter-Country Income Distribution and Transnational Enterprise*. Oxford: Clarendon.

Vernon, Raymond. 1966. "International Investment and International Trade in the Product Cycle." *Quarterly Journal of Economics* 80: 190–207.

_____ ., ed. 1970. *The Technology Factor in International Trade*. New York: Columbia.

_____ . 1971. *Sovereignty at Bay: The Multinational Spread of U.S. Enterprise*. New York: Basic Books.

_____ . 1972. *Restrictive Business Practices: The Operation of Multinational United States Enterprises in Developing Countries*. New York: United Nations.

_____ . 1974. "The Economic Consequences of U.S. Foreign Direct Investment." In *International Trade and Finance*, edited by R. E. Baldwin and J. D. Richardson, 287–90. Boston: Little Brown.

Villamil, Jose, et al. 1978. *Transnational Capitalism and National Development*. Brighton: Harvester.

Wachtel, Howard. 1977. *The New Gnomes: Multinational Banks in the Third World*. Washington, D.C.: Institute for Policy Studies.

Weber, Max. 1930. *The Protestant Ethic and the Spirit of Capitalism*. Translated by Talcott Parsons. London: Allen and Unwin.

_____ . 1947. *The Theory of Social and Economic Organization*. Translated by A. M. Henderson and T. Parsons. Glencoe, Ill.: The Free Press.

Weisskoff, Richard. 1970. "Income Distribution and Economic Growth in Puerto Rico, Argentina, and Mexico." *Review of Income and Wealth* 16: 303–32.

Wells, Louis T., ed. 1972. *The Product Life Cycle and International Trade*. Boston, Mass.: Harvard University Graduate School of Business Administration.

White, Lawrence. 1978. "The Evidence of Appropriate Factor Proportions for Manufacturing in Less Developed Countries." *Economic Development and Cultural Change* 27: 27–60.

Wolfson, Murray. 1971. *Karl Marx*. New York: Columbia.

World Bank. 1975. *The Assault on World Poverty*. Baltimore, Md.: Johns Hopkins.

———. 1979. *World Development Report*. New York: Oxford.

———. 1980. *World Development Report*. New York: Oxford.

———. 1981. *Accelerated Development in Sub-Saharan Africa: An Agenda for Action*. Washington, D.C.: The World Bank.

———. 1984. *World Development Report*. New York: Oxford.

———. 1984a. *Toward Sustained Development in Sub-Saharan Africa: A Joint Program of Action*. Washington, D.C.: The World Bank.

———. 1985. *World Development Report*. New York: Oxford.

Yeats, Alexander. 1979. *Trade Barriers Facing Developing Countries*. New York: St. Martin's.

Yhap, Lorene. 1975. "International Migration in Less Developed Countries: A Survey of the Literature." World Bank Staff Working Paper no. 215. Washington, D.C.: The World Bank.

Yotopolous, Pan. 1977. *The Population Problem and the Development Solution*. Food Research Institute Studies 16, Stanford University, Stanford, Calif.

# Index

agriculture:
  balanced expansion in, 102–3
  neglect of sector, 178–79
  role in development and trans-
    formation, 100–2
allocation:
  and the free trade model, 31–37
  of resources and scarcity, 27–28,
    40
  (*see also* market, prices,
    equilibrium)

balance-of-payments:
  concept, 73–75
  equilibrium growth rate model,
    86–88
  and the foreign exchange gap,
    85–86
  (*see also* dependency, trade)

capital:
  accumulation and wealth-
    seeking goals, 61–63
  as a complement to technology,
    93
  in demand-oriented models, 77–85
  in neoclassical supply models,
    90–91
  in relation to global accumulation,
    182, 187–88
  (*see also* investment, savings)
capital labor ratio, 94, 171
capital output ratio, 79
class:
  and the government bureaucracy,
    39–40
  international linkages of, 176–77
  role in the radical heterodox
    model, 188–89

structure and income distribution,
  44–45
competition (*see* market, prices,
  equilibrium)

dependency:
  concept of, 172–74
  systematic effects, 177–80
  (*see also* trade, technology)
development:
  human dimensions of, 115–16
  and human motivation, 41–42
  models of ideal types and
    pattern variables, 52–57
  and per capita income attain-
    ment, 4–9
  (*see also* economic growth,
    distribution)
disequilibrium (*see* equilibrium,
  exchange, market, prices)
distribution:
  of capital incomes and assets, 29,
    43
  of labor incomes, 29, 42–43
  role in meliorist development
    model, 130–36
  of world product, 7

economic growth:
  incentives and competition, 64
  and inequality, 64–65
  Keynesian model, 79
  Marxian model of, 181–90
  neoclassical model, 89–90
  sources of, 90
  stages, 57–61
  warranted rate of, 80
efficiency:
  economic, 34

# About the Author

WILFRED L. DAVID is a Graduate Professor of Economics and African Studies at Howard University, Washington, D.C. Until 1977, he was Professor and Chairman of the Economics Department at Fisk University. He also held senior academic appointments at Vanderbilt University, the University of Delaware, and Brooklyn College of the City University of New York.

Dr. David's many publications in the area of international economic development include *The IMF Policy Paradigm* (1985), "Dimensions of the North-South Confrontation" (1977), and *Planning for National Development* (1975).

Dr. David holds a B.A. with honors in economics and philosophy from London University, and a D.Phil. from Oxford University.

## DATE DUE

| SEP 02 1987 | | | |
|---|---|---|---|
| | | | |
| | | | |
| | | | |
| | | | |
| | | | |
| | | | |
| | | | |
| | | | |
| | | | |
| | | | |
| | | | |
| | | | |
| | | | |
| | | | |
| | | | |